The Mind and Art of Victorian England

THE
MIND AND ART
OF
VICTORIAN
ENGLAND

Edited by
Josef L. Altholz

THE UNIVERSITY OF MINNESOTA PRESS, MINNEAPOLIS

Preface

The reign of Queen Victoria (1837–1901) coincided closely enough with a distinctive epoch of English history so that the age bears her name with a certain inevitability: it could not have been other than Victorian. Victoria presided, earnestly if somewhat remotely, over the first industrial society in the world's history. Reaping the fruits of early industrialization, Britain enjoyed unexampled wealth and prosperity, an empire upon which "the sun never set," and the security of a *pax Britannica* which lasted with scarcely an interruption for a century. Viewing the Exhibition of 1851, a complacent Englishman could observe with satisfaction both the economic supremacy of his nation and the fact — a negative fact but an important one — that Britain had *not* had a revolution in 1848. It was an age not of revolution but of reform: political reform which admitted first the middle and then the working classes to the dominant share of the suffrage; economic and social reforms which proclaimed the triumph of laissez-faire while laying the foundation of the welfare state; moral reforms attempted if not achieved through education and religious revival; aesthetic reforms, proposed if not achieved, but adding to the richness and variety of Victorian England. It was an age whose problems cried out for reform, and despite the prevailing complacency, virtually all the great Victorians were critics of their age. Their criticisms were diverse and often mutually incompatible, but they shared with each other — and with their public — a high seriousness which gave character and substance to the flowering of their culture. Such was the Victorian age: the high-water mark of English history, the maturation of British culture, and the seedbed of our problems and our discontents.

The study of Victorian England — like the reputation of the Victorian era or the connotations of the word "Victorian" — has passed through several phases. The Victorians themselves, from John Stuart Mill's "Spirit of the Age" (1831) through Humphry Ward's *Survey of Fifty Years of Progress* (1887), had a unique self-consciousness, alternating self-criticism with self-praise. The generation which succeeded the Victorians, in its inevitable but exaggerated revolt against parents and grandparents, had nothing but criticism and sneers, as epitomized in the brilliant maliciousness of Lytton Strachey's *Eminent Victorians* (1918). A reaction in favor of a more sympathetic assessment was bound to ensue. Its landmark was the greatest piece of writing on the Victorian age, G. M. Young's *Victorian England: Portrait of an Age* (1936), which saw the "function of the nineteenth century" as the release of the "disinterested intelligence" and its operation "over the whole range of human life and circumstances." From Young's revisionism flowed two streams of thought. The first was the development of professional research on Victorian England, which reached its maturity in literary scholarship with Walter Houghton's *Victorian Frame of Mind* (1957) and in historical study with Kitson Clark's *Making of Victorian England* (1962). The second was a stream of popular interest in the period, stimulated by a postwar awareness that the Victorians had an assurance and an apparent stability that we can never retrieve, heavily laced with nostalgia and a passion for trivia, yet capable of rising to connoisseurship and a valid appreciation of the Victorian achievement. Ironically, the publication of such works as Steven Marcus's *The Other Victorians* (1966), showing the "underside" of the life of the seemingly respectable Victorians, set the seal upon their respectability in our age of permissiveness. It remains now to bring the results of the still-growing professional scholarship in this field to that wider educated public whose interest in the Victorian period has been stimulated.

This was the purpose of the lecture series on which this volume is based. The lectures were part of a "Victorian festival," including a major art exhibit, at the University of Minnesota in the autumn of 1974, which was sponsored by a grant from the National Endowment for the Humanities. This multidisciplinary endeavor involved the united efforts of faculty, students and members of the public in educating interested laypeople while producing something of lasting value to scholars.

Volumes of general essays written for both the scholar and the non-specialist form a characteristically English genre. G. M. Young's masterpiece grew out of such a volume, *Early Victorian England* (1934); and the BBC symposium *Ideas and Beliefs of the Victorians* (1949) was another landmark in the revaluation of the Victorian age. One of the purposes of this volume is to demonstrate that North American scholarship has matured to the point of being able to produce works of equal quality on English subjects. For this reason, only American and Canadian scholars were invited to contribute. (The one holder of an English chair is in fact a Canadian.)

This volume contains the public lectures of 1974, in revised form, and with some additions. Because the centerpiece of the "Victorian festival" was an art exhibit (the Forbes Magazine Collection), greater attention is given to the arts than is usual in works of this sort. On the other hand, the areas of political, social and economic history, which might well form a volume by themselves, were excluded for lack of time and space. It was possible to include one essay, on the theatre, which we were unable to fit into the lecture series. We had hoped also to include an essay on music, but no suitable author could be found. No attempt was made to impose a general theme or thesis to which the essays had to conform, and each stands by itself as the judgment of the author on his subject.

The grant from the National Endowment for the Humanities funded the printing of the pictures in this volume, so that it would be possible to bring out an illustrated book at a reasonable price. The pictures were selected by Melvin Waldfogel, who wrote the accompanying text. The index (also funded by the grant) was prepared by David Horgan.

The lecture series was arranged by a faculty committee consisting of Melvin Waldfogel (Art History), William A. Madden (English), and the editor (History). The entire "Victorian festival" was coordinated by Barbara Schissler, director of the University of Minnesota Gallery. Thanks are especially due to Lyndel King, curator, and others of the Gallery staff; Ann Pflaum and David Horgan, graduate student volunteers; and William VanEssendelft of the University extension staff. The editor also acknowledges the assistance of Glen Wilson of Macalester College in connection with the theatre section of the Bibliography, which was otherwise compiled on the basis of suggestions by the authors.

J. L. A.

Table of Contents

The Mind and Art of Victorian England

Victorian England: The Self-Conscious Society

Jerome H. Buckley

Though the idiom is not precisely ours, we should find a peculiar cogency in a late-Victorian indictment of Victorian society: "When the brightness of future ages shall have dimmed the glamour of our material progress, the judgment of history will surely be that the ethical standard of our rulers was a deplorably low one, and that we were unworthy to possess the great and beneficent powers that science had placed in our hands."[1] So concludes *The Wonderful Century,* written in 1898 by Alfred Russel Wallace, the biologist who forty years earlier had anticipated and then generously supported Darwin's theory of the origin of species. Surveying his age, Wallace may well strike us as absurdly crotchety in his attack on the practice of vaccination or in his defense of a pseudoscientific phrenology. Yet he remains practical, percipient, and timely in his warnings against the extravagant waste of petroleum oils and natural gas, the general despoiling of the earth, the alarming increase of military power, the mistreatment of subject races, and the almost systematic neglect of the urban environment. Like many other Victorians dismissed and largely forgotten in the first half of the twentieth century, Wallace has something to say directly to us.

The epithet "Victorian" in popular usage still bears some negative connotations, some overtones of self-complacency and undue propriety, but the general reaction against all things Victorian has long since sub-sided, and the term itself has acquired new shadings of approval, sugges-tions of solidity, amplitude, integrity, energy, and purpose. Scholar-critics since the late 1940s and especially in the past ten or fifteen years have thoroughly rehabilitated the major Victorians, introduced us to many unfamiliar minor ones, and given the mind and art of the age sufficient status to be the subject of a collection as wide-ranging and respectful as this one. Fresh interpretations have destroyed the stereotypes with which the most eminent Victorians were once stamped and discarded. New sympathy has established new relevance. Ruskin is no longer simply the muddled angry prophet with a command of the periodic sentence, but a serious aesthetician, an economist to be listened to, an ecologist rebuking our physical as well as moral pollution. Carlyle has recently emerged as the radical activist rather than the turgid reaction-ary. Macaulay has become much more than the naïve apologist for laissez-faire. Mill's crusade for liberty is seen to involve a sophisticated critique of liberalism. Dickens's later, darker novels now seem not the product of a tired imagination incapable of its early humor and exuber-ance, but the achievement of a mature artist with a searing vision of society. And Tennyson's *Idylls of the King*, once condemned as over-wrought escapist romance, now, in book after scholarly book, appears a masterly chronicle of a culture in moral and intellectual jeopardy. Simi-larly the best Victorian architecture, the legacy in brick and stone, is praised for bearing the seeds of modernism and occasionally respected enough to elude the depredations of the modern wrecker. Victorian painting in its turn has been rediscovered at greatly inflated prices as a sound investment in a world of decreasing options. A New York art critic has just explained that the "bad" canvases of Holman Hunt and his school are, after all, better than they seemed to be a few years ago, perhaps even "good" now — "or if not good, at least important and interesting and not all that funny."[2] At any rate, the Pre-Raphaelites, including Hunt, are enjoying more attention than they have received in decades, and the paintings and drawings of Dante Gabriel Rossetti several years ago earned the accolade of a splendid two-volume *Catalogue Raisonné*. More recently, in the summer of 1974, the work of the almost unknown mad painter Richard Dadd, who was confined for over forty years to Bethlem Hospital, drew large crowds to an impressive exhibi-tion at the Tate Gallery in London.

It is difficult to determine how self-assured, how pleased with himself, the average middle-class Victorian may or may not have been. But a closer acquaintance with Victorian literature and with the intellectual history of the period rejects the early twentieth-century allegation that the more articulate Victorians were guilty of a pervasive self-complacency. They were, it seems to me, far less self-satisfied than self-conscious — that is, less absolute than relativistic in their self-regard. Indeed we might argue that a double self-consciousness, public as well as private — by which I mean an awareness of the personal self in time and of the whole era itself as a perpetual transition — was their central attribute. Each of the major Victorians knew not merely his place in a social order but also his place in history, the roles he could or should play in a social drama of many shifting scenes. The idea of history dominated the intellectual life of the nineteenth century. All things related to the eternal process moving on; life was change, movement, growth and decline; the society itself, forever expanding and contracting, was necessarily at any given stage progressive or decadent. The recurring Victorian image of the world was organic rather than mechanical; Darwin's beautiful, irregular, ever-branching tree replaced Newton's well-ordered machine. The intellectual imagined himself and his culture in the long perspectives of human time. He asked whether present achievement adequately realized past promise and how much of value it would contribute to future progress.

Such social self-consciousness, such sense of responsibility to time, underlies Wallace's dissatisfaction with "the wonderful century," his concern with the harsh "judgment of history" in the distant brighter age to come. (As Wallace foresees it, a remote if not immediate future will necessarily somehow *be* brighter, though it is not at all clear how any future is to recover the natural resources he describes as lost through present mismanagement.) In "The Function of Criticism at the Present Time" Matthew Arnold appeals to a similar self-consciousness; "the best title to esteem with posterity," he tells his contemporaries, will be to have cultivated the critical spirit, in which alone a true culture may ultimately flourish. Elsewhere Arnold measures Victorian attitudes and sentiments not against the future but against the best that the past has thought and said, the tradition of sweetness and light he now imagines sacrificed to the rancor and prejudice and anarchy of the philistines. Carlyle, in his first major essay, "Signs of the Times," contrasts his own "mechanical" age with the "dynamical" culture of the Elizabethans; and in his best proportioned book he brings a purposeful medieval past to bear upon a confused and dreary present. Even John Stuart Mill, whose Benthamite education inculcated scant respect for history, lamented the decline of the heroic in his own time; unlike their forebears, modern English gentlemen, he said, fear ridicule, actively support no high principles, prudently retreat from engagement, with "a moral effeminacy" and "an inaptitude for every kind of struggle."[3] Newman, Ruskin, Morris, Bagehot, Disraeli, Pater — to name but a few others at random — were likewise self-consciously eager to see their age in some admonishing historical perspective. Yet each was also aware of the new and peremptory demands of the present, the difficulty of assimilating entirely new fact and opinion to established practice and belief. And none was sufficiently the "reactionary" to think he could withdraw to a more coherently ordered past and so evade the accelerating assaults of modernity, the pressures of what Arnold called "the world's multitudinousness."[4]

In an age of unprecedented discovery, invention, and innovation, few could escape personal bewilderment and perplexity. If the society as a whole seemed uncertain of its direction, where was the individual to find his own stability? A healthy self-consciousness became the mark of identity. Samuel Butler equated the individual self with memory of a private past, and the self of society with its remembered growth. George Eliot believed that to "forget oneself" was to isolate the present from one's past experience and so to threaten the integration of the personality. But in a world of drastic change it might be difficult to establish and maintain a continuity, either public or private, between past and present. Newman pointed to "self-knowledge" as "at the root of all real religious knowledge," since, he argued, "it is in proportion as we search our hearts and understand our own nature, that we understand what is meant by an Infinite Governor and Judge."[5] Self-analysis, however, was not always reassuring. Many a Victorian self-consciously discovered within himself only the divided aims of modern life, the dialogue of the mind with itself, an ambivalence, a debilitating doubt. Carlyle, who never for long transcended self-consciousness, counseled "self-annihilation" and resolute devotion to the Everlasting Yea of selfless hard work. And George Meredith, who saw in the deep probing of the self the source of many modern ills, looked enviously at the lark ascending:

Was never voice of ours could say
Our inmost in the sweetest way,
Like yonder voice aloft, and link
All hearers in the song they drink.
Our wisdom speaks from failing blood,
Our passion is too full in flood;
We want the key of his wild note
Of truthful in a tuneful throat,
The song seraphically free
Of taint of personality . . .

As the poem most central to the mind and art of the Victorians, *In Memoriam* is a striking example of both public and personal self-consciousness. Often compared to Pope's *Essay on Man* as a representative social document, it touches on a wide range of public issues and concerns, in fact on most of the large themes of this volume — science, religion, politics, art, and the role of the artist. Many of its topical allusions have required glossing in scholarly commentaries, for what was new or familiar in 1850 when the poem was published has sometimes been forgotten or superseded. Tennyson's awareness of contemporary science, however, remains of interest to the intellectual historian.

The new astronomy places the whole argument of *In Memoriam* in a plural universe of frightening vastness, "the worlds of space in the deep night," where chance may rule and "the stars their courses blindly run." Nineteenth-century geology gives it similar extension in time. Tennyson records the catastrophic theories of creation advanced by Cuvier to explain remote origins and the apparent fortuitousness of the whole process:

They say,
The solid earth whereon we tread

In tracts of fluent heat began,
And grew to seeming-random forms,
The seeming prey of cyclic storms,
Till at the last arose the man . . .

(CXVIII)

But Tennyson himself is more deeply moved by Charles Lyell's concept of uniformitarian change, the theory of ageless unending erosion, the image of streams drawing "down Aeonian hills" and sowing "the dust of continent to be"; and the scheme of geological time becomes to him a reminder of a perpetual instability and transience:

> There rolls the deep where grew the tree.
> O earth, what changes hast thou seen!
> There where the long street roars, hath been
> The stillness of the central sea.
>
> The hills are shadows, and they flow
> From form to form, and nothing stands;
> They melt like mist, the solid lands,
> Like clouds they shape themselves and go.
>
> (CXXIII)

Thomas Malthus had already given Tennyson a frightening vision of surplus population and cosmic indifference to the individual life. Lyell's *Principles of Geology*, the testimony of "scarped cliff and quarried stone," now provided evidence that in the course of long evolutionary time many "types," that is, whole species, as well as single lives, had perished. Heavily influenced by the same sources (Malthus and Lyell), *The Origin of Species* appeared nine years after *In Memoriam*, and Tennyson has been both commended for forecasting Darwin's great hypothesis and blamed for not imagining the mutability of species. Tennyson, of course, was not a scientist, but a poet drawing freely upon pre-Darwinian evolutionary theory, when he speculated on development in man and nature, and his originality as a theorist is of less importance than the intensity of his response to current ideas. His description of Nature, not as the benevolent Mother whom Wordsworth extolled, but as a sort of amoral Amazonian, fierce and predatory, "red in tooth and claw," crying, "A thousand types are gone;/ I care for nothing, all shall go," established the idiom for much later discussion of the struggle for survival and possibly even influenced Darwin's use of personification and the metaphor of "natural selection." "Nature," wrote Darwin, "if I may be allowed to personify the natural preservation or survival of the fittest, cares nothing for appearances, except in so far as they are useful to any being . . . Man selects only for his own good; Nature only for that of the being which she tends."[6]

Victorian science, however, is not the subject of *In Memoriam*, and public concerns generally are only incidental to its primary theme. Unlike the *Essay on Man*, it is an intensely personal poem, an elegy to a dead friend, a confession cast in the form of a private diary or perhaps a sequence of intimate letters to a closed family circle. Public ideas, especially the new scientific concepts, impinge upon the personal grief and place the bereaved poet in a surrealist world of infinite hollow space and inhumanly endless time. The new public knowledge, the scientific assumptions of transience and insignificance, challenge the ideal view of purpose and immortality, the very substance — or the mere illusion — of human dignity. If Nature has cared nothing for vanished types, will she ultimately in the evolutionary process sacrifice the human species, too, and all the fondest hopes of mankind?

> *And he, shall he,*
>
> *Man, her last work who seemed so fair,*
> *Such splendid purpose in his eyes,*
> *Who rolled the psalm to wintry skies,*
> *Who built him fanes of fruitless prayer,*
>
> *Who trusted God was love indeed*
> *And love Creation's final law —*
> *Though Nature, red in tooth and claw*
> *With ravine, shrieked against his creed —*
>
> *Who loved, who suffered countless ills,*
> *Who battled for the True, the Just,*
> *Be blown about the desert dust,*
> *Or sealed within the iron hills?*
>
> *(LVI)*

More immediately, though still in general terms, the poet turns self-consciously to his art. In terror of change, he rejects the brave Renaissance dream of undying poetic fame; if his poem survives at all, its durance will be brief; what hope, he asks,

> *What hope is here for modern rhyme*
> *To him, who turns a musing eye*
> *On songs, and deeds, and lives, that lie*
> *Foreshortened in the tract of time?*
>
> *(LXXVII)*

But whatever the future may think of any work of art, the poet is sensitive to the opinions of his contemporaries. In a curious dramatic vignette, he presents three passersby commenting on his grief. The first two might be voices of his personal self-consciousness in their contention that the lament is excessive or merely self-indulgent, the cry of one who "loves to make parade of pain." The third is the angry voice of public self-consciousness:

> *A third is wroth: "Is this an hour*
> *For private sorrow's barren song,*
> *When more and more the people throng*
> *The chairs and thrones of civil power?*

> *"A time to sicken and to swoon,*
> *When Science reaches forth her arms*
> *To feel from world to world, and charms*
> *Her secret from the latest moon?"*
>
> *(XXI)*

But in the depths of his despair the poet finds no solace either in the extension of democracy or in the advance of science; he is alienated altogether from the public world, and outer space is still more alarming than enticing. Concerned with the dimensions of his art, he asserts his right to court the muse Melpomene rather than Urania, that is, to be subjective and elegiac and to ignore the higher, sterner claims of dramatic or epical poetry. He indulges in lonely self-colloquy, probing his moods and motives, aware of the griefs within that remain inarticulate (the "tears that at their fountain freeze"), half-fearful that he may be distorting the personal past by remembering it as entirely "pure and perfect." Most disturbingly, in his acute self-consciousness, he questions his own sanity; has the shock of grief, he wonders,

> *stunned me from my power to think*
> *And all my knowledge of myself;*

> *And made me that delirious man*
> *Whose fancy fuses old and new,*
> *And flashes into false and true,*
> *And mingles all without a plan?*
>
> *(XVI)*

The loss of all knowledge of the self, the doubt of his own identity, this plunges him into the confusion that fails to distinguish past from present, subjective from objective reality. "But what am I?" he asks at one juncture, and then helplessly answers, "An infant crying in the night" — and a little earlier he has characterized infancy as a state without a sense of separate identity, without "the use of 'I,' and 'me,'" or the knowledge that "I am not what I see,/ And other than the things I touch." In short, his bewilderment brings him close to the condition we should now call schizophrenia.

In our time such mental and emotional disturbance has become sufficient sanction for a considerable poetry of disaffection. R. D. Laing and his followers see schizophrenia as a mode of positive release, a "healing voyage" beyond a sick society, and the schizophrenic's alienation quite possibly the healthy protest of a sensitive mind against a mad, mad culture.[7] Tennyson, however, resists the seductions of madness and any desire he may have had to rationalize his unhappy isolation, and stubbornly clings to sanity. He is painfully aware that his self-absorbed grief may distort the truth. When he dreams nightmarishly of his dead friend as alive and suffering some distress, he awakens to realize, "It is the trouble of my youth/ That foolish sleep transfers to thee." If the world had no ultimate purpose, it would be merely a delusion, a thing of

> *Fantastic beauty; such as lurks*
> *In some wild Poet, when he works*
> *Without a conscience or an aim.*
>
> *(XXXIV)*

He himself will be no such "wild" — which is to say, insane — artist. We need not here rehearse the experiences of memory and intuition that eventually give him individual reassurance, nor examine the philosophic idealism by which he reappraises modern science. We need only observe that his recovery demands his willing return to society and the abandonment of a self-indulgent subjectivity:

> *I will not shut me from my kind,*
> *And, lest I stiffen into stone,*
> *I will not eat my heart alone,*
> *Nor feed with sighs a passing wind . . .*

> *What find I in the highest place,*
> *But mine own phantom chanting hymns?*
> *And on the depths of death there swims*
> *The reflex of a human face.*
>
> *(CVIII)*

The resolution of this most representative Victorian poem rests accordingly on a realignment of personal and public self-consciousness. When the self is at last ready to join in the larger community, then time loses its terror, the "Wild Hours that fly with Hope and Fear" acquire some positive meaning, and "all, as in some piece of art,/ Is toil coöperant to an end."

Tennyson's reconciliation with his kind, however, implied no unquestioning conformity to the practice or prejudice of the age. On the contrary, his social criticism after *In Memoriam*, in the 1850s, grew only the more trenchant, as in *Maud*. But never does madness, which is indeed the key theme of *Maud*, seem preferable, as Dr. Laing would now sometimes have it, to social participation and responsibility. We may remember that John Stuart Mill feared a possible tyranny of public opinion and, in his *Liberty*, pleaded for a greater eccentricity of thought and conduct. Yet all the while Mill, too, took for granted the free individual's countervailing rational regard for the health and security of the whole society, the mature adult's essential public self-consciousness. "Liberty, as a principle," he insisted, "has no application to any state of things anterior to the time when mankind have become capable of being improved by free and equal discussion." We should then be free to pursue "our own good in our own way," but only "so long as we do not attempt to deprive others of theirs, or impede their efforts to obtain it." Later, in *Utilitarianism*, Mill made the case for social awareness even stronger. The will to belong, he said, is basic and "natural"; every man, no matter how distinctive and alienating his attributes or attitudes may be, must feel some respect for the larger public purposes of his time:

The deeply rooted conception which every individual even now has of himself as a social being tends to make him feel it one of his natural wants that there should be harmony between his feelings and aims and those of his fellow-creatures. If differences of opinion and of mental culture make it impossible for him to share many of their actual feelings — perhaps make him denounce and defy those feelings — he still *needs to be conscious* that his real aim and theirs do not conflict, that he is not opposing himself to what they really wish for, namely their own good, but is, on the contrary, promoting it.[8]

Nineteenth-century science, of course, did much to shake common preconceptions about the order of the physical world. Yet many of the most prominent scientists, notably Lyell, Darwin, Huxley, and Tyndall, all great expositors, maintained the importance of public discourse and strove to make clear, in lucid and often eloquent prose, the general relevance of the latest research. Meanwhile, men of letters, critics, poets, novelists — at least until the coming of the late-century aesthetes — accepted the primary burden of public communication, even when their visions of reality could enjoy little popular acclaim. In short, the Victorians typically — if we may generalize about a people so diverse and individualistic — sought personal fulfillment within the broad cultural context and recognized a considerable degree of accountability to the body politic.

In Victorian poetry Gerard Manley Hopkins, who had virtually no public in his own time, provides us the most conspicuous example of a distinctive originality, an idiosyncrasy of method which opened new avenues of expression. Hopkins frequently meditated on the extreme intensity of his own self-consciousness, "that taste of myself, of *I* and *me* above and in all things, which is more distinctive than the taste of ale or alum, more distinctive than the smell of walnutleaf or camphor, and is incommunicable by any means to another man (as when I was a child I used to ask myself: What must it be to be someone else?). Nothing else in nature comes near this unspeakable stress of pitch, distinctiveness, and selving, this selfbeing of my own."[9] In his later sonnets he repeatedly probed the fearful insistency of the self, the terror of lonely exile, the perilous abysses of the distraught mind:

> *I am gall. I am heartburn. God's most deep decree*
> *Bitter would have me taste: my taste was me;*
> *Bones built in me, flesh filled, blood brimmed the curse.*
> *Selfyeast of spirit a dull dough sours. . . .*
>
> *My own heart let me more have pity on; let*
> *Me live to my sad self hereafter kind,*
> *Charitable; not live this tormented mind*
> *With this tormented mind tormenting yet. . . .*

O the mind, mind has mountains; cliffs of fall
Frightful, sheer, no-man-fathomed. Hold them cheap
May who ne'er hung there.

From his isolation came, as here, a powerful self-analysis but also the loss of a public awareness which would, he felt, have disciplined and broadened his art. "What I want," Hopkins lamented near the end of his short life, "to be more intelligible, smoother, and less singular is an audience," for, as he had felt almost from the beginning of his prosodic experiments, "It is the vice of distinctiveness to become queer. This vice I cannot have escaped." [10] No considerable Victorian artist, certainly not Hopkins, deliberately denied his audience, cultivated a willful eccentricity, or celebrated the "healing voyage" of schizophrenia. Even the unhappy Richard Dadd, who sank irretrievably into the chasms that Hopkins glimpsed, left paintings remarkable less for mad allusion and arbitrary symbolism than for a continuity with his eminently sane, precisely ordered earlier work. [11]

Self-consciousness was not, of course, a Victorian discovery. Yet it was not long before the Victorian period that it became established as a cultural mode. We may properly associate its rise with the first Romantics, especially with Rousseau on the Continent and Wordsworth in England. Rousseau began his *Confessions* with a defiant sense of innovation: "I am commencing an undertaking, hitherto without precedent, and which will never find an imitator. I desire to set before my fellows the likeness of a man in all the truth of nature, and that man myself. Myself alone!" Completing the first draft of *The Prelude* in 1805, Wordsworth was likewise impressed by the novelty and temerity of his performance, for it was, he said, "a thing unprecedented in literary history that a man should talk so much about himself." [12] Much Romantic confessional poetry followed, long before Wordsworth's personal epic actually appeared, and the vogue of autobiography, usually in prose, has persisted throughout the nineteenth and twentieth centuries. But the difference between Romantic and Victorian self-consciousness is one essential difference between *The Prelude* and *In Memoriam*; whereas Wordsworth is endlessly fascinated by himself as his all-sufficient subject, Tennyson, as we have seen, is embarrassed by his tormenting self-absorption, half-apologetic for his extended self-concern, aware of the objective world, fearful that the self in isolation from society may grow wholly disoriented, become — as Hopkins put it — distinctively queer. The Romantics — typically, we may suppose — believed that the solitary self by its own intuitions could reach general and normative truths; the Victorians sought understanding and self-realization in a shared social experience.

Self-consciousness, both private and public, remains characteristic of the mind and art of our own culture, but the working relationship between the individual and the society is no longer to be taken for granted as inevitable or even necessarily desirable. Though the authority of history as a discipline has sharply declined, we are constantly reminded of our place in time and of the prospects for human survival; and the assumption of cultural decadence has become a fact of existence rather than a challenge to corrective action. At its most extreme in the graphic and plastic arts but prominent also in contemporary poetry and fiction, individual self-consciousness has led to an exploration of private fantasies and personal pathologies; the nonobjectivists, the conceptualists, the neo-dadaists, all follow the subjective impulse wherever it may lead, even at the cost of a programmed self-destruction. Victorian art, on the contrary, especially literature, but painting, too, self-conscious in its own ways, communicates its concern with a general psychology and offers us an abiding assertion of life in its multiple relations. The Victorian mind perhaps more now than ever should appeal to us by placing an essentially modern bewilderment in the perspective of a social and moral reason.

The Art of
Victorian Literature

Robert Langbaum

The subject assigned me for this volume, the "art of Victorian literature," seems impossible to encompass in so short a space. I might
more appropriately write on the *arts* of Victorian literature if I am to
cover the enormous variety of Victorian literary production in poetry,
fiction, and that highly wrought, imaginative nonfictional prose — the
prose of such writers as Carlyle, Ruskin, Pater — which is a special
feature of the age. Nevertheless, I shall attempt the impossible, I shall
recklessly court failure, because failure can, as Browning and Ruskin
taught, prove fruitful. I proceed in the hope that it may prove illuminat-
ing to see how far one can go in drawing a line through the bewildering
variety of Victorian literature, to see how far one can determine whether
there is any *formal* principle or cluster of principles by which Victorian
literature as a whole can be distinguished from the English literature that
precedes and follows it. Even if I fail, we shall, I think, have learned a
good deal about Victorian literature on the way.

Let us start then by tracing the connection with romantic literature; the
connection is clearest in poetry. The great subjects of romantic poetry are
the imagination and nature — the imagination as it transforms, and discovers itself in, nature. Instead of God, the romantic or post-
Enlightenment poet gives us nature; then he or the speaker of his poem
discovers a Godlike life in nature by discovering his own inwardness
there. After the Enlightenment had chased spirit from the world with its
destructive test of reason, nature remained, for all the English romantic
poets except Blake, the one area of objective reality where spirit could

still be found — spirit as life force, that is — because it remained the one area where objective reality could still be seen as corresponding to the heart's desire and therefore as symbolizing subjective reality, as still congenial to imagination.[1]

Contemporary society and church were not congenial, although Anglicanism appealed to Wordsworth and Coleridge in their later phase when it came to seem not a threat but an anomaly antithetical to the society, a last loosening link to the past. The societies romanticists found congenial to imagination were remote, soil-bound communities that derive spiritual force from organic connection with nature — communities, described by Wordsworth in "Michael" and "The Brothers," that were fast disappearing. Or else the romanticists found congenial those societies of the past, especially the medieval past, in which spirit had been objectively real; so that the Gothic settings of Coleridge's *Christabel* and Keats's "Eve of St. Agnes" seem objectifications of spirit, landscapes of the mind. For Keats, in "Eve of St. Agnes" and "Ode on a Grecian Urn," past societies are congenial to imagination because they come to us transmuted by art. But Keats is exceptional when he uses art objects rather than nature as the objective pole to imagination and as social surrogates. He finds no heirs until the mid-Victorian aesthetes. In English romanticism, art and society are much less important than nature as objective poles to imagination.

Coleridge in "Frost at Midnight" and Wordsworth in "Tintern Abbey" perfected a form for objectifying imagination in nature. The poet, standing in a particular place at a particular time, *sees* a natural phenomenon from his particular perspective. As a result of the particularity, the poet finds a conflict between nature and himself at that moment. In "Tintern Abbey," the returning poet finds that the landscape is the same but that he has changed, has apparently grown away from nature. In "Frost at Midnight," Coleridge's mature thoughts seem to disturb the silent processes of nature. In both poems the poet, through a dialectical interchange between himself and nature, comes by a process of association to realize that his maturation and thoughts are part of the natural process and are organically connected with his childhood sensations, that nature is alive because it includes mental operation, that inner and outer feed each other in a circular movement that makes for growth and renewal. The poet, in other words, arrives at a revelation of spirit, his spirit, in the external world, and thus spiritualizes nature while confirming the existence of spirit in himself. He thus rebuilds the world of values that the Enlightenment destroyed; the values seem valid because they emerge from the experience of a single speaker at a particular place and time. These poems move through time to arrive in the end at a stasis — in "Tintern Abbey," through memorialization of the temporal experience in the landscape; in "Frost at Midnight," through transformation of stillness as silence into stillness as motionlessness — transformation of the temporal process of frost into "silent icicles,/ Quietly shining to the quiet Moon."

Keats, in "Ode on a Grecian Urn," uses the same poetic form to find his imagination objectified in a work of art; only he reads backward from stasis to motion, from objectified to subjective imagination. In "Ode to a Nightingale," however, he uses this form to turn the nightingale's natural voice, existing in time, into the sort of timeless cultural symbol that is available to art. The poem comes to a climax in the stasis of magic casements opening on to faery seas — the timeless depersonalized audience for a timeless voice. The stasis encloses motion, but the frozen motion thaws when the word "forlorn" (the faery lands are forlorn of time-driven humanity) returns us to the world of time and the bird's departure. In all these poems the stasis that encloses movement is itself time-enclosed, since the epiphany or illumination that reveals the poem's movement as static pattern occurs at a specific moment. All poems in this new form are time-haunted. This form, which I have elsewhere called the dramatic lyric,[2] derives from the eighteenth-century meditative-descriptive poem (poems like Gray's "Elegy in a Country Churchyard"). The dramatic lyric is the distinctively new form of romantic poetry.

The romantic dramatic lyric was transformed by the Victorians into the dramatic monologue, which is the distinctively new form of Victorian poetry. The dramatic monologue — poems like Browning's "My Last Duchess" and Tennyson's "Ulysses" — can be used as a model for discovering the art of much Victorian literature, literature in all genres, because the thing that turns the romantic dramatic lyric into the Victorian dramatic monologue is the remarkably increased interest among Victorians in society. Inspired by the French Revolution, the romanticists were mainly concerned to liberate the individual from the old order and its shackling creeds and dogmas. Hence the turn to inwardness as the source of values; hence the interest in the single man alone in nature. The Victorians, instead, were in a position to recognize the emerging new industrial and democratic society; they were at once exhilarated by its possibilities and depressed by the wrong direction it was taking. The age believed above all in reform and progress; so that society became the field for individual self-realization and came to rival nature as the objective pole to imagination.

Yet the Victorian writers retained the romantic belief in inwardness as the source of values. The individual and his inner needs remained, for literature at least, the test against which society's success or failure could be measured. Carlyle, the first of the great Victorian nonfictional prose writers, called for more *inwardness* as the way to achieve a healthier *society*. For society in Carlyle's view was no mere utilitarian arrangement; it was, like nature for the romanticists, a part of *our* nature, an objectification of self that made self-realization possible. That is the meaning of the "clothes philosophy" in *Sartor Resartus*. The clothes or social institutions that objectify our inner needs must change as our needs change; but our need for clothes or social institutions remains permanent.

Carlyle and the other so-called Victorian sages — Newman, Ruskin, Arnold, Pater — were concerned in their social criticism with the *quality* of life. They were concerned with society as an aspect of culture; for culture affects and proceeds from the inner life.[3] Their social criticism is not sociology because its claim to validity does not rest on statistical proof or logical argument. Their social criticism claims validity as the sincere insight of an imaginative intellect whose passionate thought penetrates the social surface in order to illuminate both inner life and social surface. In other words, the social criticism of the Victorian sage convinces in the way creative literature does, through a whole texture of images and examples that are the sign of an inner coherence — an inner coherence deriving not from logic but from the single imagination.[4] It is because the Victorian sage's voice is not general and neutral but single and characteristic that we can believe that his social "facts" have been returned to us from inside an imagination. Each Victorian sage has his own characteristic voice, and he convinces or fails to convince through his character. For we must feel a sympathetic connection with his character, his inwardness, if we are to think passionately with him and adopt his view of the social scene from inside out. In this way of communicating through our sympathy with the single speaker, the prose writings of the Victorian sages bear a relation to the dramatic monologue.

The increased interest in society accounts for the literary program by which the earlier Victorian poets reacted against the romantic tradition they had inherited. This program called for objectivity and realism. Thinking mainly of Wordsworth and Byron, the Victorians felt that the autobiographical confessional mode was self-indulgent, that the poem would seem more valid if the poet were to keep himself and his philosophizing out of it. In calling for more realism, the Victorians were calling for more objectivity and more social notation. "Realistic" details came to mean not simply details of social vices — a traditional subject sustained by Byron and Shelley (society in Byron's *Don Juan* is vicious but still glamorous). Social "facts" came to mean facts that were uncongenial to imagination and therefore unassailably objective. And after Lyell's geology, with its extinct species in the rocks, had led to Darwin's survival of the fittest, nature itself became another uncongenial "fact."

Browning and Ruskin called for objectivity and realism. Arnold called for objectivity and architectonic structure, but not for realism, because he wanted the Victorian reaction against romanticism to take the form of a classical revival. Victorian realism had even less to do with classicism than with romanticism, since the new "facts" were even more uncongenial to the universal moral order posited by classicism than to imagination. Victorian literature represents the next phase of romanticism. Romanticism had always moved toward objectification of the subjective, and the Victorian writers were determined to maintain and intensify romantic inwardness in the face of an increasingly irreconcilable objective reality. Awareness of the split between the testimonies of head and heart made the Victorians more "scientific" than the romanticists about outer and inner reality. Victorian literature tries to contain the conflicting evidences of psychology, on the one side, and history or sociology on the other.

The dramatic monologue exemplifies the continuation and modification of the romantic tradition. Browning takes over the structure of the romantic dramatic lyric, substituting for the speaker who bears the poet's name a speaker who bears a name and character other than the poet's. To an audience brought up on romantic autobiographical poetry, Browning thought it necessary to point out — in a prefatory note to *Dramatic Lyrics*, the volume that contained his first dramatic monologues — that these poems were "so many utterances of so many imaginary persons, *not mine*."[5] As in the romantic dramatic lyric, the speaker organizes the poem according to his particular perspective; his perspective makes its imprint on the objective scene, it is his entry into objectivity. I mean by this that in the romantic dramatic lyric the ideas proposed gain validity as arising from what a particular man *sees* at a particular time in a particular place; since the speaker is Wordsworth, we assume that the poet approves the ideas. In the dramatic monologue, the ideas are proposed as simply characteristic — characteristic of the speaker and his age. It is a secondary concern whether Browning approves the ideas, and sometimes we cannot be sure. Point of view remains the channel for the reciprocal flow between subjectivity and objectivity, even if the flow no longer yields truth but only a revelation of character.

"My Last Duchess" is a great psychological study of art collecting. Browning shows that the duke's passion for art collecting proceeds from egomaniacal possessiveness and power hunger. His last duchess eluded him with her spontaneous aliveness; he could not bear to share her, so he ordered her killed. Now he has her where he wants her, in a life*like* portrait that none can see unless *he* chooses to show it. The auditor to whom he reveals the duchess's portrait and story turns out to be the envoy come to arrange the duke's next marriage. The poem's power derives from the duke's effrontery in telling such a story to such a person and to his triumphant control over the situation. His consummate poise is aristocratic, but it is also the result of his total blank in moral understanding. The duke's combination of aestheticism and amorality is the quintessence of his age, the high Italian Renaissance. It is because the duke finds his image in the age that he can so relentlessly *be* what he *is*; his character has a centrality and magnitude it could not have were he carrying on that way in Victorian London. The same can be said of that even more representative because less maniacal Renaissance figure, the bishop in "The Bishop Orders His Tomb at St. Praxed's Church."

Both dramatic monologues are, like the dramatic lyric, time-haunted. They portray a moment in a life; but they also, unlike the romantic dramatic lyric, portray a moment in a historical age — a moment that contains the whole life and age. There are no reversals, no plot in the Aristotelian sense. The poems proceed through intensification of the given to a final revelation of character — the character of the speaker and his age — which transforms movement into stasis: a stasis manifested by the statue of Neptune taming a sea horse that the duke, interrupting the action, compulsively insists in the last lines on calling to the envoy's attention; and a stasis manifested by the bishop's vision of himself in the end as already the recumbent statue on his tomb.

Approval or disapproval seems hardly relevant. And the inner life is not necessarily, as in the romantic dramatic lyric, spiritual and transcendent. The realism is psychological as well as social; hence the frequent interest in psychic and social pathology. The attitude, in other words, is "scientific," which is why we give the speaker a sympathy not measured by his moral deserts simply because we want to understand him, want to see how the world looks from his point of view. The thrill of the dramatic monologue comes from our sense of the price paid in moral judgment for our sometimes dangerous understanding. The dramatic monologue derives its special effect from the split in our reaction between sympathy and judgment.

Browning meets the Victorian condition in that his attitude is "scientific." But he mainly evades the Victorian view of society as uncongenial to imagination by setting most of his dramatic monologues in the past. This is an evasion because the past in Browning is still glamorous, still an objective counterpart to a vital, complex inner life. Here Tennyson is more modern. For Tennyson, who particularly dwells on morbid emotions, conceives society as opposed to self-fulfillment. Even in "Ulysses," which is set in the past, the aged hero finds kingship incompatible with his deepest desire, his desire to die; he abdicates his social responsibility to set sail once more on the ultimately fulfilling journey from which he will never return. In diction and imagery Browning is more modern than Tennyson. But Tennyson is more modern in that he gives more of his dramatic monologues contemporary settings. These dramatic monologues — poems like "Locksley Hall" and *Maud* — are not entirely successful because they cannot unify through action or tone their disparate reports on the speaker's inner life and social milieu. But they do show what the age was trying to accomplish in the revision of literary form, and the manner of their failure shows the problems posed for literary form by the Victorian contradictions between subjective and objective reality.

In *Maud: A Monodrama*, the brutally commercial society is so repugnant to the oversensitive, morbidly introspective speaker that his only desire is to escape social relations, to "bury myself in myself" (Part I, line 75).[6] His complete alienation leads to madness, to the psychotic illusion of being dead and buried but not deeply enough. The imagery of suicidal self-burial derives from the speaker's impassioned recollection in the opening stanzas of his father's suicide and his traumatic discovery of the body; he is haunted by the fear that he too will commit suicide. His father committed suicide not for the old tragic reasons, loss of love, land, honor, but because "a vast speculation had failed." This makes for a bad half-line of verse, verse that seems bathetic in the context of passion:

> Did he fling himself down? who knows? for a vast speculation had
>   failed,
> And ever he muttered and maddened, and ever wanned with despair.
>
> *(I, 9–10)*

The poem's flaw throughout is this disparity between the intensely lyrical passages on the inner life and the prosaic bathos of the social realism. Nevertheless, the attempt to hinge tragedy on a stock swindle is a bold confrontation of contemporary reality.

Because of his father's destruction by the old friend with whom he went into the business venture, the speaker has come to see society as a jungle where everyone wars against everyone else, where food and drink are adulterated and "a Mammonite mother kills her babe for a burial fee" (I, 45) — the instances are largely drawn from Carlyle. Nature, too — here Tennyson anticipates Darwin — is "a world of plunder and prey" (I, 125); so that the speaker cannot find even in nature the confirmation of values Wordsworth found. War against another nation would be preferable; for it would be honestly declared, would unite British society and bring out the chivalric virtues. In a world where values have become almost entirely subjective, love and war remain the only fields for the objectification of values.

The speaker and Maud fall in love, but their love is enmeshed in the web of brutal social relations. She is the daughter of the man who swindled the speaker's father; her brother, grown lordly on his father's ill-gotten gains, opposes the match as beneath her; he has chosen for her a new-made lord whose grandfather wrested the family fortune from exploitation of the women and children who worked naked in his coal mines: "Grimy nakedness dragging his trucks/ And laying his trams in a poisoned gloom" (I, 335–36). These lines are a good example of the poem's social realism.

As an example of the poem's other side, the speaker intones the impassioned lyric, "Come into the garden, Maud," while he waits for her in the garden of the manor house where within her brother is giving a Tory political dinner. The lyric reaches what is for the whole monodrama the climax of ecstasy as Maud approaches:

> *There has fallen a splendid tear*
> 　*From the passion-flower at the gate.*
> *She is coming, my dove, my dear;*
> 　*She is coming, my life, my fate;*
> *The red rose cries, "She is near, she is near;"*
> 　*And the white rose weeps, "She is late;"*
> *The larkspur listens, "I hear, I hear;"*
> 　*And the lily whispers, "I wait."*
>
> *She is coming, my own, my sweet;*
> 　*Were it ever so airy a tread,*
> *My heart would hear her and beat,*
> 　*Were it earth in an earthy bed;*
> *My dust would hear her and beat,*
> 　*Had I lain for a century dead;*
> *Would start and tremble under her feet,*
> 　*And blossom in purple and red.*
>
> 　　　　　　　　*(I, 908–23)*

Even at the climax of ecstasy, the image of burial recurs — showing the speaker's intuition that the participation of flowers in his passion is illusory, that one must burrow deeper and deeper for value, that value can never be objectified.

We learn in Part II that the brother surprised the lovers, dueled with the speaker, was mortally wounded and that the speaker fled, carrying in his heart Maud's "cry for a brother's blood" (II, 34). On the coast of Brittany the speaker, overwrought by guilt, dwells in minute detail on an empty shell. Does the shell's emptiness signify the failure of love and the dissolution therefore even of subjectivity as a last stronghold of value? Does the empty shell's survival against storms signify the sheer endurance nevertheless of meaningless phenomena? The shell lyric might be called imagist in that it presupposes a world without value in which particulars are alone valid. "Strange," says the speaker, that emotional disturbance, instead of drowning "all life in the eye," should "Suddenly strike on a sharper sense/ For a shell, or a flower, little things" (II, 106–

12). The more irrelevant these particulars, the more cut off from meaning, the more valid and therapeutic.[7]

News of Maud's death leads to the poignant lyric, "O that 'twere possible" (II, 141–238), which was written twenty years earlier in response to Hallam's death. This lyric is about the utter irreconcilability of desire and reality. As the speaker goes mad, desire itself dies. Maud turns into a dead phantom he wants to be rid of; while the world remains loveless (the social criticism goes on even in madness). Now that subjectivity is as menacing as objectivity, there is no recourse but burial. In his madness the speaker imagines himself dead and buried, but not buried deeply enough to escape the world's noise. His hallucination ends with the plea for some kind heart "To bury me, bury me/ Deeper, ever so little deeper" (II, 341–42). Here the poem ought to end — in unresolved contradiction. For *Maud* up to this point is about a sensitive man's escape into madness from an unendurable reality.

To achieve a positive ending, however, Tennyson in Part III sends his speaker into that other field for the objectification of value — war. Under the influence of Carlyle, who preached work or action as the cure for modern self-consciousness, Tennyson makes the speaker, as he emerges from madness, solve his personal problems by going off to fight in the Crimean War. The speaker even negates his own social criticism with the deplorable line: "It is better to fight for the good than to rail at the ill" (III, 57). Tennyson tries to relate war to love by arbitrarily turning Maud into a blessed spirit who sees "a hope for the world in the coming wars" (III, 11). Such reversals are wrong for the dramatic monologue since they presuppose an objective stance from which one alternative can be judged better than the other. The bad writing of Part III carries little conviction; and we of course are not convinced, we wish the conclusion away. It is a sign of the modern split between fact and value that critics so often distinguish, as I am now doing, between the genuine and fake in modern works — the fake being always those places where the author tries to impose upon values a spurious objectivity.

The split between fact and value is the essential subject of the dramatic monologue and the determinant of its form — its organization around a point of view. *Maud* goes beyond the usual dramatic monologue in its attempt to portray, along with the point of view, an extensively specified social milieu that has an interest and an existence independent of the point of view. This so-called monodrama is, in other words, dealing with just the combination of elements that accounts for the preeminence of the novel in the Victorian period. Inasmuch as the dramatic monologue deals with psychology, on the one side, and history or sociology on the other, it points toward the novel and toward the modern short story which made its appearance soon after the dramatic monologue. But the dramatic monologue differs from the Victorian novel in that it subordinates the social notation to the psychology; whereas *Maud*, like the Victorian novel, tries to give them equal attention. In its attempt to meet the conditions of the age as completely as the novel, *Maud* is the most boldly innovative poem of the mid-century. It is bolder even, though less successful, than Browning's *The Ring and the Book*. *The Ring and the Book* is also, as Henry James pointed out, novelistic;[8] but it is like a colorful historical novel rather than like the "realistic" Victorian novels of nineteenth-century life.

When we use the word "realistic" in connection with modern literature, we expect a contemporary setting. That is because "realism" in the modern sense means "facts" cut off from meaning and incommensurate with desire; it means an external world, mechanical and abstract, that belongs to another order of being from the characters. These are the recognizable conditions of society since the industrial revolution. In *The Ring and the Book*, instead, which takes place in Italy in 1698, the incommensurateness is moral rather than psychological. The society can no longer provide valid moral guideposts for the characters; but its failings are human failings, its "facts," rotten as they are, have a meaning derived from values of the *ancien régime*. The good characters can win out over a society of human adversaries who are merely obsolete; the good characters are on the side of progress. In *Maud*, instead, the society is inhumanly brutal; its "facts" are explainable only by the law of the jungle. The contradiction between outer and inner life is so wide that the speaker can only go mad or, if we take Part III seriously, succumb to society. In spite of the many good things in it, *Maud* finally fails because it cannot contain so wide a contradiction.

The manner of *Maud*'s failure helps us understand the techniques of the Victorian novel, which are designed to contain the contradiction. All the elaborate techniques of the Victorian novel — the multiple narrators, the stories within the story, the coincidences, the many narrative threads that have in the end to be tied together — all these techniques are attempts to make the psychological and social notation work together, to connect the unconnectable while making it clear that they are unconnectable. Dickens's techniques are the most elaborate, and he is the novelist who goes to the extremes laid out in *Maud* — who, on the one side, portrays the inner life to the point of madness and, on the other, the utmost social brutality.

This brings us to the art of the Victorian novel, which can to some extent be understood on the model of the dramatic monologue. The first word to be used in connection with the Victorian novel is "realism." And the first place to look for the particular Victorian application of the term is to George Eliot in her famous chapter xvii of *Adam Bede*. My strongest effort, she says, is not to improve on the facts by making them more beautiful or morally simple than they are:

my strongest effort is to avoid any such arbitrary picture, and to give a faithful account of men and things as they have mirrored themselves in my mind. The mirror is doubtless defective; the outlines will sometimes be disturbed, the reflection faint or confused; but I feel as much bound to tell you as precisely as I can what that reflection is, as if I were in the witness-box narrating my experience on oath.

George Eliot modifies Aristotle's dictum that art imitates nature, represents things as they *are*. She offers only to be true to her own *impressions*, and admits that these impressions may sometimes distort the object. But if she is true to her own impressions, she achieves as much validity as is possible in a world where we can no longer be sure what is objectively real. Here we have the principle that determines the structure of the dramatic monologue — that validity lies in the point of view, that point of view is the only entry we have into reality.

It is safe to say that Victorian realism generally is impressionist. George Eliot enunciates another doctrine of Victorian realism when she goes on to say that human feelings and values do not in life come marked with the external signs of grandeur and beauty by which we recognize them in traditional art. In modern realistic art, as in life, we cannot know human feelings and values through external signs but only inwardly, through sympathy. "All honour and reverence to the divine beauty of form!" she says. "But let us love that other beauty too, which lies in no secret of proportion, but in the secret of deep human sympathy. . . . do not impose on us any aesthetic rules which shall banish from the region of Art those old women scraping carrots with their work-worn hands."[9]

Since sympathy is the way of knowing that distinguishes the dramatic monologue and accounts for its structure, we see how the dramatic monologue, which is so obviously structured for impressionism and sympathy, is a convenient model of Victorian realism. George Eliot equates the real with the mediocre and ordinary; whereas most writers of dramatic monologues are like Dickens in that they find the real in extraordinary cases. But value in all these writers exists only inasmuch as it registers on a sensibility, is known through sympathy.

Even the rather simple concept of realism laid out in George Eliot's first successful novel, *Adam Bede*, allows sufficiently for imagination and inwardness to prepare for the more complex psychological realism of *Middlemarch*, the masterpiece that climaxes her career. In the most important of her comments in *Middlemarch* on novelistic method, George Eliot says that imagination is often considered inaccurate and fanciful when it is actually the most precise form of perception. She makes the physician Lydgate reflect on imagination in terms that apply to both scientific research and novel writing. "Imagination," Lydgate reflects, "reveals subtle actions inaccessible by any sort of lens, but tracked in that outer darkness through long pathways of necessary sequence by the inward light which is . . . capable of bathing even the ethereal atoms in its ideally illuminated space."

The reflected reality of *Adam Bede* turns into the "illuminated space" of imagination; the imagination takes the object inside itself and therefore sees inside the object. Within its "illuminated space," the imagination provisionally frames the object, "correcting it to more and more exactness of relation" and thus helping us "to pierce the obscurity of those minute processes which prepare human misery and joy." The "arduous invention" [10] that frames the object corresponds to the artifice of the laboratory experiment and the novel. Within the simplifying conditions of the frame, the penetrating imagination can analyze the processes behind psychic manifestations, but it can also operate through sympathy. The internal view of the object corresponds to the projective way of knowing that dissolves the distinction between inner and outer reality in the romantic dramatic lyric and the Victorian dramatic monologue. The internal view accounts for D. H. Lawrence's remark that "George Eliot . . . started it all. . . . It was she who started putting all the action inside." [11]

Nowadays Dickens seems to us to penetrate even deeper psychologically than George Eliot. In his own time, however, he was judged strong in external rendition, but weak in psychology because he oversimplified through caricature and the contrasting of morally black and white characters.[12] Writing in the 1950s, Dorothy Van Ghent accounts brilliantly for the apparent lack of complex inner life in Dickens's characters by showing that it is the whole point of Dickens's art to transpose inner life "to other forms than that of human character." In *Great Expectations*, Miss Havisham's inner life is transposed into the decayed wedding cake on the banquet table. Mirroring her own decay, the cake contains her desire to die and to spread death around her by making time stand still. I quote Miss Van Ghent: "'When the ruin is complete,' Miss Havisham says, pointing to the cake but referring to herself, she will be laid out on the same table and her relatives will be invited to 'feast on' her corpse." "Without benefit of Freud or Jung," Miss Van Ghent concludes, "Dickens saw the human soul reduced literally to the images occupying its 'inner life.'"[13]

It requires depth psychology to understand the sense in which Dickens is more deeply psychological than George Eliot. For we now know that the unconscious masks itself through projections into the external world, that it often appears to us as external. Thus Dickens's extravagant simplifications and objectifications — his portrayal of people as if they were things and things as if they were people — signal a concern with unconscious process. George Eliot, instead, carries on an intricate analysis of the conscious mind; and though her novels are about the interchange between private and communal life, we always know what is going on inside and what is going on outside. Her mixture within the same people of ordinary good and evil proceeds from the realm of ordinary though subtle observation. But Dickens's separation of extreme good and extreme evil in different persons proceeds from the realm of unconscious desire. His villains fulfill desires we only dream of, hence the atmosphere of hallucination, or the comedy that hovers on the edge of hallucination.

The new insights into Dickens's depth psychology have led recent critics to invert the Victorian idea of Dickens as realistic exposer of bad social conditions. Critics now suggest that external reality is in Dickens a mere projection of psychic states. Dorothy Van Ghent speaks of Dickens's "vision of a purely nervous or moral organization of reality";[14] and Hillis Miller speaks of the insubstantiality of society in Dickens, and indeed in all Victorian fiction, as a mere mirror image of imagination. To the extent that they dissolve the external world of Dickens's novels, these critics go too far; they anticipate the twentieth century by turning Dickens into Kafka. The novel remains Victorian to the extent that inner and outer reality are opposed to each other yet held in balance. The balance is most even in George Eliot, most uneven in Dickens. But Dickens's society, though fragmented, is still substantially there. That is why his novels remain comic, do not quite turn into the nightmare of Kafka's novels; for comedy turns into nightmare when the characters reach out to find that the object of attack or laughter is not there.

Miller comes closer to the mark when at the end of his perceptive little book, *The Form of Victorian Fiction*, he contradicts what he has said earlier in the book about the insubstantiality of society in Victorian novels. "The Victorian novelists," he says in the end, ". . . are unwilling to accept the notion so prevalent in fiction after Conrad and James, that no comprehensive vision of society is possible." Miller cites Dickens's notebook entry, made about the time he was planning *Our Mutual Friend*, in which he projects a story

representing London — or Paris, or any other great place — in the light of being actually unknown to all the people in the story, and only taking the colour of their fears and fancies and opinions. So getting a new aspect, and being unlike itself. An *odd* unlikeness of itself.

In the projected story, the city changes according to the perspective of each city-dweller. There is in *Our Mutual Friend* just such a multiplicity of points of view; the difference is that the *narrator*, as Miller says, "sees the city and its citizens as they really are." [15] The Victorian novelists are unwilling to *settle* for the point-of-view novel. Yet points of view are what they introduce through their multiple perspectives even while they try to maintain objective reality as a separate interest.

The Victorian novelists use points of view for the same reason that they are used in dramatic monologues, as an entry into the opaque meaningless stuff of objective reality, as a way of giving form and meaning to objective reality. Like the dramatic lyric and the dramatic monologue, the novel was from the first time-haunted; novelists established their reality through exact notations of historical and quotidian time. But Victorian novelists are increasingly preoccupied with the problematical nature of time, with the disparity between psychic and clock or calendar time, for the same reason that they are increasingly preoccupied with points of view — as a way of dissolving the opaqueness of objective reality.

The dissolution of community and communication, the dissolution into points of view, goes farthest in Dickens. Dickens's real contribution to the novel derives, according to V. S. Pritchett, from "his strongest and fiercest sense: isolation."

The distinguishing quality of Dickens's people is that they are solitaries. They are people caught living in a world of their own. They soliloquize in it. They do not talk to one another; they talk to themselves. The pressure of society has created fits of twitching in mind and speech, and fantasies in the soul. . . . The solitariness of people is paralleled by the solitariness of things. Fog operates as a separate presence, houses quietly rot or boisterously prosper on their own. . . . The people and the things of Dickens are all out of touch and out of hearing of each other, each conducting its own inner monologue.[16]

It is of course the people who find in the things the counterpart of their own alienation, thus animating the external world and making it signify solitariness. Dickens's novels might be read as a combination of dramatic monologues, with the elaborate plot a mechanism for conveying us from one dramatic monologue to another. Such a reading would account for our habit of discounting the plot in Dickens and other Victorian novelists, and believing only in the character revelation. We merely tolerate the plot — the coincidences, suspense, recognitions, reversals — as an anachronistic hangover from an earlier time when belief in a publicly objective moral order made revelation through action possible. We can see in this way of discounting plot and believing in character a split that corresponds to the split between sympathy and judgment in our way of reading the dramatic monologue. But the Victorian dramatic monologue is actually ahead of the Victorian novel in that it *settles* for point of view; it abandons plot for pure character revelation, and in this points toward the earlier twentieth-century novel.[17]

We can see why Dickens hangs on to plot and we understand the nature of Dickensian comedy when Pritchett, who describes the solitariness of Dickens's people, can also praise Dickens's "capacity for comic social generalization." In the twentieth century, Pritchett says, we "talk of novels of private life, and novels of public life. In Dickens, on the contrary, the private imagination, comic, poetical and fantastic, was inseparable from the public imagination and the operation of conscience and rebellion."[18] D. H. Lawrence defines the theme of Hardy's novels, and by implication all Victorian novels, as the individual's war against society. The theme requires that both sides be real. Even in madness, the speaker in Tennyson's *Maud* never loses his sense of social reality: society pounds upon his grave. In Dickens, the eccentricity that verges on madness is a retreat from social pressures. Society is in all the Victorian novelists a very real antagonist.

In the older literature, according to Lawrence, the conflict was with God's laws. But in the older literature society's laws were congruent with God's. In the Victorian novel, society is no longer sustained by God. Therefore its laws are relative; its voice and judgment is merely another point of view. Hardy's Eustacia, Tess, Sue "were not at war with God, only with Society. Yet they were all cowed by the mere judgment of man upon them, and all the while by their own souls they were right." This, says Lawrence, "is the weakness of modern tragedy, where transgression against the social code is made to bring destruction, as though the social code worked our irrevocable fate" [19] — as though the social code were not merely relative. Lawrence criticizes Hardy for seeming to side with society against characters like Tess and Jude with whom author and reader secretly sympathize. Lawrence is analyzing a split corresponding to the split in the dramatic monologue between sympathy and judgment, where sympathy is private, intuitive, certain and judgment is public, theoretical, uncertain.

This brings us to the most conspicuous feature of Victorian fiction, the so-called omniscient narrator. The Victorians were not the first to use the omniscient narrator. Narrators, beginning with the oral tellers of tales, have always been omniscient, have always known all there was to know about the stories they were telling. It is, however, in Victorian fiction that the omniscient narrator first becomes an *issue*, just because the omniscient voice has lost authority, no longer knows the story as God would know it. The omniscient narrator becomes conspicuous because the Victorian novelist is so nervously self-conscious about speaking with such a voice.

The omniscient narrator may represent, as in George Eliot, the author's best intelligence as he tries to understand a reality which he merely reflects and which must always therefore elude him. Or the omniscient narrator may represent, as in Dickens, Thackeray, Hardy, a collective voice whose judgments no longer command the general assent that they do in Jane Austen or Fielding; so that the judgments of the collective voice in Victorian novels often seem sentimental, timid, 'conventional.'

In *Vanity Fair*, Thackeray self-consciously parodies both omniscience —
"(for novelists have the privilege of knowing everything)" — and the
lack of it. The narrator pretends limitation of knowledge to satirize social differences (he must rely on informants when Becky rises too high
above and then falls too far below the novel's upper middle-class norm)
and to satirize prudish readers who would be shocked by details of
Becky's sexual misdemeanors. The limitation of knowledge mainly concerns Becky, on the question of whose guilt the narrator cannot pro-
nounce; for Becky is the one character whom Thackeray portrays
ambiguously, so as not to exclude the possibility of sympathy for her.
In judging the others, especially Amelia whom surprisingly he turns
against in the end, Thackeray retains omniscience. Again we are talking
about the split between sympathy and judgment; whenever the split
occurs, the omniscient narrator becomes another point of view. The
Victorian novel displays the omniscient narrator's last faltering performance, because the Victorian novelists have not yet recognized that
their novels are built around points of view. When the novel catches up
with the dramatic monologue and *settles* for points of view, the omniscient narrator turns into the central intelligence or organizing point-of-
view character in the novels of James and Conrad.

The narrator, whether he tells the story in the third or first person and
whether he seems to be the author or, like Moll Flanders and Henry
Esmond, bears a name other than the author's, is "omniscient" if he
pretends to tell the whole story, to see things as they really are. He is a
"central intelligence" or "point of view" narrator when he obviously
lacks information, when, like the speaker of the dramatic monologue, he
offers only a perspective, and in the most effective instances an obviously
biased perspective, toward the story. The first-person, point-of-view
narrative becomes a dramatic monologue only when the emphasis falls
on the speaker and the present-tense situation in which he is speaking
rather than on the story he tells, when the story exists only to advance the
present-tense situation.

The dramatic monologue, then, though it differs in this last respect
from most point-of-view novels, is a good model for understanding the
structural principle that makes Victorian literature Victorian. For Victorian literature represents that moment in the history of English literature
when the conflict between inner and outer reality is as wide as possible at
the same time that both interests are maintained. Point of view is the sign

of the tension, as is the increasing distinction between subjective and objective time. Point of view and problematical time make the cord that keeps subject and object apart and ties them together. As we move into the twentieth century, one side tends to swallow up the other. If the external world wins, then psyche yields to the apparently blank notation of externals — in certain imagist poems, in naturalistic fiction, and in what Roland Barthes calls the "objective literature" of Alain Robbe-Grillet.[20] If psyche wins, then the dramatic monologue gives way to symbolist and surrealist poetry in which objects are mere symbols of psychic states, and the socio-psychological novels of Dickens turn into the expressionist novels of Kafka and Beckett.

The Poetry of Thought

David J. DeLaura

D o poets *think*? And if they do, is it good for them and for their art?
The questions cause us to smile, and yet within them lie some of the
most sustained attitudes toward poetry and its function, from ancient
times onward. When Plato, in the *Ion*, says that the inspired poet is "a
light, winged and holy thing," who when falling under the power of
music and meter literally loses his mind, poetry is evidently not being
conceived as the result of "thinking" in any ordinary sense. On the other
hand, Aristotle was to elevate poetry by claiming that it "is something
more philosophic and of graver import than history." Whatever
"philosophic" means here, Aristotle does seem to regard poetry as *somehow* akin to intellection *of some sort.* The high and "divine" prerogatives
of the poet, building his "golden" world, were reasserted in the Renaissance by Philip Sidney. Something rather more ambiguous, also in the
Platonic mode, happens in the famous passage in *A Midsummer Night's
Dream* when we hear that "The lunatic, the lover, and the poet/ Are of
imagination all compact." But a more decisive shift in the attitude toward "strong imagination" occurs in the early seventeenth century, with
consequences reaching even into our own day. Francis Bacon,
Macaulay's hero of pragmatism and the scientific method, uses the
Platonic commonplaces in order to suggest new doubts. "Poesy," we
hear, "was ever thought to have some participation of divineness, because it doth raise and erect the mind, by submitting the shews of things
to the desires of the mind; whereas *reason* doth buckle and bow the mind
unto the nature of things." I think there is a fairly direct line from this
attempt to put poetry in its place to Jeremy Bentham's remark in 1825
that "between poetry and truth there is a natural opposition," and that

35

"the game of push-pin [pinning the tail on the donkey] is of equal value with the arts and sciences of music and poetry." [1] Later in the seventeenth century John Milton, less prejudicially, moved poetry away from "mind" by insisting that it should be "simple, sensuous, [and] passionate" — though his own poetry of course usually strikes us very differently. There are important exceptions to this kind of thinking. Coleridge, in the *Biographia Literaria*, insisted that "No man was ever yet a great poet, without being at the same time a profound philosopher"; and John Stuart Mill, a very strange bedfellow, seems to echo this view: "Every great poet, every poet who has extensively or permanently influenced mankind, has been a great thinker." [2] Moreover, apart from the great "philosophical" poet of ancient times, Lucretius, there were examples of poets in the English tradition who wrote in ways analogous to formal "thought" and argument. One thinks of Spenser's *Four Hymns*, or Pope's *Essay on Man*, or the long — and I fear rather boring — speeches of the Father and the Son in Milton's Heaven. The eighteenth century, in Akenside and in the various loco-descriptive poets, had a good deal of tolerance for versified, if unoriginal, "thought."

Still, I think it is true to say that, in the history of English taste and English thinking about poetry, poetry has not by and large been considered the vehicle or medium either for "thinking" or for "telling the truth." In fact, poetry has been much more consistently aligned with pleasing illusion (often called "idealization") — perhaps even a necessary and valuable illusion, but illusion nevertheless. A good measure of this prejudice is the surprisingly unbroken tradition, extending from the late seventeenth into the late nineteenth century, of hostility to the metaphysical poets. [3] Even Coleridge, a great reviver of interest in the seventeenth century, judged that "Our faulty elder poets sacrificed the passion and passionate flow of poetry, to the subtleties of intellect and to the starts of wit." [4] For the nineteenth century, the Augustans fell under the same ban, and we all know Matthew Arnold's dismaying judgment that the difference between "the poetry of Dryden, Pope, and all their school" and "genuine poetry" is that "their poetry is conceived and composed in their wits, [while] genuine poetry is conceived and composed in the soul." [5] Both poets and their enemies by and large have shared this prejudice: the modern "positive" intellect cannot square imagination with reason and truth, and relegates it to the pleasures of the childhood stage of the race; poets, by a curiously similar logic, have tended in modern times to stress the distance of poetry from reason in an effort to preserve poetry or the imagination as a last bastion against the rationalism and mechanism of the modern manipulative intellect.

All of this is by way of prelude to a consideration of the place of "mind" and "thought" in nineteenth-century poetry. It may startle even to suggest that nineteenth-century poets "thought" in any significant sense of the term. By simply inverting the old prejudices, T. S. Eliot, followed by F. R. Leavis and his *Scrutiny* disciples and the American New Critics, made the metaphysicals the norm, and all subsequent poetry was viewed as intellectually deficient. Leavis virtually denied significant thought to the nineteenth-century poets; Eliot's shrewder charge was that "they thought and felt by fits, unbalanced; they reflected. . . . Tennyson and Browning ruminated." "Tennyson and Browning were poets, and they think," he concedes, "but they do not feel their thought as immediately as the odour of a rose."[6] Though the presumptions of the 1920s have abated somewhat in recent years, this is still the challenge in discussions of our topic. What Eliot actually asserted is that in only two or three passages of Shelley and Keats is there an attempt at "unification of sensibility." My own view (which cannot be developed here) is that the "secret" and central history of nineteenth-century poetry is precisely a struggle for such unification, however imperfectly and intermittently achieved.

"Thought" becomes a *problem* for poetry only with the Romantic period. Both generations of Romantic poets discovered new ways to "think" in poetry, and the bulk of critics and readers, for whom the older subordination of poetry to the "truth" of ethics, philosophy, and theology was still a truism, were puzzled and dismayed by the new "uses" to which poetry was being put. The larger context for our study, then, is the quite revolutionary breaking away of poetry from the crumbling older intellectual synthesis, and the growth through the nineteenth century of poetry as an "independent" power. At least two developments among the Romantics can be discriminated. First, there was the unsettling example of Wordsworth. Though he gradually created for himself the serious audience he sought, his poetry was for many years open to a curiously paradoxical charge: Jeffrey was by no means alone in suggesting that the "absurdity" in Wordsworth consisted in "an unlucky predilection for truisms," combined with "obscure phraseology" and "mysterious and unintelligible language."[7] Even friendly critics complained that Wordsworth's quasi-philosophical "system" — the notion that whatever "exists before our senses, is capable of being associated, in our minds, with something spiritual and eternal" — was in fact (as one reader complained) "a rapturous mysticism which eludes all comprehension."[8] The important point is that, for the first time, poetry seemed suddenly "difficult" and "intellectual" and "metaphysical" and "mystical."

In the second generation, Byron and Shelley reinforced the new tendencies and added new problems of their own. As Hazlitt, himself a radical in politics, put it, Byron "goes to the very edge of extreme and licentious speculation, and breaks his neck over it,"[9] while Shelley played into the hands of the enemies of reform by "flying to the extremes of scepticism": "he utters dark sayings, and deals in allegories and riddles. His Muse offers her services to clothe shadowy doubts and inscrutable difficulties in a robe of glittering words, and to turn nature into a brilliant paradox."[10] In fact, Hazlitt is at one with the most conservative and even clerical critics of the day in judging that "poetry moves best within the circle of nature and received opinion: speculative theory and subtle casuistry are forbidden ground to it."[11] Neither Byron nor Shelley were "original" thinkers of course; the bulk of their unsettling speculations and paradoxes were the stock-in-trade of eighteenth-century rationalists and radicals. But Byron's *Cain* (1822), especially, brought the issue of the social consequences to a head: as critics saw, the "philosophical" and religious doubts, difficulties, and perplexities raised by Byron, though familiar to cultivated readers, were now for the first time being promulgated, and in a popular form that precluded rebuttal, among "hundreds of minds that might never otherwise have been exposed to such dangerous disturbance."[12] Although we know that even into the 1840s, Romantic practice and thought had little effect on the tastes of a large number of readers of poetry,[13] the most perceptive critics of the thirties and forties saw that the most interesting recent poets had become unprecedentedly "difficult," and as even a liberal like Leigh Hunt complained in 1842, the new trend to "think" in poetry, and even to think originally and exuberantly, had indeed gone too far.[14]

The bulk of early- and mid-Victorian critics resisted the new varieties of "thought" in poetry, and many current presuppositions worked against it. Again and again we are told that poetry is a matter of "feeling" rather than of "argument," a matter of "heart" and not "subtlety of thought." [15] And by "thought" they increasingly meant precisely "modern" thought, the troubling thought that some of the Romantics had brought into poetry. Above all, they had a strong sense of the exclusiveness of "poetic ideas" and a "poetic manner." [16] They accepted the lyric norm, and tended to put a high premium on clarity, musicalness, and simplicity. [17] The constant harping on "lofty and noble sentiments," "lofty thought," a "sustained tone," [18] led to a rejection of "realistic" and everyday detail (such as was suddenly flooding into the novel), and a perennially offended rejection of Browning's poems as "grotesque." [19] Even Tennyson ran into the objection at times, for example, in "St. Simeon Stylites" and *The Princess*. [20] Behind all this, I think, was a growing terror that a newly liberated poetry would cease to yield the familiar "spiritual" truth about things. Hence the continual complaints about the pessimism and hopelessness of contemporary poetry. [21] Hence, conversely, the emphasis on "profound moral harmonies," and praise for "poetic thinkers who have not been conquered by the problems of their age," and who have a "faith in the victory to come." [22] As the older theological and philosophical norms seemed less and less able to fit the case, there developed a vague minimalist criterion that the poet must at least show that (in Kingsley's words) "There is a moral law independent of us," or that "The Powers [that govern the universe] are just." [23]

The early Victorians, men as different as Carlyle and Macaulay, feared the imminent extinction of poetry, as its subject matter and attitudes were crowded out by science and the modern rational spirit. At the same time many placed unprecedented new burdens upon poetry, and numerous figures, major and minor, sought to instruct and lead the age in a time of growing doubt and confusion. [24] The topic I want to center on in the rest of this essay is the not easily understood fact that in the years just before and after 1850, Matthew Arnold and Arthur Hugh Clough, joined temporarily by the older poets Robert Browning and Alfred Tennyson, achieved a relatively successful "poetry of thought" that found new ways in which to explore and to some extent master contemporary "speculative doubt" and spiritual distress. I want to try to understand the rise and fall of this sort of poetry. I am thinking of the bulk of Clough's verse, as well as the "troubled" poetry of Arnold, mostly from the Sturm und Drang period after 1849 and contained in the 1852 volume: such poems as "Empedocles on Etna," "Tristram and Iseult," the Marguerite poems, and two slightly later poems, "The Scholar-Gipsy" and "Stanzas from the Grande Chartreuse." To these I would add two other important poems of 1850: Tennyson's *In Memoriam* and Browning's *Christmas-Eve and Easter-Day*. Significantly, the reviewers very early associated Arnold and Clough with the two older poets.[25]

To understand why the "poetry of 1850" (as I would like to call it in a kind of shorthand) should have risen to excellence then and not before requires a look at the early Victorian period, the time of Tennyson's and Browning's first poems. The most powerful formulator of Victorian demands on the poet was Carlyle, who defined poetry as the expression of "*musical* thought . . . one spoken by a mind that has penetrated into the inmost heart of the thing; detected the utmost mystery of it, namely the *melody* that lies hidden in it; the inward harmony of coherence which is its soul."[26] Now, to speak briefly, by insight into the mystery, melody, and harmony of things Carlyle means substantially what Matthew Arnold was later to call a religious or "interpretative" view of things, in an at least implicitly providential universe.[27] But after the early thirties Carlyle became much less certain that such a view of things was now possible; two centuries of slogging through the Stygian mud of modernity would be required before such a serene and uncontentious vision could be expected. As a result, contemporary poetry was largely mere "dilettantism," so much meter-mongering, unworthy of a serious man's efforts or attention. Hence Carlyle's advice, freely given to all the poets he knew, to give up poetry in favor of prose. *Now* was the time for "Prophecy" and Fact, not "Art" and Fiction. By "Prophecy" Carlyle seems to mean — and again I speak very summarily — the denunciation of contemporary evils, a direct wrestling with the difficulties of the day, and the assertion of a final, if distant, spiritual clarification.

Obviously, the bulk of poets, by definition, did not heed Carlyle's injunctions against poetry literally, although the most serious did indeed take the new "prophetic" role of the modern Man of Letters seriously. But it seems certain that the more or less explicit pattern of experience that critics and poets alike felt called upon to approximate — though in more Christian terms — was that of *Sartor Resartus*: the passage through the rough straits of modern doubt (though pausing to shout No to the temptation of nihilism), through the doldrums of the Byronic Center of Indifference, and on to the affirmation of the Everlasting Yea. That pattern was most anxiously observed in the successive volumes of Tennyson's poetry, by reviewers (often his well-placed friends from Cambridge days) who sought evidences of "development." There had been a time of indecision, near the beginning. Arthur Hallam, in his famous review of 1831, defended Tennyson's earliest "aesthetic" and proto-symbolist poetry as a "sort of magic," depending for its effect on "music" more than on conventional meaning or ideas. In that argument, Hallam denied, against the admirers of Wordsworth, that "the highest species of poetry is the reflective."[28] But we know from "The Palace of Art," begun later in the same year, that Tennyson and Hallam recoiled from that dizzyingly antinomian vista, which was many decades ahead of its time, and climbed back onto the Wordsworthian and Victorian high-road.

In a sense Tennyson had already invented the "subject" of the poetry of 1850, modern doubt and vacillation in a highly personal context, and its hero or anti-hero. For in the 1830 *Poems* had appeared "Supposed Confessions of a Second-Rate Sensitive Mind Not in Unity with Itself" (whose title tells much of its story of a weak-minded nineteenth-century Hamlet).[29] The sympathetic W. J. Fox judged: "Such topics are more in accordance with the spirit and intellect of the age than those about which poetry has been accustomed to be conversant; their adoption will effectually redeem [poetry] from the reproach of being frivolous and enervating."[30] Similar rather ponderous "philosophical" poems of the 1842 volume evoked admiration as further evidence of Tennyson's spiritual progress. His friend Spedding approved that overly long poem, "The Two Voices," as the proper successor to the "Second-Rate Sensitive Mind," and praised Tennyson's manner in precisely Wordsworthian terms: the best poems, Spedding explains, are "a genuine growth of nature, having its root deep in the pensive heart — a heart accustomed to meditate earnestly, and feel truly, upon the prime duties and interests of man."[31] John Sterling, yet another member of the Cambridge Apostles, praised Tennyson's "thoroughly speculative intellect" and judged that in the "reflection proper to an age like ours," only Wordsworth surpasses Tennyson. But the "thought" of Tennyson that Sterling singled out for praise turns out to be that most influential of all Victorian "visions," in "Locksley Hall," ending:

> For I dipt into the future, far as human eye could see,
> Saw the Vision of the world, and all the wonder that would
>   be;

> Saw the heavens fill with commerce, argosies of magic sails,
> Pilots of the purple twilight, dropping down with costly bales;
>
> Heard the heavens fill with shouting, and there rained a ghastly
>   dew
> From the nations' airy navies grappling in the central blue;
>
> Far along the world-wide whisper of the south-wind rushing
>   warm,
> With the standards of the peoples plunging through the
>   thunder-storm;
>
> Till the war-drum throbbed no longer, and the battle-flags
>   were furled
> In the Parliament of man, the Federation of the world.[32]

Still, this was not quite enough to vindicate the "prophet's" mission, as the contemporary chronicles of doubt and spiritual shipwreck began to proliferate. 1848 brought J. C. Hare's two-hundred-page memoir of John Sterling, one of the "failed" talents of Tennyson's circle, who had abandoned the Anglican clergy for a life of literary journalism and verse writing, and who had finally divided his allegiance strangely between Carlyle and Goethe, while never permitting his still serious though undermined religious interests to come to any decisive issue. Sterling's career was immediately seized on by reviewers as "typical of a large and interesting class of intellectual persons in the present day."[33] George Gilfillan, an eager Scottish clerical reader of the signs of the times, pictured Sterling as the representative of "that strange new form of scepticism, which has seized so many of our higher minds." Quite unlike the skeptics of the eighteenth century, this new class, "while sorely perplexed about the supernatural part [of Christianity], and even the genuineness and authenticity of many of the documents, are smit to a passion with the grandeur and heavenliness of the system." (In fact, though he was thinking of Sterling and perhaps Froude, this is an only slightly exaggerated description of the actual skepticism of Arnold and Clough, who were about to break upon the scene.) A sorely perplexed Gilfillan cries out:

Never was there an age when there were so many young, ardent, and gifted spirits — never was there an age when they more required wise guidance. The desideratum may be thus expressed, 'Wanted, a tutor to the rising age; he must be a creedless Christian — full of faith, but full of charity — wise in head and large in heart — a poet and a priest . . .'

This advertisement has not yet been fully answered. The work of Carlyle and Emerson has been principally negative, and it seems now nearly perfected. We wait for a new teacher, who by uniting the spirit of Christianity to that of philosophy, shall present us with a satisfactory whole — with nothing less than which our eager inquirers will rest contented.

The still rather astonishing fact is that, for seventeen years, Tennyson had indeed been working precisely to meet this burdensome demand, in *In Memoriam*, published in 1850. Or at least an exultant Charles Kingsley so explained Tennyson's progress to the world, and perhaps to Tennyson, in one of the most remarkable reviews of the nineteenth century.[34] Kingsley fixed Tennyson in the Carlylean pattern of doubt, suffering, and final victory, rendered now in Christian terms. *In Memoriam*, Kingsley judged,

brings the development of his Muse and of his Creed to a positive and definite point. It enables us to claim one who has been hitherto regarded as belonging to a merely speculative and peirastic [experimental, tentative] school as a willing and deliberate champion of vital Christianity, and of an orthodoxy the more sincere because it has worked upward through the abyss of doubt; the more mighty for good because it justifies and consecrates the aesthetics and the philosophy of the present age.

Kingsley is especially pleased that the young men at the universities, who he claims idolatrize Tennyson, will learn that their hero is "not ashamed of Faith," and that their own needs will be satisfied by rising "from the vague though noble expectations of 'Locksley Hall,' [as Kingsley says, "the poem which has had the most influence on the minds of the young men of our day" — and he quotes the familiar prophetic passage again] to the assured and everlasting facts of the proem to *In Memoriam*." In short, the "earnest seeker," who had already found in "Locksley Hall" a way beyond Byronic and Shelleyan "selfish sorrow," into "faith in the progress of science and civilization, hope in the final triumph of good," could now in *In Memoriam* cap this same forward movement by a "faith in God."

Of course this review deserves a lecture of its own. For one thing, we know that the ringing tones of the prologue to *In Memoriam* are not characteristic of the poem as a whole, in which the recovery from doubt, even in such a central matter as immortality, and the assertion of faith, are far less confident. But apart from Kingsley's not overly scrupulous opportunism, two of his phrases deserve special attention. Kingsley's key claim is that, having expressed in "Locksley Hall" "faith in the progress of science and civilization, hope in the final triumph of good," Tennyson in *In Memoriam* further "justifies and consecrates the aesthetics and the philosophy of the present age." Kingsley's hope — shared by a host of others — was that, having denounced and overcome the mammonism, selfish ambition, and class snobbery inherent in the new activities, Victorians could now achieve a "higher" and more "spiritual" view *of the very same activities*; that is, that with a purified moral vision, colonialism, railways, and the conquest of physical nature would prove to be exactly the vehicles, as they careened down "the ringing grooves of change," for spiritual advancement and obeying the will of God.[35]

No matter that Tennyson had not been so affirmative as this, and that he eventually turned fiercely against the more vulgar contemporary hopes for "progress" through machines and heedless activity. The value of Kingsley's review to us is that it captures in so pure a form the deepest hope of the age, for a satisfying deliverance from modern "doubt" that would not at the same time require a revolution in their habits of thought and action. But the mood of 1850, for some of the most thoughtful and talented among the "cultivated" young, was in fact that of neither "Locksley Hall" nor *In Memoriam*. For them, it was already too late for such morally and intellectually suspect affirmations. For the "poetry of 1850" is essentially the poetry of Arnold and Clough, who, to put it briefly, raised the very issues that Carlyle, Gilfillan, Kingsley, and Tennyson had sought to capture for their own purposes, but found themselves unable to give the desired answers. And it was, above all, the poetry of Oxford. There were of course others. Members of the older generation like Browning and Tennyson, as I have said, were late and temporary participants in the mood; and, as we have seen, after his death the perturbed spirit of Sterling was fought over by men of all parties; and Francis Newman, brother of John Henry, published in 1850 his spiritual autobiography, *Phases of Faith*, the record of a lonely and even eccentric journey into skepticism that caused its own little whirlwind of controversy.

But it was especially those who had felt the full blast of the Oxford Movement, and the jolting rebounds from it after 1845, who experienced the agonies of the forties, a period of disillusionment that can only be compared to the 1790s and the collapse of the Revolutionary hopes.[36]

Apart from the collapse of the Oxford Movement, which, as one friend of Arnold's and Clough's put it, was a storm that "cast the wrecks of [Oxford's] intellects on every shore,"[37] the 1840s saw the height of Chartist agitation and ended with a series of European revolutions. Among the receptive young men at Oxford, a chief force working against a "Christian" solution was precisely the new kind of ethically elevated "spiritual" skepticism, detached from the familiar norms and settings, that found its most powerful expression in Goethe, Carlyle, Emerson, and George Sand. Even more desolating was the emergence, long before Darwin, of a first version of scientific naturalism, symbolized in a book like Robert Chambers's *Vestiges of Creation* (1844). But it happened too, and more disturbingly, that the very forces pressuring these young men toward a more traditional allegiance turned out to be themselves unsafe oracles, once the miasma of doubt had seeped into their consciousness. For example, the curious mixture in John Henry Newman of dogmatic assertion and a deep skepticism about the "rationalizability" of religion contributed, I think, to the detachment from attempts at a rational theology. Even more important, those who had felt the direct influence of Thomas Arnold — notably his son Matthew and Clough — found that the Rugbeian emphasis on honesty and conscientiousness could rebound on itself. The Evangelical concern for "truth" dissolved before Clough's eyes as reality was perceived to be in endless flux, that required a Montaignean concern for the "ondoyant et divers," an almost Paterian eagerness not to miss any nuance of truth. The result was the very reverse of Thomas Arnold's call to decision and action. The reversal is summed up in three of the best lines Clough ever wrote, as the firm voice of Thomas Arnold modulates into a more baffled tone perhaps never previously heard in England:

> I will look straight out, see things, not try to evade them;
> Fact shall be Fact for me, and the Truth the Truth as ever,
> Flexible, changeable, vague, and multiform, and doubtful.[38]

In these circumstances, it is not surprising that a new kind of morally sensitive and "intellectual" hero should appear by mid-century. Tennyson's anguished heroes, up through *Maud* (1855), share the emotional torments of Goethe's suicidal Werther as well as the more "speculative" distress of Goethe's Faust.[39] Bailey's *Festus* (1839), ecstatically greeted by many critics and readers, was a more hysterical (and more Christian)

English Faust.[40] The genealogy of the hero of 1850 would also include, especially for Arnold, a French tradition of "meditation" and "reverie," going back to Rousseau, and including Chateaubriand's *René* and Senancour. And behind all of these suffering intellectual figures is the ever-present Hamlet analogy.[41] Moreover, as Kathleen Tillotson and others have pointed out, the forties saw the rise of the novel of "ideas," fiction with a purpose, as the great new popular form became an instrument in the religious, political, and social wars of the decade.[42] But when it came to presenting actual intellectuals, poetry was far ahead of the novel. Two novels of 1850, Dickens's *David Copperfield* and Thackeray's *Pendennis*, presented intellectuals and artists as heroes, but the actual content of their minds and of their work is evoked in a merely shadowy way.[43] It might be added that, formally and generically, the poetry of 1850 also has close ties to the newly serious "meditative" essay of the period, notably Carlyle's essays of the late twenties and thirties (first collected in 1839), in which the intellectual and spiritual stresses of the time were rehearsed in a body of passionate verbal art, with a strong implicit reference to the speaker's own experience, and with a panoramic explanation of modern history that affected nearly all intellectuals of the age.[44]

The result of this climate of intense unsettlement was that about 1850, a great many people, drawn from two generations, were ready to tell their story. Apart from Arnold and Clough and those already mentioned, perhaps the most ambitious telling was that of James Anthony Froude, whose *Nemesis of Faith* fluttered the dovecotes of Oxford in 1849. But Froude's oracles were highly ambiguous, and though the book has remained an interesting document of nineteenth-century "unconversion," its uncertain literary and spiritual power did not allow it to rise into genuine authority and clarity. Carlyle spoke for a great many more conservative readers when he complained: "What on earth is the use of a wretched mortal's vomiting up all his interior crudities, dubitations, and spiritual agonising bellyaches, into the view of the public, and howling tragically, 'See!' "[45]

What I want to suggest here are some of the qualities that enabled the best poetry of Arnold and Clough, as well as *In Memoriam* and *Christmas-Eve and Easter-Day*, to rise above the dubitations and howlings of the day, and to turn "spiritual . . . bellyaches" into permanently and independently valuable art.[46] Of course it would take several essays to characterize "the poetry of 1850" adequately. Let me here merely suggest in summary form some of its major characteristics and the reasons for thinking it deserving to be called in a special sense "the poetry of thought."

The four poets of 1850 — Arnold, Clough, Tennyson, and Robert Browning — do in the poems we have mentioned form a distinguishable group, concerned with a common set of problems. In fact, an argument might be made that there was a more or less conscious dialogue among them. For example, I believe that Arnold's ironic "praise" of modern activism in "The Grande Chartreuse" (lines 163–68) is a conscious response to the much-quoted visionary lines in "Locksley Hall." Further, it has been suggested that Arnold's "Empedocles" is a kind of counterstatement to Browning's *Paracelsus*, and Browning's "Cleon" seems even more clearly a rebuttal of "Empedocles."[47] One of the most important, and too little understood, topics of the age is the elaborate interchange of poetry between Arnold and Clough, including Clough's only recently published indecent parody of Arnold's "Resignation."[48] Finally, there is evidence that Browning's meeting with Clough in Florence, just after Clough had written "Epi-Strauss-ium" and "Easter Day, Naples, 1849," may have propelled Browning into the writing of *Christmas-Eve and Easter-Day*.[49]

Next, in an age saddled with an unnourishing range of philosophical options and a decayed and increasingly irrelevant theology, the poetry of 1850, supplemented perhaps by Wordsworth, was a vehicle for ethical and quasi-philosophical reflection better than what the "professionals" were then providing. Though we tend today with some justice to deplore the various moral and religious burdens placed on Victorian poetry, and though there have been numerous discussions about whether these poets can be considered *original* thinkers, in the best sense such poetry provided a "service" to the culture. The highly sensitive John Campbell Shairp, who had himself gone through the Oxford ordeal of the forties and had returned to an unsectarian Christian orthodoxy, judged in 1867 that recent literature had indeed taken over the work of the "regular philosophers." As he put it, of late literature had "broken into deeper ground of sentiment and reflection," by "an unveiling of the most inward . . . feelings" of men, and that "This bringing to light of layers of consciousness hitherto concealed . . . has . . . enriched our literature with new wealth of moral content."[50] Despite the old-fashioned rhetoric of this passage, I for one thoroughly agree. The poetry of 1850 was in the first place a poetry of self-revelation and self-definition, a thinking out of philosophical problems in a highly personal context. It involved genuine originality in the sheer range of new thoughts, new arguments, and new emotions it discerned. Moreover, because of its complex examination of "fundamental" issues that were also the pressing issues of the moment, and because of the new demands made on the reader's close cooperation in the act of understanding, it inevitably became a mode of self-understanding for the reader as well.

The experiment involved was to convert "speculation" into "meditation," and "meditation" into "wisdom" and perhaps a kind of partial affirmation. By "speculation" I mean that the poetry of 1850 chose for its characteristic subject matter exactly those disturbing "new" topics introduced into English poetry by "the Satanic School" in the age of Byron. I refer also to a subtle and persistent tie that developed between speculation on "forbidden" topics like first principles, a "Byronic" skepticism and cynicism as to the worth of human values and activities, and an abiding contemporary preoccupation with the problems of self-involvement, self-analysis, self-consciousness, and self-revelation. To this was increasingly added the special problem of troublesome "modern" thought, a scientifically supported naturalism that steadily pushed aside the teleologies of the older metaphysics. None of these were of course strictly "new" subjects; many of them were familiar to the Greeks and to the writers of the Old Testament. But they became more acute and moved to the forefront of human consciousness through the nineteenth century, as the "external" framework of society and its institutions, as well as the most basic human relations, seemed suddenly without support and were subjected to close scrutiny and "analysis." We have learned to call this situation the death or disappearance of God.

By the conversion into "meditation" I mean the novel attempt to treat this troublesome subject matter of the pathology of thought, hitherto either inimical to poetry or made the vehicle of an antitheological view of life, in a new spirit, in order to wring poetry from what Arnold called the "unpoetrylessness" of the modern situation itself. The attitude is to be clearly distinguished from that of the more positive skepticisms of the eighteenth-century *philosophes*, of Byron, and of Swinburne in the next decade. For the poetry of 1850 — though the four poets range from the nondogmatic Christianity of Browning to the clearly post-theological position of Arnold — is everywhere conducted in an antirationalistic and

even "conservative" spirit. Their implicit shared program, and their originality, is the attempt to exorcise the demon of doubt by "taking
thought," by "thinking about thinking," by the most grimly truthful
inspection of traditional moral and intellectual complacencies — a species
of homeopathic medicine — precisely in order to achieve a "higher"
point of view from which to comprehend and master personal "division"
and intellectual doubt.

It is important to stress that the age generally resisted this mixing of
intellectual modes. Carlyle set the tone for reviewers of all parties when,
in "Characteristics" (1831), he contrasted "the region of meditation"
with both "Metaphysical speculation" and unhealthy self-consciousness.
The approved words, *meditation* and *contemplation*, had become standard
from the time of the first defenders of Wordsworth. Over against this
desired ruminative and reflective tone, the critics constantly opposed a
battery of negative terms, notably "speculation" and "skepticism," along
with their even more disreputable cousins, "doubt" and "unbelief."
"Argument," it was agreed, was not the proper mode for poetry;
"analysis" was as thoroughly suspect as it became later in Mill's *Autobiography*; and the word "philosophy" itself became one of the outlaw terms
as it took on a disturbing connotation, implying "radical" and unsettling
thought. Even the word "criticism" took on a dark hue, and mid-
Victorians had a great deal of difficulty in welcoming satire, parody,
irony, and what they called "casuistry." The reviewers were equally
nervous when confronted with the "confessional" mode so central in
Romantic poetry, which was now frequently rejected as overly "self-
conscious" or "unhealthily introspective."[51] In short, the climate of critical opinion was far from preparing readers for this new and "mixed"
mode I am attempting to describe, since the subject of the poetry of 1850
was precisely that melancholy "return of the mind upon itself" described
by Hallam in 1831, precisely that skeptical "dialogue of the mind with
itself," "the allegory of the state of one's own mind," which by late 1852
Matthew Arnold was, in a terrible act of self-suppression, attempting to
put out of his poetry.[52] What they had sought to recover, in effect, was
some share of the Wordsworthian "meditative" mode, the "philosophic
mind," "Reason in her most exalted mood," even when — as with
Arnold and Clough — their philosophical views should logically have
forbidden it.

Editors continue to call the Victorians anti-intellectual, and each of the

four poets of 1850 in one way or another did finally put aside the dialogue
of the mind with itself, in favor of a solution or at least an attitude that
goes beyond reason — "the heart," as they learned, "has its reasons."
Their novelty, and their integrity, lie in their having prefaced these conclusions by a remarkably full inspection of the intellectual impediments
involved. Their range of moods is, finally, neither that of Voltaire nor of
Montaigne, but of Pascal; though they did not know him well, they were
in effect aware of the force of his dictum, "Seeing too much to deny and
too little to trust," and in the great new extension of cosmic space and
time, they had experienced the metaphysical shudder, Pascal's version of
the dangling man who is terrified "to see himself suspended in a body
which nature has given him, between the two abysses of the infinite and
of nothingness" — in the profoundest sense, between two worlds.[53]
Their thought, then, is far from being a hindrance to our four poets,[54]
and long before English had words for the new experiences, they had
each, in a different configuration but in each case with an adequate
intellectual foundation, explored the personal correlatives of doubt — the
pain, alienation, and dread that are what we call the "existential" basis
and background of all human consciousness. And they did so without
that indifference to the communal dimension that characterizes much
modern existentialist thought.

With more time, we might explore the revealing conjunction of
specific themes and attitudes in the four poets of 1850. Apart from the
pained interrogation of "metaphysical" and "transcendental" topics
promptly noted by the critics, the poets explored other key issues of the
day in revealingly similar ways. Like the novelists of the period, they
could on occasion affirm the redemptive and healing power of love and
marriage, the supreme mid-Victorian solution for doubt and irresolution.
But they are all, if in different ways, surprisingly unorthodox, and in this
they go well beyond the bulk of the novelists, in realistically scrutinizing
the emotions and states of love, and their attitudes could range variously
across the ironic, the humorous, the erotic, the skeptical, the antinomian,
or the despairing. Even more revealing would be a study of their complex attitudes toward society and participation in the work of the contemporary world. That is, they were all, in varying degrees, both of their
time and highly critical of it; they all accepted one aspect of the prophet's
role, that of the judgment of the age according to a higher or "religious"
standard. Not even Tennyson, as I have suggested, comfortably ac-

quiesced in Kingsley's demand for sanctifying the age's program of action and aggrandizement.

This deep ambivalence about action helps explain, not only why the poetry of 1850 could not be maintained, but, more broadly, why imaginative literature as a whole gave up by and large the newfound and still inchoate aspiration (in Walter Bagehot's words) to be "a deep thing, a teaching thing, the most surely and wisely elevating of human things"[55] — that is, literature's bold proposal to assume a role of spiritual and intellectual *leadership* in the new society. For although all four poets used poetry as a means of achieving their own spiritual equipoise, the patterns of their experience, like that of *Sartor Resartus*, transcended the merely personal and were implicitly "representative" experiences of the age; as a result, their various solutions inevitably struck readers as possible models for coming to terms with the *mal du siècle*. But the confrontation with "self" in the poets of 1850 remained immobilizingly interiorized; not one of the four poets was able to create a convincing example of high character in fruitful relationship to modern society. The Romantic poets had, in the collapse of the Revolutionary hopes, despaired of achieving an earthly paradise, and had turned inward in search of a precariously maintained spiritual or mental equilibrium that had continually to outface the specter of alienation and paralysis.[56] A similar realization seems to me to explain much of the mood of 1850 and its aftermath. The poets, along with Dickens (who pursued this realization even farther than the poets) and soon after, Ruskin, sought to endorse the Victorian hope for the restoration of true community through benevolent *action*. But these hopes founder in a deteriorating and darkening critical situation — dark amidst even the excessive brightness of the Crystal Palace. Growing doubt about the possibility of social renewal, along with a version of Empedocles' failure to achieve high self-consciousness in a healthy interaction with external influences and society, led the literary culture toward aestheticism and the reality of the artist immured in a cork-lined room. This "failure" of the experiment of 1850, even before the culture at large could grasp its intent or significance, had anticipated that "terminal" cultural crisis from which, I believe, we have never succeeded in extricating ourselves.

Perhaps most revealing are the interrelated questions of the proper style for modern poetry and the use of "modern" ideas in poetry. Here, the four divide, but even their dividing helps define the issues of 1850.

Arnold and Tennyson do not break with the tradition of "beauty" that dominated English poetry from the time of Spenser and Milton; in effect, both find an elevated style, almost in detachment from "content," precisely the "means" for establishing the new "meditative" mode. Clough and Browning, in contrast, are far more radical, and anticipate twentieth-century experiments, in implying that beauty — which for Victorian readers was virtually the "poetry" of poetry — is a kind of premature and illegitimate *escape* from intellectual perplexity and the contrarieties of ordinary experience. Both Clough and Browning could of course, on occasion, rise to a kind of sublime serenity and simplicity. But perhaps Browning's notorious "obscurity" should be regarded almost as a strategy for not giving in too easily to the prophetic demands of the age, for maintaining a kind of reserved place where the most "dangerous" thoughts could be entertained without being forced to premature conclusions and affirmations. Similarly, Clough's refusal "to clothe [the Deity] in any mythological or objective form"[57] is of a piece with his refusal to exploit the resources of style.

Following again, I think, the lead of Carlyle in *Sartor Resartus*, Clough and Browning experimented with a poetry laced with irony, the grotesque, even the earthy — that mixing of levels of style and perception, even in "sacred" subjects — that so disturbed contemporary critics. Religiously the grating tone of Browning and the unadorned texture of Clough seem to imply a desire to establish a region of discourse apart from both the softer and more complacent side of Victorian pietism and the brutal simplicities of contemporary moralism. Clough in effect refused to be the mere "artist" and belletrist that John Sterling had tried to make himself; he attempted to remain "the poet and the thinker" together,[58] at whatever cost to his art. For both Clough and Browning, "poetry" itself — the tradition of beauty, euphony, and "movement" in verse — was, in a startling reversion to the Puritan standard, a kind of "temptation," obscuring direct engagement with truth. John Addington Symonds's description of Clough's "Easter Day" and its Wordsworthian avoidance of the "allurements" of art might apply equally to Browning: "The poem owes nothing to its rhythm, or its rhymes, or the beauty of its imagery, or the music of its language. . . . But the emotion is so intense, and so thoroughly expressed — the thought is so vigorous and vital in every line — that the grandest poetry is wrought out of the commonest materials, apparently without effort, and by the mere intensity of the poet's will."[59]

Matthew Arnold reflected on these matters more fully and more explicitly than the other poets of 1850. The story is now a familiar one.[60] During the period of their greatest creativity, Arnold's letters to Clough keep up a drumfire of criticism of Clough's attempt to go "to the bottom of an object," or "to *solve* the Universe," which excites merely "curiosity and reflexion."[61] Against the "multitudinousness" of Clough and Browning, Arnold insists on the need for "an Idea of the world," and upholds the standards of beauty, form, sensuousness, and the "grouping of objects" (*LC*, 98–99). Arnold pursued this joint attack on controversial thought and lack of beauty beyond the grave, in "Thyrsis," where he rather cruelly implies that Clough's poetic — and even actual — death was caused by his taking on the "stormy note" of modern intellectual conflict. And in general, Arnold's prose criticism also depreciates the role of ideas in poetry.[62]

Though in fact Arnold resembled Clough in condemning the richness of diction in the Elizabethans, Keats, Shelley, and Tennyson, and claims that his own ideal of style is that of a Wordsworthian "plainness of speech" (*LC*, 124; October 1852), he was permanently preoccupied with "the grand moral effects produced by style," as the "expression of the nobility of the poet's character," and declared that Sophocles' style "supports me and in some degree subjugates destiny" (*LC*, 101) — again suggesting, as I think Tennyson hoped, that elevation of style was to work its own spiritual effect, establishing an emotional and intellectual standing ground quite above the level of contemporary conflict and opinion. These complications in Arnold's poetics tend to simplify after 1853, as he gave up the struggle to keep faith with his own deepest perceptions.[63] But it has long been evident that most of the supposed defects that Arnold rather coldly pursued in Clough were the problems of his own best and most troubled poetry; and it is somehow comforting to hear Arnold, in the very act of giving up his own "stormy note," responding to, while virtually acknowledging, Clough's charge that Arnold's own poetry is unstrung and hopeless: "But woe was upon me if I analysed not my situation: and Werter[,] Réné[,] and such like[,] none of them analyse the modern situation in its true *blankness* and *barrenness*, and *unpoetrylessness*" (*LC*, 126; December 1852). These are some of the matters that a closer inspection of the situation of poetry in 1850 would reveal.

But the poetry of 1850 — the attempt to "meditate" and reflect on the deepest human questions in a richly personal context, and yet to achieve a standpoint distinct from that of the older orthodoxy *and* that of modern secularity and mere "denial" — passed. Tennyson and Browning found the conditions for this kind of poetry only in a very limited segment of their highly varied work.[64] It was Clough and Matthew Arnold who, in rather different ways, lived out the program of, as one contemporary critic called it, the poetry of the new "irreligious religiosity." But both ended very shortly, in a kind of "silence," their personal and poetic resources spent; perhaps no one could have gone very much further with the "poetry of skepticism."

But this is not to say that a taste — indeed, a need — for such a poetry did not exist. There is a deep pathos in reading, for example, the intensely felt essays of the 1850s and 1860s by David Masson, the Scottish critic, as he seeks to define the qualities of a jointly "meditative" and "speculative" poetry, brooding on the deepest questions regarding "man, his origin, and his destiny," and conducted in a broadly Christian but undogmatic context. To join Shakespeare and Wordsworth, his models of "melancholy" pensiveness, he eagerly welcomed precisely Browning's *Christmas-Eve and Easter-Day*, *In Memoriam*, and Clough's "speculative theology."[65]

But while the need remained — and to some extent remains still — the conditions for such a poetic mode passed quickly. The universities and the culture at large were moving rapidly toward a much blanker and more terminal skepticism, and poetry soon gave up the attempt to master, in a joint act of imagination and undogmatic intellection, the spiritual and intellectual problems of the age. The testimony of Henry Sidgwick, the Cambridge philosopher, is particularly valuable in this respect. As he said late in the century, after 1860 and the kinds of doubt symbolized by *Essays and Reviews*, his own views and those of his fellow undergraduates were already less Christian than the views expressed in *In Memoriam*. In fact, Clough's poetry was especially satisfying as the expression of Sidgwick's own non-Christian theism. But *In Memoriam* remained important nevertheless, as he explains, at a level *below* "the difference between Theism and Christianity," that is (and here his language is close to Masson's), "in the unparalleled combination of intensity of feeling with

comprehensiveness of view and balance of judgment, shown in presenting the *deepest* needs and perplexities of humanity." But in retrospect, he
sees with dismay that the sought-for freedom from the "Hebrew old
clothes" of the older theology had proven a doubtful boon: it was now
the day of "atheistic science," and "the faith in God and immortality,
which we had been struggling to clear from superstition, suddenly seems
to be *in the air*," and he now felt that in seeking "a firm basis for this
[residual] faith" they were once again "in the midst of the 'fight with
death' which *In Memoriam* so powerfully presents." [66]

For myself, the unity of the poetry of 1850 not only goes "deeper down
than the difference between Theism and Christianity," but it encompass-
es all those who (whether or not they make a positive theistic affirmation) shared a world of discourse — unquestionably drawn, however
fragmentarily, from the older culture — on precisely those "*deepest*
needs and perplexities of humanity," while it excludes those for whom
(in Arnold's words) the question of "faith" is simply "a dead time's
exploded dream," and the pain of nineteenth-century loss "a past mode,
an outworn theme." There have been later poets of "thought." Thomas
Hardy, a more "advanced" skeptic who learned a good deal from the
form and subject matter of Clough, tore a pained music out of the ancient
conundrums. William Butler Yeats, despite his early deprecation of ideas
and his greater separation from the older religious tradition, resumed
some of the supreme "existential" themes in a body of fierce rhetoric.
And T. S. Eliot, in *Four Quartets*, explored the paradoxes of the old
theology in a highly original "meditative" strain. But they are exceptions, and such themes have tended to find their way instead into the
often semi-poetic reflections of twentieth-century philosophers:
phenomenologists, existentialists, personalists.

Swinburne spoke for the new mood of the sixties, and there is no
doubt some justice in his ringing scorn for what he called this recent
"poetry of the intellect." In 1867 he insisted that verse is not the medium
of "reluctant doubt, of half-hearted hope and half-incredulous faith"; and
he took shrewd aim at the fact that such poetic agonies had been under-
gone, even by freethinkers, as if there was "nothing before Christ or
beyond Judaea" (Dawson, pp. 168, 165). He was right; the poetry of 1850
was very English, very provincial, lacking in any final boldness; and in
the case of Tennyson and Arnold, at least, it was too solemn and unironic
for the taste of a later generation.

But Swinburne does not, I think, have the last word. In the preceding year, John Morley struggled to express his resistance to Swinburne's own kind of poetry. Morley is a valuable witness, since as a freethinker himself he was not preoccupied with the "blasphemy and paganism" that troubled more conventional readers. With no theological ax to grind, Morley nevertheless takes exactly the Pascalian or existential view of man's situation as his standpoint, and says that there are two ways in which the poet can treat the terror of existence. "He can transfigure [men's] baseness of fear into true poetic awe, which shall underlie their lives as a lasting record of solemn rapture. Or else he can [like Swinburne] jeer and mock at them." [67] This search for what Morley calls "enlarged meditation" and "impassioned thought" obviously has little to do with one's explicit belief, but rather with an openness to a special range of experience and "intellectual" emotion, facilitated by submitting onself to a process of reflectiveness that can only be called an aspect of character. Morley again invokes Pascal as well as Novalis, in a later review, contrasting Byron's "elegant" melancholy with "the deep and penetrating subjective melancholy" of those alive to the tragedy of the human situation. [68]

In short, something *had* gone out of English poetry, and with surprising swiftness: a seriousness, a depth, an adultness. [69] A number of recent critics, including Frank Kermode and Meyer Abrams, have called for a post-symbolist and "public" poetry that can "think," a poetry in which men can speak to men again about matters of shared importance. [70] Despite their own solemnities and confusions, the poets of 1850 (as I have been calling them) strove for something very similar: a fullness of self-revelation that was not the mere impertinence of personal confession, and which linked itself with intellectual themes of high importance. As modern readers we are convinced that literature is somehow a special mode of "knowledge"; I would add that the poetry of 1850 demonstrated that, even in areas of thought previously reserved for formal philosophy, poetry could, without losing its own earthly body in a mass of abstraction, become not only a *vehicle* of knowledge and understanding but a genuine *source*. [71]

It should be made clear that although the poetry of 1850 could only be sustained for a short time, Tennyson alone found his audience at once; English readers were not by and large ready in 1850 for Browning, Arnold, or Clough, and each had gradually to win a newly serious audience in the succeeding decades. The chief originality of all four poets helps define their continuing claim upon us. Though variously within and without traditional religion, they were defining, virtually for the first time in English, the complex intellectual and emotional crosscurrents thereafter present to the religious consciousness of almost all sensitive and reflective people. I refer to the inevitability of "doubt" in all acts of faith and belief, the deep underlying presence of "skepticism" as the backdrop of all such conscious affirmations. Or perhaps it is more accurate to reverse the figure, and say that the poets of 1850 in effect discovered and conveyed the fact that affirmation in the modern world will necessarily be only intermittently conscious and for the most part will remain "latent," while across the more perceptible levels of consciousness march and countermarch the confused armies of the modern night battle. For such reasons, all four poets continue to speak to many contemporary readers, in a peculiarly intense way, especially to the large number of men and women who, even as we enter the last quarter of the twentieth century, find themselves permanent residents of the no-man's-land between two worlds, exiled from the older culture yet resistant to the blank and "poetryless" secularity of the future.

The Warfare

of Conscience

with Theology

Josef L. Altholz

T he most important thing to remember about religion in Victorian England is that there was an awful lot of it. The nineteenth century was marked by a revival of religious activity unmatched since the days of the Puritans. This religious revival shaped that code of moral behavior, or rather that infusion of all behavior with moralism, which we still call, rightly or wrongly, "Victorianism." Above all, religion occupied a place in the public consciousness, a centrality in the intellectual life of the age, which it had not had a century before and did not retain in the twentieth century.

That is the second important thing to remember about the Victorian religious revival: that it did not last. It was not merely that the churches lost, or rather had never had, the growing working classes of their increasingly urbanized society; they could hardly be blamed for being defeated by demographics. But the striking thing about the decline of the Victorian religious revival is that it took place, in the latter decades of the century, within that very middle class whose virtues it sanctified. Most importantly, those special segments of the middle class which served as culture-bearers to their age and shapers of the next, the intellectual and professional classes, had their faith eroded in a distinctive and decisive manner.

The crisis of intellectual faith, which may be dated about 1860, had a deceptive appearance of suddenness. The 1850s had been a period of relative religious calm, in which unquestioning churchgoers had little to trouble them except the growth of Popery and ritualism, the dissidence of Dissent, and the strange absence of the poor from the churches. Then in 1859 appeared Darwin's *Origin of Species*, the most famous but not the most important of the challenges to faith, which questioned both the literal accuracy of the first chapters of Genesis and the argument from design for the existence of God. In 1860 appeared a book entitled *Essays and Reviews*, six of whose seven authors were clergymen of the Church of England, which brought to Britain the techniques and startling hypotheses of German biblical criticism. In 1862 the Mosaic authorship of the Pentateuch was denied by no less than a bishop, John William Colenso. In 1864 and 1865 the courts decided that nothing could be done about these subversives within the Church, and in 1869 one of the Essayists and Reviewers became a bishop. Naturalistic, non-miraculous lives of Jesus appeared: Renan's *Vie de Jésus* in 1863, J. R. Seeley's *Ecce Homo* in 1865. Meanwhile the scientists pressed their challenge: in 1863 Huxley's *Man's Place in Nature* and Lyell's *Antiquity of Man*, and finally in 1871 Darwin's *Descent of Man*, stripped away the uniqueness of mankind. To retain a traditional Bible-centered faith in the 1870s, an educated man had either to deny the findings of biblical criticism and natural science, supported by an increasing mass of evidence, or else to re-create that faith on a new basis which few were able to construct.

Because this crisis was brought on and highlighted by challenges external to orthodox faith — because the normal posture of the churches during the crisis was one of denial and resistance in the face of the triumphant advance of science and criticism — it is natural to see these events in terms of the inevitable progress of the human mind and the advancement of science. Certainly, if we understand by "science" what the Germans call *Wissenschaft*, not merely the natural sciences but social and humane studies scientifically treated, what transpired was a victory for science. This is the traditional approach to the subject, immortalized in the phrase of Andrew Dickson White, "the warfare of science with theology." This approach presupposes a clear and direct confrontation between geological, biological, and historical science on the one hand and religion on the other, with science ultimately prevailing because of its intrinsic merits.

I wish to propose an alternative approach, which treats the conflict not as a struggle of faith against its external enemies, but as a crisis within religion itself. The real point of the conflict was not the challenge of science but the response of religion. The scientific challenges laid bare certain weaknesses of the Victorian religious revival, and the victory of science was largely due to elements within the religious position. The most important such factor was the latent conflict between the sensitivity of conscience stimulated by the religious revival and the crude and harsh statement of the dogmas to which such sensitive consciences were expected to give their allegiance.[1] The spokesmen of orthodox faith narrowed the ground on which Christianity was to be defended and allowed their scientific opponents to appear more honest than themselves. In these conflicts, the position of orthodox doctrine was, as presented by its upholders, not only less valid but less moral than that of irreligious science. As events unfolded, not merely the intellect but the moral sense, particularly the sense of truthfulness, revolted against orthodoxy. This may be called "the warfare of conscience with theology."[2]

It is possible to analyze this conflict as a "class struggle" of sorts, if this be understood not as a struggle between classes but as a struggle within the middle class, between the clergy on the one hand and the secular professions on the other, for the minds of the rising generation.[3] The nineteenth century saw the rise and definition of the professions, including the clerical profession itself. The eighteenth-century clergyman could not be said to have had a vocation. He was a country gentleman, or hoped to be one; his few religious duties left him ample time to mingle in society, to be a magistrate, a naturalist, an essayist, or a sportsman. If he did not much improve his world, he was very much a part of it. But the evangelical revival changed all that. The evangelicals (the "serious" Christians, as they called themselves) insisted that clergymen be serious, attend to their religious duties, and expand the definition of those duties until they were capable of absorbing their entire time and energy: two sermons on Sunday, weekday services, frequent visiting of the poor. To this the tractarians added the sense of a distinct vocation and separation of the priesthood from the laity. By the 1840s, even among those who were neither evangelical nor tractarian, the professional ideal of the clergy had won out.

All Victorians were earnest; it was important to be earnest; but clergymen were distinctively and preeminently earnest. They hunted not, nor did they attend the theater; they wore black unrelieved by the slightest hint of gray; and from the 1860s they adopted that ultimate badge of clericalism, the dog collar. Such a hard-working clergy accomplished much and deserved to have accomplished more. But this professionalism came at a price. Fully occupied by work which was absorbing but specialized, concentrating their minds on the "one thing only" that mattered, most of the clergy withdrew from that wider intellectual life of England of which they had once been a central part. At the very time that Coleridge formulated his ideal of the "clerisy" to embrace all the educated classes, the clergy was separating from the "clerisy" and withdrawing behind the impregnable fortress of Holy Scripture and Paley's *Natural Theology*. A closed mind had become, as much as the black coat, part of the professional equipment of a clergyman.

At the same time the secular professions had also developed their distinctive specialized training and functions and esprit de corps, and the physical and natural sciences, though still largely in the hands of amateurs, were beginning to develop similarly professional standards. Now what distinguishes these sciences, and their aspiring brethren in the social sciences, is a preeminent concern with fact — fact that is verifiable and applicable. To the gentlemen of the factual professions, it was galling to see the precedence and prestige accorded to a clergy which had come to define itself by the blinkers it wore. In their struggle to impress scientific ideas, and, more important, the idea of science itself on the minds of the rising generation of intellectual young men, it was inevitable that they would come into conflict with the obstacle of clerical narrowness. And in this conflict they found themselves armed with a weapon which even clergymen were taught to fear, the weapon of truth.

It is difficult to avoid the conclusion that these rival professionalisms — the growth of an Anglican clericalism coinciding with the awakening of a self-conscious intellectual laity — provide necessary predisposing conditions for the conflict that was to develop. However, there are certain difficulties which limit the usefulness of this class analysis in terms of conflicting elements in the intellectual middle classes. The first arises from the professionalism of science itself: scientific facts require scientific minds to appreciate them, and they could have only a peripheral effect as long as education remained classical rather than scientific. Second, as we shall see, the heaviest blows to clerical orthodoxy were dealt, not by scientific outsiders, but by dissident clergymen, those who felt entrapped by the narrowness of their profession and sought to break out to a broader culture. After all, Lyell's geology and Darwin's biology, even if absolutely true, affected only a few chapters of Genesis, leaving the rest of the Bible untouched; but biblical criticism, even in the hands of devout clergymen, affected the whole text and inspiration and authority of the Bible and perhaps of the Christian faith. Most important, however, is the fact that what ultimately alienated the rising intellectual generation was, not the external challenge of science or criticism, but the response of the spokesmen of orthodox religion. It was the failure of orthodoxy, not the strengths of heresy or infidelity, which lost the intellectual classes to religion.

The orthodoxy of Protestant England, common to Anglicans and most Dissenters, was the product of the evangelical revival. It is impossible to overstate the pervasiveness and intensity of the moralism which the evangelicals had infused into every aspect of Victorian life. Indeed, what separates us from the Victorians is, not so much the difference in our moral judgments, as their readiness to make moral judgments and our readiness to suspend them. Our objectivity is their immorality. The sensitivity of conscience thus produced, the self-consciousness and introspection thus fostered, were awesome things; and the moral crises which are so frequent in both the literature and the life of the educated classes did not always pass through the approved channels of evangelical conversion and a strenuous but safely moral life.

One of the moral virtues most frequently inculcated (and regarded as distinctively English) was the virtue of truth. Now truth is a two-edged sword. For one thing, there was a fundamental confusion in the Victorian concept of "truth." In one sense the word refers to objective truth, the factual reality; in another sense it means truthfulness, that is, the honesty of a person. It is characteristic of the Victorians that they were more interested in truthfulness than in truth; they were more concerned with the moral character of the speaker than with the factual correctness of his statement. A result of this attitude is that the debates over biblical criticism have a curious ad hominem character. Thus, criticism is opposed because it seems to impugn the truthfulness of God as the author of the Bible;[4] or the Essayists and Reviewers are condemned as dishonest because the conclusions they reached contradicted the promises they made at their ordinations. The trouble with this mode of reasoning is that it draws attention to personalities and away from the actual issues of debate; it is the practice of evasion in the name of honesty.

This practice was not uncommon among the clergy. It contributed, in the middle decades, to a growing (though rarely articulated) distrust of their preaching, a loss of influence which paralleled their increasing professionalism. This is best stated by a Broad Church clergyman, Arthur Stanley, later Dean of Westminster:

> I believe that the besetting sin of the clerical profession — that to which its peculiar temptations may lead — is indifference to strict truth. . . . There is also a habit of using words without meaning, or with only a half-belief, or for the sake of a convenient argument and of filling up an awkward gap, or with a love of things established . . . which leads in part, I am convinced, to that deep-rooted indifference to sermons, and that vast separation between faith and outward belief, and that distrust of all that the clergy say, and that intolerable arrogance which so many of them feel towards lay people.[5]

Stanley's friend Benjamin Jowett put it more concisely: "I never hear a sermon scarcely which does not seem equally divided between truth and falsehood."[6] Preaching, to be sure, has problems as well as temptations; there are a limited number of conclusions which may safely be arrived at in an unlimited number of sermons, and facility in achieving this may correlate negatively with religious depth. By 1860 it was noticed that the really ablest men were no longer proceeding to holy orders; and Frederick Temple, like Jowett an Essayist and Reviewer, was struck by the "extraordinary reticence"[7] on religious matters of the young men at the universities.

Part of this reticence, this reluctance to express and examine doubts and perplexities in religion, was the frequently inculcated belief that religious doubt was in itself sinful. The duty of avoiding doubt, whatever intellectual operations might be needed to accomplish this, was put with characteristically eloquent crudity by Samuel Wilberforce, later Bishop of Oxford:

> Whilst irreverence and doubt are the object of your greatest fear; whilst you would glady retain a childlike and unquestioning reverence by abasing, if need were, your understanding, rather than gain any knowledge at the hazard of your reverence; you are doubtless in God's hands, and therefore safe. . . . Fly, therefore, rather than contend; fly to known truths.[8]

As his biographer remarked, "In an age that pressed desperately for the answers to all sorts of questions, Wilberforce believed they were better left unasked."[9]

One reason for the non-asking of questions was the belief that doubt was not only sinful but that it rendered the doubter miserable in this life as well, the absence of faith producing emptiness and unhappiness. Men of much faith projected what they would feel if deprived of their faith; and no factual evidence of serene agnostics and happy atheists could shake their conviction that doubt was a state of misery. Even the usually sensible Newman could exclaim, "Consider the miseries of wives and mothers losing their faith in Scripture."[10] It became a duty to prevent this, to suppress one's own doubts and discourage the doubts of others. But could the rising generation, self-consciously devoted to truth but increasingly aware of disturbing facts, be expected indefinitely to contain their doubts and profess an assurance which was decreasingly real? This was the point of tension, the poison in the theological atmosphere which had to come out.

The issue on which the intensity of Victorian religion first began to turn inward on itself was, not an external challenge of science or criticism, but a felt conflict between the morality which the evangelicals had cultivated and the theological doctrines which they taught. Victorian morality was not merely stern, it was also humanitarian; though the evangelicals doubted whether the mass of mankind could be saved, they preached the duty of active benevolence; they freed the slaves and improved the conditions of factory labor. There was already a discrepancy here between the essentially otherwordly character of their faith and the contemporary aspirations, in which they often shared, towards the progress and improvement of human society. More important, the humanitarian values thus engendered were incompatible with the commonplace theology of the day. Here we must note that the word *theology* is and was used loosely; nineteenth-century England was not a home of systematic theology as Germany was; the best of its religious thinkers were self-taught amateurs. The theology espoused by most evangelicals, and generally accepted by most others, was a sort of unsystematic and semiconscious quasi-Calvinism, positing the Atonement rather than the Incarnation as the central fact of Christianity, and stressing the sterner and harsher Christian doctrines: original sin, reprobation, vicarious atonement, eternal punishment. The unbalanced emphasis of these essentially unattractive themes was bound to come into conflict with the sentimental and humanitarian spirit of the age, itself largely a product of the religious revival.

The conflict between humane ethics and rigorous dogma was responsible for some of the more spectacular losses of faith in the 1840s. How could a benevolent and sensitive conscience accept the morality of a Jehovah who behaved, as the young Darwin put it, like a "revengeful tyrant"[11] and who condemned the majority of his human creatures to an eternity of torment disproportionate to their wickedness or based on no personal fault at all? These were the issues which provoked theological crises in the 1850s. F. D. Maurice, perhaps the most prophetic mind of the century, was deprived of his professorship in 1853 for questioning the eternity of punishment. Jowett's 1855 commentary on St. Paul, denouncing the conventional presentation of the Atonement, brought a storm of criticism foreshadowing the later denunciation of *Essays and Reviews*. Let me quote Jowett to show the depth of the indignation which Victorian quasi-Calvinism could produce in a usually calm mind: "God is represented as angry with us for what we never did; He is ready to inflict a disproportionate punishment on us for what we are; He is satisfied by the sufferings of His Son in our stead. . . . The imperfection of human law is transferred to the Divine." After this Jowett "cannot but fear whether it be still possible so to teach Christ as not to cast a shadow on the holiness and truth of God."[12]

The erosion of faith caused by this ethical revulsion against cruel dogmas crudely stated is perhaps the clearest example of what I have called "the warfare of conscience with theology."[13] The classic statement of this revulsion is that of John Stuart Mill: "I will call no being good, who is not what I mean when I apply that epithet to my fellow creatures, and if such a being can sentence me to hell for not so calling him, to hell I will go."[14] This sentiment was not confined to such eminent cases as Darwin, Francis Newman, James Anthony Froude, or George Eliot; it can be found in many elements of society.[15] The apparent immorality of the Bible and the Creed provided stock arguments for atheists; more important, it provided grounds for that perplexity of faith about which professed believers were so unwholesomely reticent. It is possible that the science and criticism of the 1860s had such effect because they provided stimuli and rationales for minds already unsettled and alienated on these

moral grounds. At any rate, the ethical challenge preceded and transcended the scientific challenge. Perhaps the Victorian religious revival
had made men too moral to be orthodox, too humanitarian to be Christian.

The ground was thus prepared for the first onslaughts of science and
criticism. Biblical criticism, to be sure, was slow to reach England; it was
a German product. But science, especially biology and geology, had a
respectable English pedigree. Country clergymen observed plants and
animals; country gentlemen looked at rocks; and so we have biology and
geology. But the close observation of nature produced some problems.
How could these geological strata and fossils of extinct species be squared
with a six-day Creation dating, according to Archbishop Ussher's
chronology printed in the margins of the authorized Bible, from only
4004 B.C.? The question was focused by Sir Charles Lyell in his *Principles
of Geology*, which advanced the convincing hypothesis that geological
formations were the results, not of sudden catastrophes such as Creation
and the Flood, but of the slow operation of uniform processes of change.
The uniformitarian hypothesis required a much longer time-span than
seemed to be allowed by the biblical account of Creation. The response
of churchmen was not, in the 1830s, directly hostile; rather they sought
to show that the biblical texts could be harmonized with the new science.
Unfortunately, the various "harmonies," such as those which treated the
"days" of Genesis as geological eras, proved to be nearly as incompatible
with the developments of geology as the literal biblical text itself. And
those fossils, which suggested transformations in biology as vast as those
in geology, were awkward to get over: a religious scientist was reported
to have concluded that fossils had been deliberately placed by God to test
man's faith.

More serious problems would arise when the concept of development
was extended from geology to biology. The idea of evolution, though
not yet acceptable to most biologists, was in the air. In 1844 Robert
Chambers, an amateur, published anonymously a book called *Vestiges of
the Natural History of Creation*, which maintained that each species had not
been specially created by God but had evolved according to general laws.
This rather unscientific work, a sort of Darwin without discipline, was
written in a reverent spirit. It was received, however, with a storm of
theological criticism which anticipated the more famous debate later ex-

cited by Darwin. The book was criticized by scientists no less strongly than by clergymen, but many sensitive laymen were curiously attracted by the idea of evolution. The storm over *Vestiges of Creation* was a sign of the uneasiness of the times, the unsettlement of minds produced by the scientific picture of impersonal nature functioning without direct divine interposition, a picture difficult to accept, yet increasingly difficult to resist. The poet Tennyson was one of the fascinated readers of *Vestiges of Creation*, and *In Memoriam* shows both its influence and the problems it posed:

> *Are God and Nature then at strife,*
> > *That Nature lends such evil dreams?*
> > *So careful of the type she seems,*
> *So careless of the single life;*
>
> *That I, considering everywhere*
> > *Her secret meaning in her deeds,*
> > *And finding that of fifty seeds*
> *She often brings but one to bear,*
>
> *I falter where I firmly trod,*
> > *And falling with my weight of cares*
> > *Upon the world's great altar-stairs*
> *That slope through darkness up to God,*
>
> *I stretch lame hands of faith, and grope,*
> > *And gather dust and chaff, and call*
> > *To what I feel is Lord of all,*
> *And faintly trust the larger hope.*
>
> > > > *(LV)*

In Memoriam, published in 1850, stands as a monument of the Victorian mind at equipoise, unable to deny the results of science, yet hopefully (if "faintly") placing its faith in "the truths that never can be proved."

But these first glimmerings of doubts and difficulties did not produce a direct conflict between science and religion. Indeed, it was almost an article of faith that such a conflict could not occur, that the conclusions of reason would ultimately harmonize with the dicta of revelation, that the facts of nature discovered by science could not contradict the Word of God who was the creator of nature. A clear position on this matter had been worked out in the conflicts with the rationalists of the eighteenth century, when it was the glory of the Church of England that its thinkers had met the deists and freethinkers on their own rational grounds and more than held their own. A line of Anglican apologists, from Berkeley through Butler to Paley, had used the language of the Enlightenment to justify the ways of God to man. The culmination of this process came, at the end of the eighteenth century, in the work of Archdeacon William Paley. His *Natural Theology* (1802) demonstrated the existence of God by the argument from design. As the existence of a watch proves that there must have been a watchmaker, so the complexity and perfect interrelationships of nature prove that it must have been designed by an intelligent creator. The smoothness and closeness of Paley's arguments had a certain fatuous charm, and the abundance of his detailed illustrations from nature impressed the young Darwin and may have influenced his style. Another of Paley's works, *The Evidences of Christianity* (1794), rested the case for the specific Christian revelation primarily on the argument from miracles. These works became standard textbooks at the universities and provided the staple apologetic theology for generations of clergymen.

The argument from design and the evidence of miracles and prophecies seemed to have met not only the challenge of eighteenth-century rationalism but all future argumentative needs, enabling the clergy to disregard most external challenges to religion. Paradoxically, the success of the Paleyan apologetic was to prove disastrous in the 1860s: it was precisely the argument from design and miracles and prophecies (the "external evidences") that were devastated by the new science and criticism. But evangelicalism and tractarianism had turned the clerical mind from more original researches in apologetics to matters internal to the Church. The one exception, the Bridgewater treatises of the 1830s, proved to be restatements by religious scientists of the argument from design.

Meanwhile philosophy had moved beyond the positions of the Enlightenment to new rationalisms, whether the utilitarianism of Bentham and Mill or the German metaphysics of Kant and Hegel. The external evidences for Christian faith on which Paley had relied were being pushed aside by a new emphasis on inward religious experience, more profound but less verifiable, whose spokesman in England was Coleridge. In his distaste for the formal evidences and dogmas of Christianity, Coleridge spoke for many sensitive religious intellectuals, and he provided the philosophical underpinning for much of later Broad Church biblical criticism. Orthodox clergymen were vaguely aware of these challenges to their position, but they were unable to respond with more than denunciations.

Then, in 1858, emerged a new champion of orthodoxy who seemed to have finally refuted all unbelievers and heretics with the most up-to-date philosophical weapons. H. L. Mansel, in his Bampton lectures on *The Limits of Religious Thought*, employed the then-current philosophy of Sir William Hamilton to place the Christian faith permanently beyond the reach of rational challenge. Mansel argued that the Absolute, the Unconditioned, the Infinite (in other words, God), was utterly beyond the power of human reason to understand, either to defend or to deny. He thus dismissed summarily both Paley's demonstration of the existence of God and the rationalists' attempts to disprove it. From this supreme skepticism, Mansel immediately passed to the most complete orthodoxy. What man's reason could not do, God could do and did in his revelation. Regardless of intellectual or ethical difficulties, man must accept revelation as God gives it; he can examine not its contents but only its evidences. And the evidences Mansel offers are none other than the external evidences of Paley: miracles and prophecies. We must accept revelation on these evidences and we must accept it in its entirety, with no exceptions or qualifications.[16]

This now-forgotten book of 1858 is important because it shows the state of mind of the most intelligent upholders of orthodoxy on the eve of their most formidable challenges. Mansel's book was hailed as having definitively put down rationalism, with the result that the "religious world" was in a state of false security just before the crises of 1859 and 1860. His admirers could perhaps be excused for not having anticipated that Hamilton's philosophy of the Unconditioned, on which Mansel's logical structure depended, was shortly to be demolished by John Stuart Mill. They were more culpable for disregarding the ease with which Mansel's philosophical skepticism could be accepted by those who, like Herbert Spencer, saw no need to proceed beyond it to Christianity. But the great danger in Mansel's argument was that it identified the Christian faith with the text of the Bible and rested the authenticity of the Bible solely on external evidences such as miracles and prophecies. While removing faith safely beyond the reach of philosophy, Mansel had exposed it directly to the attack of science and biblical criticism. The prevailing acceptance of the Paleyan evidences made Mansel and others blind to the vulnerability of a faith which rested solely on such external supports.

Mansel's successor as Bampton lecturer was to assert that the Bible was, as history, "absolutely and in every respect true." Another held that every word in the Bible was "the direct utterance of the Most High." [17] The clear implication of such statements was that, if any text of the Bible could be shown to be scientifically or historically erroneous, not only that text but the entirety of revelation must be given up. Never had traditional Christianity been so self-confident or so vulnerable.

We may now turn to the first of the great challenges to orthodox Christianity, the publication of Darwin's *Origin of Species* in 1859. This work became the most successful exposition of the doctrine of evolution because, first, it offered a coherent and detailed presentation of the evidence and, second, it provided for the first time a satisfactory explanation of the mechanism of evolution, the theory of natural selection. Although Darwin hesitated to apply his theory to the case of man, its applicability was immediately recognized and became the focus of the public debate. "Is man an ape or an angel?" asked Disraeli; being a politician, he was "on the side of the angels." [18] While some scientists found objections to evolution, the attack on Darwin turned on his denial of the special creation of each species by direct divine action and his refusal to assign to man a unique place distinct from the rest of animal creation. Philosophically Darwin was even more subversive: his concept of random variations challenged not only the literal text of Genesis but also the argument from design of Paley and the deists.

The controversy over the *Origin of Species* took the unfortunate form of a direct confrontation between religion and science. The great majority of religious spokesmen condemned the doctrine of evolution, often without regard to its scientific merits, on the ground of its repugnance to the text of the Bible and its tendency to degrade man to the level of the beasts. A majority of scientists, on the other hand, accepted evolution as at least a probable hypothesis, and some, notably Huxley and Tyndall, were goaded by their clerical opponents to take an increasingly anti-religious position. Both sides seemed to identify the substance of Christianity with the text of Genesis.

The most famous confrontation occurred at Oxford in 1860. Samuel Wilberforce, a fine bishop but an over-ardent controversialist, went beyond the scientific arguments in which he had been briefed to refute evolution by sarcasm, asking Huxley "was it through his grandfather or his grandmother that he claimed his descent from a monkey?" Huxley's reply was simple but devastating: "He was not ashamed to have a monkey for his ancestor; but he would be ashamed to be connected with a man who used great gifts to obscure the truth."[19] The audience (largely clerical) applauded. By relying on the supreme virtue of truthfulness, Huxley turned Victorian morality against Victorian orthodoxy. When it came to the test, the defenders of orthodoxy were not interested in truth, and the defenders of truth were not interested in orthodoxy.

The direct effects of this debate have been exaggerated, but it holds a great symbolic significance. The clergy in the audience may have merely applauded a good debate, or they may have enjoyed the put-down of a bishop whose outspokenness had made him many enemies; but the young laymen saw the contrast between the shallowness of a reverend bishop and the reverence for truth of an irreligious scientist. It was this contrast, more than the actual issues of the debate over evolution, which gave rise to the feeling that science was the wave of the future and religion a thing of the past. The effect of the victory of science in the evolution debate was not a headlong abandonment of faith by those who had previously been religious, but rather a confirmation of doubts that already existed and a general turning of attention to the more meaningful issues of the secular world.

The challenge of evolutionary biology, serious though it might be, was superficial compared with the challenge of biblical criticism, which ranged over the entire text and interpretation of the Bible and touched more deeply the sources of the Christian faith. This was an internal problem, not an external one. While textual criticism was relatively uncontroversial, the same could not be said of the so-called higher criticism, the analysis of the authorship, sources, motivation, and accuracy of the biblical writings. The results of such analysis might well disconcert those who believed in the direct and literal divine inspiration of the biblical writings; and the cool and detached manner of historical research seemed hardly compatible with a lively faith.

What was worse, biblical criticism was un-English, lacking in native roots and challenging the prevailing insularity. It was a German product. Hardly anybody read German; most did not think it worth reading; and what they heard of German thought was not encouraging. Virtually the first work of German criticism which reached England was D. F. Strauss's *Life of Jesus*, which treated the Gospels as mythological rather than historical and scandalized even Germans; translated by George Eliot in 1846, it affected a few sensitive, already doubting souls, but served for most who heard of it as a warning that criticism led to infidelity. England was unprepared for biblical criticism; "the Bible, and the Bible alone" was the watchword of English Protestantism. The extreme sensitiveness to any questioning of the authority of the Bible was exacerbated in the 1860s by the coincidence of the arrival of biblical criticism with the challenge of evolutionary science.

Seven men, six of them clergymen of the Church of England, sought to break through the reticence of the educated on matters of faith by "a free handling, in a becoming spirit, of subjects peculiarly liable to suffer by the repetition of conventional language, and from traditional methods of treatment."[20] The resulting composite volume, modestly entitled *Essays and Reviews*, was published in 1860. The five essays and two reviews, independently written, varied in character and quality: one was a rewritten sermon, another a learned, cold, but unexceptionable historical monograph. The one layman wrote a devastating critique of the attempted "harmonies" between Genesis and geology. Rowland Williams, a feisty Welshman, wrote a provocative essay on Baron von Bunsen in which "justification by faith" was turned into "peace of mind." Baden Powell, a mathematician, flatly denied the possibility of miracles. H. B. Wilson gave the widest possible latitude to subscription to the articles of faith and questioned the eternity of damnation. The entire work was capped by Jowett's tremendous though wayward essay "On the Interpretation of Scripture," in which he urged that the Bible be read "like any other book" and made an impassioned plea for freedom of scholarship: "The Christian religion is in a false position when all the tendencies of knowledge are opposed to it."[21]

Much of what the Essayists and Reviewers wrote is now commonplace theology, and the work would not have attracted much attention even in 1860 but for the fact that its authors were clergymen. Once again the ad hominem element prevailed. How could a clergyman hold such views consistently with the Thirty-Nine Articles and his ordination vows? Once again Samuel Wilberforce led the attack, supported by evangelicals and High Churchmen in a rare display of unanimity. From all quarters the volume was denounced: some 150 replies fill three pages of the British Museum catalogue. Wilberforce pressed for a synodical condemnation by the bishops, which he obtained tentatively in 1861 and formally in 1864. Williams and Wilson, the two Essayists who were subject to deprivation, were prosecuted in the church courts and partially condemned in 1862. But here the peculiarities of the English legal system intervened, demanding a strict construction of church formularies while giving the most liberal interpretation to the accused writings, and the conviction was reversed by the Privy Council in 1864. The Privy Council, someone quipped, "dismissed Hell with costs, and took away from orthodox members of the Church of England their last hope of eternal damnation." [22] Ironically, the liberty of thought within the Church of England was saved by the subjection of the Church to the state.

Hard on the heels of the clergymen of *Essays and Reviews* came a bishop, albeit a colonial bishop, with a more direct though less competent attack on the literal interpretation of the Bible. John William Colenso had been brought up to believe that every detail of the Bible is literally true; he had a simple, numerical mind which led him to write textbooks of arithmetic; sent out as bishop to Natal in 1853, he was an effective missionary among the Zulus. Natives, however, lack the knowledge given to civilized men that certain questions ought not to be asked; and so, when they were translating the story of the Flood, one African innocently enquired: "Is all that true? Do you really believe that all this happened thus?" Colenso was an honest man; and he knew, having read Lyell, that geologists had disproved the universal Flood. He began to reexamine the first books of the Bible, with the aid of a few German works and a lot of arithmetic, and he found that the statistics given in the Bible, with their magnificent oriental rotundity, were simply impossible. His method was absurd, but his conclusion was irresistible: the Pentateuch was unhistorical, and most of it was written by someone other than Moses. He had to speak out, though many would be shaken by such statements from a bishop: "Our duty, surely, is to follow the Truth, wherever it leads us, and to leave the consequences in the hands of God." So he published *The Pentateuch Critically Examined* in 1862, telling a shocked England that "the Bible itself is not 'God's word'; but assuredly 'God's word' will be heard in the Bible, by all who will humbly and devoutly listen for it." [23] Having said this, he claimed the right to remain a bishop of the Church of England.

Pious ears were offended; orthodoxy was outraged. The prevailing sentiment was expressed by Bishop Lee of Manchester: "the very foundations of our faith, the very basis of our hopes, the very nearest and dearest of our consolations are taken from us when one line in that Sacred Volume on which we base everything is declared to be unfaithful or untrustworthy." [24] Bishops demanded the removal of their heretical colleague. The Bishop of Cape Town, who claimed jurisdiction over Natal, held a synod which deposed Colenso. Colenso appealed to the Privy Council, where the matter was promptly diverted from a religious question to the technical issue of the legal status of colonies. In the end, without ever resolving the doctrinal issue, the Privy Council held that Colenso could not be deposed. The Bishop of Cape Town, acting on his own, consecrated another bishop for Natal; most of his clergy repudiated Colenso; but he held on, and the result was a local schism which lasted for decades.

The legal judgments on *Essays and Reviews* and Colenso made it not illegal for a clergyman to deny the literal inspiration and infallibility of the Scriptures, but that did not mean that it was tolerable for him to do so in the eyes of most of the clergy and many even of the laity. There was a double standard of belief, or rather of honesty, for clergymen and laymen. Indeed it is possible that the outspokenness of the Essayists and Reviewers actually retarded, by provoking so powerful a reaction, the advent of that freedom of thought in matters of faith for which they strove.

The turning point came when Temple, the least offensive of the Essayists and Reviewers, was nominated to be Bishop of Exeter in 1869 and consecrated despite strong efforts to prevent it. Eventually the theological climate would change: evolution became generally acceptable in the 1880s and, with the publication of *Lux Mundi* by a group of High Churchmen in 1889, it became evident that even conservative clergymen would have to deal with the problem of biblical criticism. But by then it was too late. What clergymen had belatedly discovered, intellectual laymen had known all along.

There had been something exaggerated and even slightly comical in the reaction against biblical criticism. Here, as with the response to Darwin, it seemed as if the defenders of orthodox faith were afraid of the impartial search for truth. As Tennyson said: "There lives more faith in honest doubt,/ Believe me, than in half the creeds."

The Essayists and Reviewers, Colenso, and a few others such as F. D. Maurice and Archbishop Tait — not doubters themselves, but critics — were concerned to bridge the gap separating professed faith from the frank inquiry of educated laymen. One of these laymen, the philosopher Henry Sidgwick, spoke for many when he wrote: "What we all want is, briefly, not a condemnation, but a refutation. . . . A large portion of the laity now . . . will not be satisfied by an *ex cathedra* shelving of the question, nor terrified by a deduction of awful consequences from the new speculations. For philosophy and history alike have taught them to seek not what is 'safe', but what is true." [25]

The failure of the spokesmen of orthodoxy to respond to such appeals, to enter into a creative dialogue with the new ideas, was more important than the new ideas themselves in alienating the rising intellectual generation. As Jowett said: "Doubt comes in at the window when inquiry is denied at the door." [26] From the 1860s, the intellectual leadership of England turned, first tentatively and in single cases, then in a growing flood, away from that deep concern with matters religious which had characterized mid-Victorian England. I am not speaking of that minority which, as in previous generations, was naturally attracted by philosophical radicalisms. I speak of those who yet retained much of the evangelical heritage, particularly in morality, but who, becoming increasingly suspicious of an orthodoxy so ineptly defended, drifted away from formal Christianity. A novel of 1888, *Robert Elsmere* by Mrs. Humphry Ward, tells the story of a clergyman who, because he can no longer believe in the creed of his church, resigns his office and devotes his life to social service. Robert Elsmere was the type of many young men of the late nineteenth century, some maintaining an outward conformity while thinking freely, others leaving organized religion altogether. Christianity had now become an "open question." [27]

As the natural sciences, soon joined by the social sciences, continued their progress, a limited number became outright atheists, needing no religion to explain a universe which could now be understood in purely natural terms. More common, though not always articulated, was the position for which Huxley invented the term "agnostic." As Huxley described it, there was a good deal of residual Christianity in agnosticism:

"a deep sense of religion was compatible with the entire absence of theology. . . . Science seems to me to teach in the highest and strongest manner the great truth which is embodied in the Christian conception of entire surrender to the will of God. Sit down before the fact as a little child, be prepared to give up every preconceived notion, follow humbly wherever and to whatever abysses nature leads, or you shall learn nothing." [28]

Truthfulness had replaced belief as the ultimate standard; but the abandonment of faith did not necessarily represent an abandonment of morality. Indeed it was an outraged moral sense that had led in many instances to the rejection of the Christian faith; and Victorian morality could, at least among the elite, survive the collapse of the Victorian creed. In the writings of George Eliot, as in the practice of numerous positivists, agnostics, and atheists, a humanized evangelical morality — the creed of duty, service, and love — stood alone and triumphant, unsupported by belief in God or the hope of personal immortality:

> O may I join the choir invisible
> Of those immortal dead who live again
> In minds made better by their presence; live
> In pulses stirred to generosity,
> In deeds of daring rectitude, in scorn
> For miserable aims that end with self,
> In thoughts sublime that pierce the night
>   like stars,
> And with their mild persistence urge man's
>   search
> To vaster issues.
>   So to live is heaven:
> To make undying music in the world,
> Breathing as beauteous order that controls
> With growing sway the growing life of man.
>
> . . . .
>
>   May I reach
> That purest heaven, be to other souls
> The cup of strength in some great agony,
> Enkindle generous ardour, feed pure love,
> Beget the smiles that have no cruelty —

Be the sweet presence of a good diffused,
And in diffusion ever more intense.
So shall I join the choir invisible
Whose music is the gladness of the world.

In such pure expression, the morality of the unbelievers could rival that of Christianity. The search for truth in science and in life is an activity as religious in spirit, if not in form or object, as the search for truth in religion. Thus one may speak of the "religion of unbelief" — the faith of those who found the prevailing orthodoxy incompatible with the truths of which they were convinced, and who followed the truth they saw wherever it led them. The heritage of the Victorian religious revival had passed to those who had kept the morality when they could not keep the faith.

But they were living on the ethical capital of the Christianity which they had abandoned. In the long run, as the defenders of orthodoxy had pointed out, it was impossible for any but a small elite to sustain a morality without the foundation of faith. By the twentieth century, Victorian morality had gone the way of Victorian orthodoxy. But it did not go with joy: after the first flush of release, there was a sense of loss, a feeling of failure. We can "hear the ghost of late Victorian England whimpering on the grave thereof"[29] in the words of Oscar Wilde: "I would like to found an order for those who cannot believe; the Confraternity of all the Fatherless I might call it, where on an altar, on which no taper burned, a priest, in whose heart peace had no dwelling, might celebrate with unblessed bread and a chalice empty of wine."[30]

Thoughts on
Social Change and
Political Accommodation
in Victorian Britain

John M. Robson

*T*he *Spirit of the Age, Characteristics, Signs of the Times, Tracts for the Times, Hard Times,* even *The Nineteenth Century* — such titles imply an awareness of identifying marks that distinguish the nineteenth century from other ages, and may be taken to imply also, behind the awareness of change and history, an uneasiness about at least some of the marks. Political and social historians have tended to dwell on the elements of change, using such terms as the age of reform, the age of improvement, an expanding society, a period of reconstruction and progress; literary critics have tended to dwell on the element of uneasiness, seeing anxiety, hesitation, alienation, and despair. The tension between optimism and pessimism has led to speculations about the distance between public and private behavior — has led some to simpleminded accusations of hypocrisy. Without denying that the tension existed, or even trying to explicate it, I shall be taking a different approach, arguing that awareness of social change induced attitudes favorable toward, or at least accepting of, political and social accommodation of change.

It is not just change, but awareness of change that is significant. When social modes and institutions are seen to be shifting, people are disturbed unless there are explanations of the origins and directions of the new modes that are consonant with an understanding of the world and man's place in it. The rage for order, which can easily become an outrage at inexplicable change, includes a passion for prediction and for its concomitant, postdiction.

Looking back at nineteenth-century Britain, one can isolate many major factors (causes and effects both) that are sometimes described as revolutionary, though probably it is wiser to reserve that term for significant sudden changes. Mere mention of some of them will suffice: technological and organizational developments in industry and agriculture, population growth, major demographic and occupational shifts, increased opportunities for communication, secularization, broadening of educational availability and curricula. The concomitant and resultant changes in life and manners were, as I've suggested, not sudden or suddenly visible to all — indeed earlier codes and customs continued for some well into the twentieth century. Nonetheless, the changes were unquestionably startling and disturbing. Consider the effect on a large scale of the shift from a life circumscribed by narrow territorial bounds and habitual mundane cares to a life bustling and busy with many new and unknown faces and issues; from a life where manners and customs were accepted as a matter of course, being ingrained by centuries of repetition, to a life where new mores were forged daily by the necessities of adaptation; from a life where status was inherited as a social stabilizer to a life where economic function determined one's place, which hence could move downward dramatically and move upward even if slowly; from a life, in short, where change was an exception to a life where change was the rule. It seemed to many, looking at the radical alterations in human relations, that human nature itself was undergoing a mutation.

These drastic changes could not have gone unnoticed of course, but certain factors related to the awareness of change have special explanatory significance. First, awareness of change goes hand in hand with a sense of history, a sense that the present time is different from the past and, presumably, from the future, and yet is part of a process. One's judgment of the present depends in large measure on the kind of process that a study of history reveals. Once the ground has been cleared a bit, I shall return to this matter; the point being made here is simply that a sense of the past heightens one's awareness of the present and focuses attention on specific differences and similarities between periods. Similarly, it should be noted, an awareness of other cultures — and of other languages — heightens awareness of one's own.

A second major contributing factor to the awareness of change was the culture-shaking improvement in communication, about which I shall say little, though the importance, for instance, of Manchester's knowing in a few hours what London was doing must not be minimized. Recall the comparative isolation of social groups from one another at the beginning of the century, and then consider the effect of hard-surface, all-weather roads, branching canals, speeding and topography-altering railways, reliable and rapid steamships, space- and culture-bridging telegraphs, fact- and opinion-spreading printing technologies, libraries, and popular newspapers. These vast changes were themselves much commented on in the period, as was their effect in making available information about, and personal acquaintance with, the other great changes mentioned above. Isolation was gradually broken down, and what might be described as British "societies" began to become British "society." Not only were new social relations created, but older ones were seen in a different and a national light, especially as "intelligence" of and from other nations and cultures was broadcast more widely and quickly. Furthermore, as similar situations and like attitudes were perceived among those who had been isolated geographically and culturally, new social and political groups found strength in numbers.

Yet another effect of improved communications, the increased visibility of social problems, for example through discussion of them in the major periodicals, can also be viewed as resulting concomitantly from a third major factor, the development of the "social sciences," a new term for a new approach. It will be recalled that the traditional division of speculative studies in Britain was between Natural Philosophy and Moral Philosophy. The former became Natural Science, a term still in use. The latter, dealing with man, in becoming Moral Science took a more dramatic turn in the transformation from Philosophy to Science. That switch indicates a methodological change, the full effect of which was seen when Science became Sciences, and individual studies began to hive off. Though "moral" had a different meaning in that usage than we assign to it, there was a strong normative bias in Moral Philosophy, while its progeny, the new social sciences, sociology and anthropology, and the quickly changing older one, political economy, moved from normative to descriptive and analytical bases, and statistics started to package experience in persuasive if odd ways.

I am not implying that one can easily separate out normative from descriptive from analytical bases, but only that the shift in tendency is noticeable and significant. Description, especially in statistical form, and that kind of analysis that attempts to disguise its abstract nature can have disconcerting effects, for, though they undoubtedly fit into large metaphoric and epistemological systems, they tend to wrench accustomed patterns of belief by putting the "normal" into unfamiliar frames. They also, by their mere presence, promote a search for even more facts. One need not refer to recondite methodological constructs, but only to such unsophisticated compilations as the Blue Books or Henry Mayhew's mid-century accounts of the London poor (which he halfheartedly tried to present in anthropological terms). That is, apart from the effects of looking at social phenomena in a scientific framework, with anticipations of explanation, prediction, and control, the raw data themselves were a revelation. Not that people were previously unaware of poverty, to choose a dominant example, but that these "facts," gathered and presented as they were, took poverty out of its traditional context and so had a special effect on society's awareness of itself and its developments. Once made visible in these unfamiliar ways, social conditions became social problems, and while conditions may simply exist, problems demand answers. To put the matter in other terms, once new light is thrown on something (as Marshall McLuhan might say, once an artist makes an environment visible), there is an open invitation to planned intervention. Furthermore, while Moral Science tended to assume retrospection and continuity, the Social Sciences tend to concentrate on the here and now, and so to induce a feverish concern for panaceas.

Let me briefly recapitulate: at least three significant factors contributed to (and also reflected) an increased awareness by Victorian society of itself as changing. These are: first, a sense of history; second, vastly improved communications; and third, the development of the social sciences. Each of these, in calling attention to change, was unsettling, but also provided opportunities for coherent responses.

These responses were attempts to ensure beneficial continuity that took account of change. Mere continuity itself is reassuring, but continued development of the beneficial and essential is more reassuring.

Social cohesion was seen as both essential and beneficial; however, some evidence suggested that the social bonds were undergoing not change, but destruction. The image of two nations, the rich and the poor, which had great imaginative and pragmatic force, mirrored not just fact but fear, fear of class strife that would permanently rend the social fabric.

What were the essential social bonds? One potent view of social union derives from Edmund Burke, the eighteenth-century authority on these matters most quoted in the nineteenth century. I shall take some sentences from a well-known passage that rewards fuller study.

> Society is indeed a contract. Subordinate contracts for objects of mere occasional interest may be dissolved at pleasure — but the state ought not to be considered nothing better than a partnership agreement in a trade of pepper and coffee, calico or tobacco, or some other such low concern, to be taken up for a little temporary interest, and to be dissolved by the fancy of the parties. It is to be looked on with other reverence; because it is not a partnership in things subservient only to the gross animal existence of a temporary and perishable nature. . . . As the ends of such a partnership cannot be obtained in many generations, it becomes a partnership not only between those who are living, but between those who are living, those who are dead, and those who are to be born.[1]

This vision may safely be taken as having normative force throughout the Victorian period, but its continued realization was threatened by the tendency for mere "partnership agreements" — what Carlyle termed the "cash nexus" — to become the strongest and perhaps the only bond among citizens, with the state as a convenience for market transactions. The worth of the nation, many complained (among them Mill and Arnold, as well as Carlyle), was judged by a maximization of what we would call the G.N.P. (Carlyle would see this as cognate with the G.H.P., the "greatest happiness principle" of the utilitarians — and perhaps one should note that Bentham introduced the word "maximization" to the language.) This switch to an economic view of social relations is now thought to be one of the most marked features of the period, as status gave way to contract, role to function. That is, the unifying forces in society were no longer those deriving from religion, ethics, and tradition, but from political economy, the "dismal science" that viewed man abstractly as motivated principally and constantly, if not uniquely, by the desire for personal aggrandizement.

There were of course those who promoted the economic view: one is familiar with them negatively through the effective satire of Dickens, as well as through the misrepresentation involved in the current use of the stereotyped label, "liberal." Their justification of the market as model is found repellant by many because it seems to condone suffering: that is, they believed that in the long run the "hidden hand" of Providence produced optimal good from the apparent conflict of individual and group interests. (We know that Keynes pointed out that in the long run we are all dead.) Choosing James Mill as an extreme advocate of this view, one can see that in fact the justification of the classical model is more complex, for while advocating laissez-faire, he scarified those whose "special interests" dominated over the "general interest" of the nation, yet he was far from arguing for any Rousseauistic concept of the collective will.

But Mill (whose commonplace books, incidentally, are studded with quotations from Burke) was not a "seminal mind" (to use his son's phrase) for the period, largely because his speculations were abstract and fundamentally un-Romantic. He tended to see history in Enlightenment terms, as a record of crimes and follies to be avoided, and to look for perfectibility through clear reason rather than for progress through accommodation of all the elements of human nature. It remained for his son, who was much more susceptible to Romantic and conservative impulses, to modify the philosophic radicalism of the early century into a liberalism that was less uncompromising, less vitriolic, and more attuned to British modes of thought and action. In particular, John Stuart Mill strove to relate individual freedom to collective good through a more subtle consideration of historical and social change, and of human nature.

My argument then is that, in considering Victorian responses to change, one should specially bear in mind the Burkean position, which influenced thinkers and politicians of almost all colors. In defining history as the known march of the ordinary providence of God, and in defining the ideal statesman as one having a disposition to preserve and an ability to improve, he spins several threads that run through the succeeding period. First, there must be continuity, based on a true understanding of historical development. Second, the state of a nation at any time grows from its own past, and so foreign and abstract models should be rejected. Third, there is change, providentially provided and therefore beneficial, which statesmen must accept. Fourth, change being incremental, new policies must be carefully studied, and cautious pragmatism should govern particular decisions. Further, it should be emphasized that Burke's views developed not in the study but the arena: his attitudes toward the constitution and the social contract are most vividly articulated in writings dealing with the American and French revolutions, or with important political issues, however much he reveals his Christian and classical background. But there is no hint of the "situational ethic" in his judgments, marked though they may be with circumstantial considerations.

With this background, we can understand some of the features that the nineteenth century sought in a philosophy of history that would provide for continuity and also accommodate change. In the abstract, philosophies of history may be imagined schematically, in forms that have been accepted at various times by various cultures and individuals. For example, there are discontinuous views, such as the Christian, which sees, at least on the level of grace, history as initial fall and final regeneration, and that of the apocalyptic revolutionary, which sees the Augean stables as needing one drastic, but one only, cleansing. Of continuous philosophies, the most easily described and subscribed to are the circle, the rising line and the falling line, the ascending and descending helixes (which combine the circle and the line), and the undulating wave (which essentially is a tilted helix rendered in two dimensions). (In fairness to some of our contemporaries, it might be mentioned that a random, meaningless scattering of dots may be seen as the true vision, as may a basically timeless stasis.)

For the Victorians, process was continuous and tended to imply progress, and it was a hard market for salesmen of apocalyptic or downward teleologies. The strong Christian tradition provided less opposition to progressivism than might be anticipated, for on the level of nature, if not on that of grace, God's providence could collaborate with Dr. Coué's prognosis — every day in every way, things are getting better and better. The almost equally strong classical tradition was not unequivocal on these issues, and the simple cyclical views could be wed to the rising line to produce the ascending helix, while descents from a golden age to a bronze one could be refuted empirically by "improvements" to be seen on all sides.

Nonetheless, both the Christian and classical traditions were based on a backward look to ages that had markedly attractive features, and so they hindered general acceptance of an uncomplicated Couéan view. In the event, the most widely adhered-to position was that the present age was transitional, that the transition was from worse to better, that better periods were not finally stable, and that history, in its broadest scope, revealed repetition. Without exactly replicating earlier periods, ages revealed similar patterns, open to heuristic interpretation. History, then, is best represented as an irregular ascending helix, sagging at one side. The low periods (troughs if one unbends the helix) are ones of confusion, strife, disunity; the high ones (or peaks) are those of clarity, agreement, cooperation; the periods connecting the low to the high, of which the nineteenth century was one, are strenuous — but promising. Matthew Arnold, for instance, with all his hesitations, saw his age as one of "expansion." (It may be remarked that people have generally ever since tended to view their own periods as transitional.) For an understanding of the coming synthesis, all agreed that clues were to be found in earlier societies that had followed the same pattern; they did not, of course, agree on where one should look or what one would find.

Those who accepted such a view, though they differed in their recommendations of policy, could accommodate change within their systems of belief. For example, Carlyle and Mill, who diverged widely in belief and a fortiori in policy, were attracted by the Saint-Simonian form of this scheme. Both longed for an "organic" age, and both saw their own age as "critical," transitional from a collapsed society to a new vital one. Looking backward, they saw elements in past organic ages that could serve as incentives (for Carlyle, even as actual models) for the coming synthesis. For some, of course, the organic past was so vitally conceived that little improvement seemed necessary: for example, the short-lived "Young England" movement of the 1840s in which Disraeli played a large part, and to which he gave fictional embodiment in *Coningsby* and *Sybil*, provides perhaps the most unqualifiedly rosy picture of an organic society transplanted, *Deo volente*, but also *noblesse oblige*, to the nineteenth century. Other manifestations are well known: the sweeping current of Romanticism in Victorian England carried with it medieval models found in Carlyle, Ruskin, and Morris, as well as in the architecture and art of the period.

As already suggested, different groups looked to different nutritional nodes in the roots of history; a glance at some of them is instructive. Remembering that only selected features of such periods are seen as both exemplary and imitable, we may see these periods as models.

British history provided several. The rather vague notions of pre-conquest Britain served to support national pride and a sense of continuity with the "freedoms" of the antique Anglo-Saxon constitution, especially favored by radicals. The medieval period, which was seen as Gothic, enriched by feudalism and by the guarantees of Magna Carta, and pervaded by Christian ideals, fired the imagination of many, especially conservatives. The Elizabethan age, viewed as the first full tide of British glory, in literature as in science, in naval force and commerce, had perhaps less power as a political and social guide, except when seen as continuous with the earlier Tudor age, and/or the Stuart ones. For High Tories, the Stuart periods had strong emotive pull in monarchical and religious terms; the Commonwealth period between the two Stuart ones was an inspiration politically to radical groups and religiously to some Dissenters. To many, however, both the Stuart and Commonwealth periods seemed to be aberrations from the desirable flow of British political history, and so could not have major imaginative force on the main body of gradualists. Much more significant was the model derived from the Glorious Revolution of 1688, which was judged, at least, by the Whigs, to have been both a return to the true constitution and an opening to the future. (It should here be noted that the absence of a codified constitution, with social as well as legal and political connotations, prevents the British from fixing firmly on one period or one document as normative.) Apart from those Whigs who saw the eighteenth century as a proper, if somewhat unexciting and perhaps too German, constitutional continuation from 1688, it was, according to the normal rule that preceding times are seen as causing contemporary problems, generally viewed as not very attractive — the Romantic rejection of supposed neoclassicism having much to do with this judgment.

As already indicated, along with these native models one should consider the naturalized ones, classical and Christian. While the battle of the ancients and the moderns had virtually and apparently permanently been won by the moderns, the traditions were powerful. The Greek city-state, in particular, in its great fifth-century flowering, reverberates through the discussions of the age, its use as a political commonplace revealing less a considered weighing of alternatives than the dominance of the classics in gentlemanly education. The appeal of Christian social and political models was even more widespread, but more mixed. The Oxford Movement, at the one extreme, reinforced the appeal of both the medieval and Stuart models, as well as that of Christian Rome (eternal more than temporal, but centered on the early Church), while, at the other, the Dissenters, champions of voluntarism and congregational organization, were more likely to favor the Commonwealth, the nonecclesiastical aspects of the early Church, and, to some extent, the Jewish polity of the Old Testament.

Given the strong adherence to, and the often reverential dwelling on, native and naturalized models, there was comparatively less interest in foreign ones. Nonetheless they had some adherents, and specific aspects of contemporary and near-contemporary societies had fascination. Particularly in the earlier part of the period, the French and American experiments (such they were often seen to be) attracted comment from all sides. In both cases, the fact of war with Britain and, in the latter, the feeling of kinship, complicated both perception and judgment. In general, however, French political democracy was viewed as mobocracy, with its tyrannical consequences, while American political democracy was seen as mediocracy, with another kind of tyrannical consequence, the unconsidered rule of an unthinking majority. Those, however, who hated monarchical and, more strongly, aristocratic rule looked less (in Paine's image) at the plumage than at the dying bird, and, while often deploring "excesses" (not just for prudential or rhetorical reasons), saw threads of silver among the red. (Similar comments are applicable to attitudes towards the later Continental revolutions.) With the advent of sociologically oriented studies of America and France, the picture becomes blurred, as the more open societal mores and institutions were judged by some to promote freedom, and perhaps not in fact to be entailed precisely by political forms. Later in the century admiration of the rise of Germany to prosperity and powerful nationhood, an admiration reinforced by popular royal intermarriage, the supposedly common Teutonhood, and the traditional dislike of France, gave a new twist to speculations and feelings about political models; even the imperial competition of the late century, while it promoted jingoism and chauvinism, also encouraged envious admiration of others' successes. (The celebration of the Elizabethan age also took on new power, for similar reasons, with the additional parallel seen in the triumphant and long reign of another queen, whose role, just because more symbolic, safely enhanced the national image.)

It may simply be mentioned that in the more exotically imaginative years of the late century, and into the twentieth, the imperial experience had unexpected payoffs in the form of foreign cultural models — such as the Arabian — that attracted particularly the rebels against Victorianism.[2]

This consideration takes us a little far afield: the main impetus through the period, I am maintaining, was a search for organic elements in past native and naturalized models that could establish continuity and give assurance. Yet another kind of historical explanation can be seen in a similar way: evolutionary theory. Continuity with apes rather than angels was of course a disturbing notion, but gradual improvement was not, especially as expressed in the tautological catchphrase "the survival of the fittest." Just as the Newtonian physical model (and, in our times, the Einsteinian) prompted extrapolations in other areas, so the Darwinian biological one induced theories of social, political, cultural — even literary — evolution.

Like the patterns of historical development we have been looking at, this model was not univocal: in considering present society, for example, different people could isolate different elements as being "fittest" or "unfittest" and therefore "fitting" or "unfitting" for survival — and for imitation. Also, a fatalism about further development was produced in some, while others were exuberant about future prospects. Whatever the specific attitudes, however, the model had for many a positive explanatory function; in the terms I am arguing, it put change in a comprehensible frame.

Having looked broadly at the awareness of change and the search for patterns of reassurance, let me turn to some remarks about practical accommodation. For that majority unwilling to accept fatalistic and quietist philosophies, the challenge was apparent: something could be done, and should be done, to preserve and strengthen the social union. If social change can be predicted, then political means can be employed in an attempt to control. In view of modern attitudes to control, it should be said that while the desire for control over people may have motivated some, what I see as more characteristic is the felt need for control over tendencies; strong as the appeal of the status quo is for those in favored positions, if one believes the coming age will be different, one cannot expect the power balance to be constant though one may well hope that it will not be fickle. So with the questions about what should be done goes the question about who should do it.

In framing this question, it will be noted, I have used "should" rather than "would." I shall touch on the latter issue in a moment, but first shall spend a moment on the question of ideal leadership. While leaders may be sui generis, they are far more likely to arise from cultural groups that provide the proper environment for, and training in, foresightedness and dedication to national goals. Good insights into the value attached to this environment and training may be gained by again contrasting Burke and James Mill. In passages regrettably too long for quotation here, Burke gives a near-rhapsodic account of "a natural aristocracy" as bred to estimation, habituated to public inspection and to command and obey, attentive to public opinion, enabled to take large views and to associate with the wise and learned — all this and more — while James Mill describes the "middle rank," the "most wise and the most virtuous part of the community," as forming and directing those below it, providing models for them, and giving "to science, to art, and to legislation . . . their most distinguished ornaments," as well as being the "chief source of all that has exalted and refined human nature."[3]

Such views of class excellence lost much of their sheen during the century, though not everyone would go the length of Matthew Arnold in identifying the aristocracy as barbarian and the middle class as philistine. His account of the populace, however, as at best enamored only of beer and fun, reflected widespread attitudes. Enlightened leadership was necessary as never before — and where could it be found or nurtured? For many there was appeal in Arnold's view, less despairingly offered by others, that hope lay in a subset of the middle class, who were not enemies of light, and had some of the graces Burke saw in the barbarians. The class origins of leaders, while significant in the past, would become increasingly less important in the future egalitarian society, but the essential characteristics would endure. Exemplars, therefore — without muttonchop whiskers and black coats — could be sought in past model societies whose courses had been determined by pilots who knew both anchor and sail. Partly because historical records tend to preserve the actions of the leaders, the "heroes," and partly because human psychology dictates reverence and a need for protection, exemplary individuals or groups were seen as dominant in model societies. An imitation ethic, religious and secular, was widespread — is it ever not? — and many and diverse qualities were isolated as characteristic of those by whom successful past societies had been guided. Rather than list those qualities, I shall take the easier and shorter path of mentioning a few characteristics that did *not* mark heroes. These would include a blindness to consequences, trivial and evanescent willpower, indolence, narrow interests, and ignorance. And these were just the qualities perceived in the numerical majority. (Notice that I say *perceived*; I do not here question the rightness or wrongness of the perception, remarking only that ideological spectacles, as Carlyle would say, are all distorting, and that modern conceptions of elitism are, at best, extremely odd.)

Herein lay a tortuous problem for Victorian reformers attempting pragmatically to shape change in desirable ways. The questions were, as already suggested, who would and who should have power, and much effort went into finding one answer to both questions. The tendency seemed clear: history portrayed power moving slowly, but steadily and probably inexorably, into the hands of a numerical majority. That majority, if it came to see itself as a class, with interests separate from those of the nation as a whole, would contrive to dominate all social and political life.

In saying social *and* political life, I am implying yet another question the reformers had to deal with: over how much of life should political power have hegemony? One of the major changes in the period was a gradual widening of political issues to encompass more and more social problems. I am not arguing that social legislation was invented in Victorian Britain — far from it — but merely that the scope of such legislation at the beginning of the period was far narrower than it was at the end, and that the administration of social policy became much more a central concern. One may say that awareness of facts (descriptive) became awareness of problems (normative); solutions were sought and governmental operations expanded — albeit slowly, and almost always in the face of stern opposition. Examples will spring readily to mind: the New Poor Law, Public Health Laws, the Factory Acts, the Municipal Acts, and so on. Perhaps a current issue among some historians may be used to cast light on the conflict over such legislation: Is that Parliament best which passes most laws, or that which finds it unnecessary to pass many? Clearly the amount and kind of legislation enacted is a guide to the relation perceived between government and society, both when one considers the degree of responsibility central government should assume for social problems, and when one considers the ways in which government should be a mirror in small of society at large.

As government increasingly became a force for social change, so demands for correction of its mirror image increased. (Again one sees that change and awareness of change lead to more and greater change.) Through the century the franchise was broadened for males, first to include more of the middle class, and then to include the working class, in line with the increase in social legislation, and with the dictum of the younger Mill that political power cannot long fail to reflect social power without a convulsion.

In the brief list of revolutionary changes given earlier in this essay, I made no mention of a "political" revolution. Actually the incremental political changes, including diminution of aristocratic and religious influence, and the concomitant shift of power from Lords to Commons, the development of a party system, the increased power of the cabinet vis-à-vis the Commons as a whole, the move toward professionalism in the permanent civil service, the importance assumed by Parliamentary committees and commissions, as well as the broadening of the franchise and the consequent (though slow) alteration in the composition of the House of Commons (as well as of local governing bodies) — these changes certainly were, in the long view, as transforming as and more durable than a sudden transfer of power from one class to another would have been without other changes. But of course British political thought and life in the period were haunted by the specter of revolution, in particular the French Revolution of 1789 but also that of 1830, and the European ones of 1848. Cynically, one can view the Reform Bills, and indeed the social legislation of the period, as *tout court* an attempt to concede as much, and only as much, as was needed to keep the lower orders passive if not contented. But to do so is to glorify one's own motives or ideology at the expense of the Victorians', or to adopt a distorted and cramped model of human motivation. Hypocrisy, especially unconscious hypocrisy, is a hard charge to prove post hoc.

It seems better, rather, to assume that gradualism and accommodation were genuine beliefs, founded on a conception of the optimal national good that, even if one wishes to reject it, is respectable as well as comprehensible. One may well ask with the Victorians not merely in whose hands political and social power will lie, but why it should be there found or confided.

Here then was the principal task of political accommodation to social change. But the models were not reassuring. Abstract and normative considerations suggested an inexorable broadening of the franchise, but observation showed a mass society not fitted to rule itself. None of the native models, except the Commonwealth, or the naturalized ones, except some aspects of the Greek and, for a few, the primitive Christian, could be thought of as democratic, and even the exceptions were open to qualification; the American and French were suspect, as foreign, for most. Knowledge of the mass of people then living was far from reassuring. Nonetheless, Tennyson's vision of freedom slowly broadening down from precedent to precedent was a generally acceptable one, as was John Stuart Mill's, of a free society in the future that would incorporate the necessary conditions of order. That is to say, visions of the coming silver age (almost no one thought of it as golden) nearly always encompassed a wider and more equal distribution of social goods and greater individual self-determination. The coming of social and political democracy, after the "finality" attitude to the First Reform Act had faded, was seen as an inevitable outcome of the development of civilization; though inevitable, it could and should be shaped, not merely accepted, to provide enjoyment.

As John Stuart Mill said, however, the issue was not merely control over one's own destiny, but over the destinies of others. The coming masters, those who would have power — or better, share in it — needed shaping. It being thought evident that they could not or would not shape themselves, they needed education and exemplars. Education — moral, intellectual, political, and physical — would enable those who were capable and motivated to take their place among the new "best," an aristocracy not of blood but of talent. Equality, a highly valued goal for many, should be of opportunity, not of function or possession. The political franchise was seen as in itself valuable, for full citizenship was properly educative for leadership as well as participation. But should not, as Coleridge suggested and Mill reiterated, men and opinions be weighed as well as counted? Many concluded that an equal franchise was unwise, at least until education was equal. The process of education would include — and the literature of all kinds in the period is crammed with illustrations — an exposure to worthy exemplars; indeed there was a heavy demand that individuals and groups from the dominant middle class should exhibit heroic qualities so that, in Matthew Arnold's phrases, culture, the humanization of man in society, and right reason could generally prevail in social and political life. Once again, cynically, one can hear the refrain, Why can't the poor be more like us? Realistically perhaps, but in any case in Victorian terms, one can say, In most respects, wouldn't they — and the nation — be better so?

Whatsoever the moral judgment, one can see this attitude as a response to the reality of accelerating and newly visible social change. God's providence may be trusted, but why not help to ensure that change is progress? Quietism was not a popular answer to the distress, often near despair, that faced the Victorians as social facts surfaced, became problems, and cried for political solutions. One can see beneath the muddling-through, the pragmatism, even beneath that more dispiriting parliamentary transition from humbug to humdrum, a conviction that, left to itself, broadening meant leveling, while determined but unprecipitate intervention could lead to greater social justice and a wider sharing of goods, without debasement, or loss of distinctiveness, dignity, and direction. Present change, when seen as part of a controllable transition from past to future, was less a threat than a challenge.

Science by Candlelight

Leonard G. Wilson

On a Sunday afternoon in February 1853 in her house at 11 Harley Street, London, Lady Lyell began a letter to a friend in the United States. "I am now writing," she said, "by candlelight & the fog was just now at 2 o'clock as dark as night. It came on very suddenly after we returned from church, & has put a stop to my walk." [1] Lady Lyell was the wife of Sir Charles Lyell, the most eminent geologist in Victorian Britain, and in the comfort of her London town house, where Lyell wrote and revised the successive editions of his geological books, they were in 1853 accustomed to use candles for lighting. In 1801 Philippe Lebon had given a public demonstration of the use of gas for lighting at Paris, and at London a Gas, Light and Coke Company was chartered in 1812. Gas lighting was adopted quickly for factories, public buildings, and larger shops, but the presence of sulphur and other impurities in gas, the leaky joints in gas pipes, and the poor fittings available prevented the use of gas in small rooms and therefore in private houses. Gas was not practicable for domestic lighting until after the invention of the incandescent gas mantle in 1885, very late in the Victorian period. [2] In private houses candles and later oil lamps were the primary means of lighting throughout the Victorian period. Science in Victorian England was pursued almost entirely by individuals working at home. In the evening, whether in a London house or in the country, the Victorian scientist read and wrote by candlelight. His thoughts and achievements must be seen against the shadows thrown by the flickering flame of a candle.

When we contemplate science in Victorian England we observe a scene essentially different from that revealed by Victorian art, architecture, literature, politics, or religion. In each of the latter fields there has been some question, often asked with prejudice, of the permanent value of

Victorian achievements. Until recently Victorian art has been regarded as an unfortunate combination of sentimentality and vulgarity — the apotheosis of bad taste. Such judgments were extreme and may have been seriously mistaken, but they have been widely held. When in 1918 Lytton Strachey wrote *Eminent Victorians*, he did so in a tone of amused condescension. Cardinal Manning, Florence Nightingale, Thomas Arnold, and General Gordon were presented each as distinct individuals, slightly eccentric — and slightly absurd.

Strachey did not describe any Victorian scientist. He knew very little of science. He probably thought it equally unimportant. But if Strachey had had sufficient scientific knowledge to discuss the work of any major Victorian scientist, his condescension might soon have given way to awe. The scientists of Victorian Britain were truly great. The names of Faraday, Joule, Kelvin, and Maxwell in physics, of Lyell in geology, and of Darwin and Wallace in biology will ring down the ages so long as science is studied and taught.

The Victorian scientists attacked fundamental problems — the nature of matter and energy, the history of the earth and of life on earth, the origin of the human mind, of reason, and of instinct. Their achievements in the solution of scientific problems were enormous. The questions the Victorians left unanswered are in many instances still unanswered, or scientists are still wrestling with them.

Our judgment of the validity of certain Victorian scientific achievements has changed drastically over the past forty years. It is now evident that some of the great Victorians saw more clearly and built their theories more wisely than they were given credit for early in this century. In two sciences, geology and biology, many scientists about 1910 thought that the views of Charles Lyell and Charles Darwin had been seriously discredited. Lyell's view that mountain ranges had been elevated very slowly and gradually, by the same kinds of earthquakes and volcanic eruptions that occur periodically in various parts of the world today, was considered by many geologists quite outmoded.[3] Geologists of 1910 thought that, at particular periods during the geological past, earthquakes and volcanic eruptions had tended to occur on a much greater scale than anything that we may observe in the modern world. Such extraordinary convulsions, they considered, were needed to account for the large-scale movements of the earth's crust that had occurred in the elevation of mountains. In developing such catastrophic theories geologists of the early twentieth century followed lines of reasoning which eighty years earlier Lyell had warned were unsound.[4]

In the half century after 1910 two profound changes occurred in geology. The discovery of radioactivity in the 1890s, and its application by Ernest Rutherford to geology, showed that the earth was not a cooling body, with a constantly diminishing internal heat, but that instead the earth possessed within itself a steady and unending source of heat from radioactive processes. Scientists needed no longer assume, therefore, that the age of the earth was limited to the time required for it to cool from its presumed original incandescent state to its modern form. The earth might be indefinitely old.[5]

When methods were developed for the radioactive dating of rocks, such methods showed further that various massive formations of igneous rocks in mountains, which some geologists had assumed had been formed within brief periods of time, had in fact required long periods of geological time for their accumulation. As a result the igneous formations of mountain ranges are now seen to represent the products of volcanic forces of the past no more extensive nor violent than those occurring today. Then, since 1950, the theory of continental drift has been joined with a wealth of new data about the floors of the oceans in the theory of plate tectonics.

In plate tectonics the crust of the earth is conceived as subdivided into large plates. The plates move laterally over the earth's surface in response to convection currents within the interior. The movements of the plates are very slow, but very steady, depending as they do on a steady production of heat within the earth by processes of nuclear chemistry. The movements of the plates produce in turn the whole array of structural geological changes — the formation and separation of continental areas, the formation of ocean basins, the elevation of mountain ranges, and the subsidence of other areas.[6] All such structural changes in the earth have proceeded very slowly and steadily, in an essentially uniform way, throughout the history of the earth. In its emphasis on the steadiness and uniformity of structural change through geological time, the theory of plate tectonics has brought geology back into essential conformity with the concepts of uniformitarianism presented by Charles Lyell in 1830 and defended by him until his death in 1875.

Despite his much more limited means of observation, Lyell's theory, like the theory of plate tectonics, was based on subtle but rigorous reasoning from complex geological evidence.[7] The concept of uniformitarianism made the age of the earth extend indefinitely into the distance of the past and suggested that, throughout its long history, conditions on the earth's surface had been essentially similar to those existing today. Uniformitarianism thus bore directly on the question of the conditions under which plants and animals lived during the geological past.

In 1910 Charles Darwin was likewise considered a partially discredited scientist. Although biologists generally accepted that species of plants and animals had originated by evolution, they tended not to accept Darwin's theory of the mechanism by which that evolution occurred, namely, the theory of natural selection.[8] There were various reasons for the reluctance to accept natural selection. The selection of small variations did not seem to fit with the larger discrete characters of Mendelian genetics nor with the mutations described by the Dutch geneticist Hugo De Vries. The deepest dislike of natural selection, however, stemmed from its denial of design in nature. The colors of flowers, the plumage of birds — all the intricate, elaborate, and beautiful features of plants and animals were explained by Darwin's theory as the result of natural selection acting on random variations. Natural selection replaced divine providence with blind chance.

By 1930 the work of J. B. S. Haldane, R. A. Fisher and others on the inheritance of genes in populations had shown that minor variations were genetically determined and that natural selection, acting on a population, could and did determine its genetic constitution. During the 1930s taxonomists, ecologists, and geneticists applied the genetic theory of natural selection to the process of species formation and by 1942 a new synthesis of Darwinian natural selection with genetic theory had clearly occurred.[9] In 1959, on the centennial of the publication of Darwin's *Origin of Species*, biologists were confident of the validity of evolution by natural selection and felt a renewed respect for the accuracy of Darwin's scientific insight. In the perspective of modern biology Charles Darwin was clearly one of the greatest founders of the science.

Even when the fortunes of natural selection were at their lowest ebb in the period from 1900 to 1920, Darwin's stature as a scientist remained very high. He had established the theory of evolution and of the origin of man by evolution; he had made many fundamental contributions to geology, natural history, and plant physiology. To a large extent biologists in 1900 were investigating problems which had been originally defined by Darwin. Darwin's collected works filled a whole shelf, and occupied the shelves of most professional biologists.

There was less tendency in the immediate post-Victorian period to depreciate the work of a scientist like Michael Faraday. Faraday's simplicity of character, honesty, and goodness made him universally liked in his lifetime, and his work presented no obvious challenge to religion. Moreover, the impact of Faraday's discoveries on the industrial use of electricity, and therefore on the conditions of life, became ever greater as the nineteenth century progressed. Faraday's discovery of electromagnetic induction in 1831 made possible immediately the development of both the dynamo and the electric motor, although their practical application would require many years. Similarly the development of an electric telegraph, in the United States by Samuel Morse in 1835 and in Great Britain by William Fothergill Cooke and Charles Wheatstone in 1837, followed closely upon Faraday's discovery of electromagnetic induction. The electric telegraph and the submarine cable, first laid across the Atlantic in 1866, opened the era of rapid communication between the most distant parts of the world. It was one of the great technical achievements of the Victorian period.[10] Faraday's discovery of the laws of electrolysis, and his introduction of such terms as electrode, anode, cathode, anion, and cation, suggest what a large part of our knowledge of electricity he helped to establish.

Faraday himself was not greatly interested in the practical application of his scientific discoveries. He sought the answer to deeper questions. Faraday was concerned with the nature of electricity. He showed that electricity was not a fluid that flowed through matter but that it was inherent in matter. He thought that matter itself should be considered not as made up of solid atomic particles, but as fields of force surrounding points in space. He developed the concept of the electromagnetic field as far as he could with his very limited knowledge of mathematics. It remained for another Victorian scientist, James Clerk Maxwell, to develop the field equations needed to express the meaning of Faraday's results.

The revolutionary significance of field theory in physics was that it denied the possibility of action at a distance. The ability of atomic particles, as well as larger bodies like planets, to influence each other across intervening empty space was a concept fundamental to Newtonian physics. In the early Victorian period the memory of Sir Isaac Newton was revered and the assumptions of Newtonian physics seemed to be established unshakably. In the concept of field theory Faraday and Maxwell were initiating a revolution in the foundations of theoretical physics.[11] The Victorian period was thus not only a time of very rapid development in science, but also a time when scientific views that had seemed firmly established for two centuries were radically transformed.

The scientific achievements of Victorian Britain were so impressive that it is natural to ask what made them so. The question is complicated by the lopsided character of Victorian science. Despite the brilliant individual achievements of such men as Lyell, Darwin, Faraday, and Maxwell, there was relatively little experimental research carried out in England before 1870. There was very little science taught at Oxford and Cambridge and almost no scientific research performed. The British government gave little support to science beyond a small grant to the Royal Society of London and the support of such institutions as the National Astronomical Observatory at Greenwich. In 1836 the government established the Geological Survey, which thereafter provided several full-time positions for geologists, and in 1841 the Royal Botanic Garden at Kew was founded as a national institution with Sir William Hooker as its director. There were also a small number of scientific curatorships at the British Museum.

On the whole, however, scientific research in Victorian Britain was carried on by amateurs. Some of the scientific amateurs were rich. With an independent income they could devote their full time to scientific pursuits. Among physicists, James Prescott Joule and James Clerk Maxwell both possessed inherited wealth which gave them leisure.

In the fields of geology and natural history, Lyell and Darwin possessed independent incomes. Both were heirs to fortunes created in the eighteenth century. Both grew up in country houses with well-furnished libraries. Both received the same kind of classical education, Lyell at Oxford, Darwin at Cambridge, and science was for both at first a pastime. Lyell and Darwin both read widely, traveled widely, and were deeply influenced by their respective travels. Despite the fact that they began as amateurs, both worked at science with an unrelenting intensity equal to that of the best professionals. Their many books were the product not only of leisure but also of many hours of sustained labor and deep thought.

Yet most of the scientific amateurs were not rich. Many were physicians who pursued science in the odd hours remaining from a busy practice. Gideon Mantell, surgeon, in practice first at Lewes in Sussex and later at Clapham on the edge of London, discovered the iguanodon and other fossil vertebrates in the Wealden formation of Sussex. Mantell was a leading authority on the geology and paleontology of southeast England until his death in 1852.[12] Some scientific amateurs were clergymen, especially country clergymen. The Reverend Leonard Jenyns, who was vicar at Swaffham Bulbeck in Suffolk from 1828 to 1849, wrote valuable works on zoology and corresponded extensively with other naturalists, including Charles Darwin. Other scientific amateurs worked in banks or offices. Joseph Jackson Lister, who developed the optical system for the achromatic microscope, was a wine merchant; so too was the geologist Joseph Prestwich until at age sixty-two he became professor of geology at Oxford. The naturalist John Lubbock, later Lord Avebury, who wrote on the instinctive behavior of ants, bees, and wasps, carried out his scientific investigations while going daily to work in his family's bank.

William Pengelly was a schoolmaster who earned his living by teaching private pupils in his house at Torquay in Devonshire through most of Victoria's reign. He also was a geologist who without pay supervised the excavation of the floor of Kent's Cavern at Torquay, completed in 1880. For fifteen years Pengelly visited Kent's Cavern almost every day and spent on an average five hours washing and labeling bone specimens and keeping records of the excavation. In the end the excavation produced nearly fifty thousand fossil bones, as well as many flint tools and pins, needles, and harpoons of bone, the household effects of Paleolithic man. The excavation of Kent's Cavern was one of the most accurate and complete excavations of a Pleistocene cave.[13]

Some scientific amateurs such as Philip Henry Gosse, Henry Walter Bates, and Alfred Russel Wallace actually made their living from science itself — by collecting scientific specimens in foreign countries for sale on the London specimen market and by writing scientific articles for popular magazines and scientific books. Books on science and natural history, especially books on the natural history of strange and distant countries, had a strong appeal to the Victorian reader.[14] But Gosse did something even more remarkable. He interested Victorian readers in the variety of animal life to be found along the seashores of Britain.[15]

The characteristic that such Victorian scientific amateurs — whether private gentlemen, physicians, surgeons, clergymen, merchants, bankers, schoolmasters, travelers, or popular authors — shared in common was that they were serious scientists. They published original research and frequently achieved sufficient distinction to be elected fellows of the Royal Society. They might even become very great scientists; they were seldom dilettantes.

In addition to the large group of amateurs there was in Victorian Britain a much smaller group of professional scientists, men who were paid to devote their full time to scientific research. At London the Royal Institution, founded in 1799 by Benjamin Thompson (later Count Rumford), was from the beginning a center of scientific research. Humphry Davy, the first director, was succeeded in 1825 by Michael Faraday; in 1855 Faraday was succeeded by John Tyndall. Between 1868 and 1875 Tyndall carried out at the Royal Institution his series of experiments on spontaneous generation which culminated in the discovery of the heat-resistant bacterial spore and of sterilization by discontinuous heating. As director of the Hunterian Museum at the Royal College of Surgeons from 1836 to 1856, Richard Owen devoted his full time to studies in comparative anatomy and became the leading vertebrate palaeontologist in England. In 1856 Owen was appointed superintendent of natural history at the British Museum. There he worked with great energy to develop the natural history departments and in 1880 succeeded in obtaining a new Natural History Museum at South Kensington. But despite a small number of such professional scientists, the great majority of Victorian scientists were amateurs.

As befitted an activity carried on largely by amateurs who possessed the independence of private citizens, the characteristic institution of Victorian science was the scientific society — particularly, the specialized scientific society. The greatest of the English scientific societies, the Royal Society of London, dated from the seventeenth century, but it was of limited importance to the development of science in Victorian England. Far more significant were such organizations as the Linnean Society (founded in 1788), the Geological Society (1807), the Royal Astronomical Society (1820), the Zoological Society (1827), and the Royal Geographical Society (1830), all of which were flourishing at the beginning of Victoria's reign.

During the Victorian period many new scientific societies were founded. In 1839 a small group of enthusiasts met at the home of the Quekett brothers in London to found the Microscopical Society. Joseph Jackson Lister, inventor of the achromatic microscope, was one of the founding members. In 1841 the Chemical Society was established in London and in 1843 the Pharmaceutical Society. Also in 1843 the Archaeological Association and the Archaeological Institute arose simultaneously from an immediate schism of the founding groups of archaeologists, and Dr. Thomas Hodgkin started the Ethnological Society. The Anthropological Society was not founded until 1863.

The specialized scientific societies had certain features in common. They held meetings regularly where members read scientific papers. Some societies, the Geological Society for example, also had an annual dinner at which speeches were made, prizes were given, and the year's progress in the science was reviewed. Soon after their founding most societies began to issue a journal, usually called transactions or proceedings, in which the papers read at meetings were published. Sometimes, as in the founding of the Hakluyt Society in 1846 or the Palaeontographical Society in 1847, the whole purpose of the society was to support publication. In their early stages smaller societies usually met either at the home of a member or in the rooms of some other society. When a society could afford to do so, it usually rented its own rooms and began to accumulate a library and perhaps a museum. Some groups, for instance the Geological Society and the Linnean Society, were given rooms in public buildings at London, at first in Somerset House, later in Burlington House.

Of unique value to the development of Victorian science was the British Association for the Advancement of Science. Founded in 1831, the British Association met during the summer of each year in some provincial city. Its membership was large, so the discussion at meetings was divided into various sections according to subject. Because it had few expenses, the British Association was able to accumulate funds from which it could make small grants for the support of scientific research. Such a grant supported the excavation of Kent's Cavern at Torquay, for instance. The association regularly commissioned reports on the state of the various sciences and some of the reports emerged as useful scientific monographs.

Victorian scientists, belonging to so many diverse, specialized societies, and in so many cases earning their living outside science, were characterized by great variety, independence, and vigor. The freedom to express ideas was reflected in the frequency of debates. Orthodox opinions were challenged fearlessly. The absence of any large cadre of professional scientists meant that there was less temptation for young men to flatter their seniors by supporting their views in order to gain professional advancement. By contrast such toadyism was not unknown within the governmental scientific establishment at Paris. Perhaps most important, the independence of scientists and scholars permitted the free discussion of even the most inflammatory scientific issues.

Freedom of scientific discussion was particularly important in the debates over geology and evolution. At Paris French scientists such as Louis Pasteur sometimes asked the Academy of Sciences to appoint a commission to investigate a scientific question in dispute. The findings of such commissions almost invariably proved later to be either mistaken or inconclusive. The loose structure of English science left all scientific questions open to debate.

The independence of British scientists, which in so many ways was their strength, was also their weakness, for it implied very few professional scientists and little direct support for science. There was little governmental support for science, few teaching positions for scientists in universities, and little scientific research. Experimental research requiring expensive laboratories and special equipment was most severely restricted. The situation actually grew worse as Victoria's reign progressed. From 1860 to 1870 almost no physiological research was carried on in Britain.[16] A similar situation existed in experimental physics and chemistry. Meanwhile in France, and to an even greater extent in Germany, experimental physics, chemistry, and physiology made enormous strides during the middle decades of the nineteenth century. In Germany the centers of scientific research were in the universities. The German university envisioned its function as the creation of new knowledge. Ideally each German university wished its professors to be the most productive scholars or scientific investigators in their respective fields. Among the nineteen universities in Germany there was keen competition for professors. An outstanding German scientist could make the provision of a separate research institute a condition for his acceptance of appointment, as Carl Ludwig did when he moved from Vienna to Leipzig in 1865.

The English universities, by contrast, felt little responsibility for the creation of new knowledge. They saw their function as the transmission of existing knowledge, in traditional forms. The curriculum at Oxford and Cambridge remained in 1850 essentially a grammar school curriculum. Oxford emphasized Greek and Latin authors, while Cambridge stressed mathematics. The teaching was done for the most part by fellows of colleges. Since the colleges forbade fellows to marry, most young men gave up their fellowships as soon as they could obtain a decent position elsewhere, usually in the church. There was nothing to encourage a college fellow to develop his knowledge in any branch of learning or to do original scholarship. Despite its emphasis on classics, Oxford made no contributions to classical scholarship. Cambridge was similarly uncreative in mathematics. Yet at Oxford and Cambridge the colleges possessed rich endowments that could have provided the support needed for both humane scholarship and scientific research. There was in fact no way that an adequate number of positions could be created for scientists in England until the teaching of science could be made part of university education at Oxford and Cambridge.

Oxford and Cambridge were also restricted to students who belonged to the Church of England. The sons of Jews, Catholics, and all dissenting Protestants, such as Methodists, Baptists, and Quakers, were excluded. In response to the demand for university education among excluded groups, and to the need for a less expensive mode of higher education, the London University (later University College London) was founded in 1826. From the beginning it included the natural sciences and such modern studies as history and economics in its teaching. When King's College was founded in London in 1828 as an Anglican counterpart, for the purpose of providing inexpensive university education for the sons of Anglicans, it too felt obliged to offer instruction in science and other modern subjects as part of a Christian education. In 1836 the two institutions were considered to be sufficiently alike in aim and purpose to be joined together in the University of London. Thus through the nineteenth century University College London and King's College provided a number of positions for scientists, although their resources were too limited to permit them to support extensive scientific research.

Both Oxford and Cambridge had made efforts at internal reform, but their attempts were seen to be so ineffectual that in April 1850 the prime minister, Lord John Russell, announced the government's intention to appoint a royal commission to study the two ancient universities. The commission's report in 1852 recommended a broadening of studies at both universities, the appointment of additional professors and a staff of university lecturers who should be permitted to marry, and the provision of new lecture rooms, laboratories, and museums.[17] In 1854 and 1855 acts of Parliament implemented some of the reforms recommended by the royal commission. There were in subsequent decades further royal commissions and acts of Parliament which ultimately resulted in the removal of religious barriers to admission to the universities, permission for the fellows of colleges to marry, and an expansion of both teaching staffs and areas of study at Oxford and Cambridge.

In 1870 Michael Foster was appointed, at the age of thirty-four, prelector in physiology at Trinity College, Cambridge. The Natural Sciences Tripos had been established at Cambridge in 1851, and Foster's appointment represented an effort to provide better instruction in physiology for students preparing for that examination. Foster began to teach a course in general biology, the first such course offered in any university. His broad biological approach to physiology was reflected in the research carried out during the next thirty years in the physiological laboratory which Foster created at Cambridge.[18] By 1900 the work of Foster's students had given the Cambridge laboratory a position of world leadership in physiological research. Walter Holbrook Gaskell had demonstrated the myogenic nature of the heart beat; John Newport Langley had carried out his fundamental investigations of the autonomic nervous system; and Charles Sherrington was carrying out the researches on which he based his concept of the integrative action of the nervous system. The distinctively biological character of Cambridge physiology owed much to the deep influence of Charles Darwin.

In 1871 James Clerk Maxwell was appointed Cavendish Professor of Experimental Physics at Cambridge. His first task was to oversee the construction and furnishing of the Cavendish Laboratory where he worked to create a center of research in physics. After Maxwell's death in 1879 Lord Rayleigh became director of the laboratory, and in 1884 he in turn was succeeded by Sir J. J. Thomson. By 1895, when Ernest Rutherford came from New Zealand to study at the Cavendish, the laboratory contained an active group of investigators.[19] The researches of the Cavendish Laboratory gave England at the close of the Victorian period the same kind of leadership in experimental physics which it possessed in physiological research as a result of the work of Foster and his students.

The rapidity with which Britain moved from a state of almost total neglect of experimental science in 1870 to a position of world leadership in at least certain areas of science by 1900 requires some explanation. The development of research at Cambridge occurred so quickly, as soon as relatively small amounts of money and relatively few men were devoted to it, as to suggest that Britain possessed other resources of a less easily definable kind which helped to make her extraordinarily creative in science. In England in the seventeenth century, although science seemed to develop independently of the universities, it was largely created by men who had been educated at Oxford and Cambridge.[20] Much the same thing was true during the nineteenth century, if one makes due allowance for the influence of the Scottish universities and the University of London. Almost all the scientific amateurs were educated at one or another of the universities; many of them were educated at Oxford or Cambridge. Men educated in the universities set the tone of intellectual and social life in the scientific societies. For all their faults Oxford and Cambridge had set a value upon learning for its own sake and they imparted a respect for learning to their students.[21] The study of science may not have been part of the curriculum, but it was an avocation fitting for an educated man. Lyell at Exeter College, Oxford, in 1816, Darwin at Christ's College, Cambridge, in 1828, and Clerk Maxwell at Trinity College, Cambridge, in 1851 — all surrounded themselves in their college rooms with books reflecting their scientific interests and made scientific pursuits one of the chief activities of their leisure. Influenced by the ancient traditions of university life they took for granted that scientific learning was worthy of cultivation.

During the Victorian period the scientific amateurs maintained the scientific life of Britain when science did not form a part of regular university instruction. They created the scientific societies and through the societies gave to science essential social, financial, and moral support. Moreover, those amateurs who became great scientists gave to scientific learning in Britain a richness and depth that laid the foundations for the rapid development of a corps of professional experimental scientists after 1870. The scientific amateurs worked privately in their homes. In the evenings they read by flickering candles, but they nonetheless envisioned scientific problems in a light of penetrating intensity.

Going on Stage

Michael R. Booth

I n 1827 the elocution teacher and handbook writer Leman Rede estimated "there are supposed to be about six thousand individuals that are
known to possess claims to the titles of actor and actress — or, in more plain
terms, who thoroughly know their business; the number of persons claiming those honours are perhaps nearly seven times that number."[1] Rede admitted that this was a "rough calculation," but if it is anywhere near the
truth the figures indicate a sizable employment market. This is not surprising, since the British theatre in the period from 1820 to 1843 was
becoming an entertainment industry of considerable proportions: Rede
lists forty-six managements of theatrical "circuits" (a regional chain of
theaters in a particular area under one management) that paid fixed
weekly wages, and eight "sharing" managements (in which actors shared
box office revenue), not to mention the numerous itinerant troupes of a
lower class and the respectable fairground companies — the most famous being Richardson's — that played in large booth theaters and
moved from fair to fair every spring, summer, and autumn.

Of this great number of theatrical performers, a significant minority
must have been novices. Indeed, it was to advise them that Rede wrote
The Road to the Stage. At the beginning of the Victorian period the stage-
struck young man pondering his future career could, if he were fortunate,
follow the same path to success as his predecessors for generations past;
that is, obtain an engagement with a small country company, rise in the
provinces until he became a leading player with an important stock company, possibly make a summer engagement at the Haymarket in London,
and then secure a permanent position in the metropolis, either at Drury
Lane or Covent Garden. Such a course had been taken by eminent performers like John Philip Kemble, his sister Sarah Siddons, William

Charles Macready, Edmund Kean, and Samuel Phelps. Kemble first appeared at Wolverhampton in 1776, and after successive engagements at Liverpool, York, and Dublin went to Drury Lane in 1783. Sarah Siddons acted with her father's traveling company, was noticed at Cheltenham, and given an early engagement at Drury Lane in 1775. There she failed, spent some years on the circuits, moved to the most respected of provincial companies at Bath, and returned to Drury Lane in 1782. In 1809, at the age of fifteen, Macready had to leave school at Rugby to look after his father's Birmingham circuit because of the latter's financial difficulties. He made his acting debut with his father's company in 1810, went later to Bath and Dublin, and came out at Covent Garden in 1816 with a three-year contract in his pocket. Both Kean and Phelps took rather longer to reach London. Kean began at Sheerness at fifteen shillings a week in 1804, when he was only fourteen; nine years later after many hard knocks on many circuits, he was making only two guineas a week at Dorchester. From there he went on to make his sensational debut as Shylock at Drury Lane in 1814. In 1826 Phelps gave up a job on a London evening newspaper at a respectable three to four pounds a week to take eighteen shillings on the York circuit. Not until 1837 and a successful Exeter season was he offered a position in a London theater, and in the meantime, like Kean, he and his family had suffered much poverty and hardship.

Several points emerge from an examination of the early careers of these performers that are relevant to the whole business of going on stage in the Victorian period. Obviously, it made a great deal of difference whether or not the actor's parents were themselves of the theater. To a considerable degree the eighteenth and nineteenth century stage was populated by theatrical families extending over many generations, of whom the most talented and influential, like the Kembles and the Terrys, assumed the power and importance of great dynasties. Seven of the twelve children of Roger Kemble went on stage; four — Sarah, John, Charles, and Stephen — became famous. Although Sarah acted from childhood, John was not intended for the theater; he abandoned uncongenial religious studies at Douai to begin acting. Similarly, although his father was a manager, Macready was meant to go on to Oxford and the bar and only left school because of his father's problems. Kean did not come from a theatrical family, but his mother and his adoptive aunt were actresses, and he learned to recite, sing, dance, fence, and somersault while still a child. Phelps, on the other hand, had no theatrical background. His father was a naval tailor, and after his death Phelps's elder brother, a wine and spirit merchant in Devonport, looked after him. Thus Phelps had to sneak off from home to act in afterpieces at the local theater, and when he decided to become an actor he had no connections to help him.

An actor's connections were invaluable at the outset of his career; to be born into a theatrical family and intended for the stage — from which even as a child he could add to the family income — meant that his beginnings were automatically ensured. A very large number of nineteenth-century actors started in this way. Even if the actor took a late decision, like Kemble, to go upon the stage, his way could be smoothed for him by family influence and recommendation. Fanny Kemble, the daughter of John's brother Charles, began acting at nineteen only to rescue her father from impending bankruptcy. Since he was manager of Covent Garden at the time, her debut was easily made, but since she was a Kemble she could have made it anywhere. As it happened, her appearance as Juliet in 1829 was an enormous public success, and she did indeed, acting for three seasons, save her father and the theater. Although *his* first appearance at Drury Lane in 1827 was a disastrous failure, the young Charles Kean, who left Eton at sixteen to make it because his father Edmund refused to support him any longer, was only offered a respectable three-year contract (he had never acted before) because of his father's name.[2]

These family means of going on stage remained an important part of the Victorian theater. As a child of eight in 1856, Ellen Terry — whose mother, father, and five brothers and sisters were theatricals — joined Charles Kean at the Princess's Theatre and acted with his company for three years. Madge Robertson (later Kendal) first acted in James Chute's Bristol company with her mother and father; the latter had been manager of the recently defunct Lincoln circuit. Marie Wilton, whose parents were traveling players, began reciting and acting with them in 1843 or 1844 when only four or five years old. Lester Wallack, a member of another well-known theatrical dynasty, acted with his father James on the latter's starring visit to Bristol and other provincial towns in 1839; he had previously acted only at school. Then he joined his uncle Henry's company at Rochester. Helen Faucit and George Vandenhoff walked straight into major London engagements on the strength of their connections. Although her mother, father, three brothers, and a sister were already on the stage, it was decreed that Helen Faucit was not to follow them, and she was kept away from the theater. Tutored, however, by her friend and mentor Percy Farren (himself bearing the name of a family prominent on the British stage for over two centuries), she appeared at Covent Garden in 1836; a year later she was Macready's leading actress. In 1839, at the age of twenty-six, Vandenhoff abandoned the post of solicitor to the trustees of the Liverpool Docks and applied for a position in Madame Vestris's new company at Covent Garden. He was engaged at eight pounds a week, without ever having been on the stage, or having studied anything but law books. The fact that his father John was still a noted London tragedian must have done him no harm. The same thing happened to Charles Mathews, Jr., who, talented though he was, was taken into Vestris's Olympic company in 1835 partly on the strength of his father's reputation; he had acted only as an amateur.

Other actors, not so fortunate in their connections or their teachers, had to make their own way. The objective of most young actors, London, was held in common and the means the same, whether or not they came from theatrical families: an apprenticeship in the provinces sufficient to obtain the necessary experience and training in order to attract the favorable attention of a London manager. Very few were able to begin their careers successfully in London. Kemble, Siddons, Kean, Macready, Phelps, and scores of well-known Victorian actors followed this road. Before 1843 and the formal abolition of their monopoly privileges, Drury Lane and Covent Garden possessed the only major companies that could offer employment at the highest salaries for the winter season; therefore it was to Drury Lane and Covent Garden that actors aspired most. After 1843, when permanent companies were virtually a thing of the past and an actor who had reached his metropolitan goal could no longer expect to spend the rest of his career safely under the roof of one theater, any one of a number of West End theaters might offer tempting engagements, if only for the run of a play, and there was a good deal of moving about between theaters.

A small provincial company was, then, the appropriate place to begin one's career. In order to obtain an engagement, the actor — if he did not have family or friends to recommend him — wrote to country managers, applied to theatrical agents, advertised in the *Era* (first published in 1838), or answered advertisements himself. A beginning of this kind was usually poorly paid; a new actor could hardly hope to receive more than the minimum salary. Leman Rede is informative on salaries in the 1820s. The best provincial companies, like Liverpool, Edinburgh, and Dublin, paid little more than a guinea a week to the novice; on lesser circuits, such as Twickenham-Cobham-Mitcham-Wimbledon-Henley, he could receive as little as fifteen shillings.[3] These figures are exclusive of the income from an annual benefit that could net a reasonable sum for an established performer; the new actor, however, would share a benefit with several others and gain little. Starting salaries did not change much over the years. In 1794 Charles Mathews, Sr., left an apprenticeship with his father, a bookseller, to begin his acting career in Dublin for a guinea a week, and four years later was receiving only one pound from Tate Wilkinson at York. Dublin and the York circuit then played a significant role in provincial theater.[4] Edmund Kean, as we have seen, began for fifteen shillings at lowly Sheerness. In 1839 Lester Wallack got one pound at Rochester.[5] In 1845 John Coleman, dismissed at the age of fifteen from a district surveyor's office, had previously paid to act in a private theater. He then played for nothing at the Standard in Shoreditch, finally obtaining twelve shillings a week for general utility parts at Windsor and moving to a guinea on the Lincoln circuit. In 1861 Squire Bancroft, who at the age of nineteen had written numerous letters to country managers applying for a position, was engaged at the Theatre Royal, Birmingham, for a guinea. Robert Courtneidge in 1879 threw over a steady job as bookkeeper to a sewing-machine firm in Manchester at two pounds a week to go on as a supernumerary in the Christmas pantomime for one shilling and sixpence a performance. It was from such humble and badly paid jobs as general utility and walking gentleman that the beginning actor hoped to work his way up to more lucrative positions like first low comedian, first light comedian, or tragedian,[6] and in the process remove to better companies with higher salaries.

Having hopefully established himself as a performer of provincial distinction, a process that commonly took several years, the actor would normally look expectantly toward London. But this was not always the case. Through lack of desire, ambition, or talent, the vast majority of Victorian actors either never reached London at all or else appeared there fleetingly and unnoticed. Seymour Hicks, who began to act in the provinces in 1888, observed of them:

The thing that struck me most about the regular provincial actors whom I knew was, in most cases, their absolute indifference as to whether they ever appeared in London or not. For nearly fifty-two weeks year in and year out they journeyed from town to town quite contentedly, and indeed holding, I daresay quite rightly, the London actor in contempt, as cramped in his methods, and feeling that the breaking of a teacup in some tragic scene was about the most violent emotion he was capable of.[7]

Actors like Bancroft and Henry Irving deliberately turned their backs on London in order to gain more experience in the country, and some stars — the tragedian Barry Sullivan was one — appeared infrequently in London but enjoyed an immense reputation in the provinces. Well-established and popular provincial players often considered carefully and bargained protractedly before accepting London offers. Writing from the York circuit in 1802, where he was a leading actor, to George Colman of the Haymarket, who had offered him an engagement for his summer season, Charles Mathews, Sr., said:

I am so fortunate as to be in great fame on this circuit, in possession of the first cast of characters, and on the best of terms with my manager. It is indeed in every respect a most valuable situation, and it is only on very advantageous terms that I shall be induced to quit it. I most undoubtedly wish to perform in London, but must look for an ample compensation for resigning a lucrative situation, for an engagement of only four months. I shall be obliged to you, sir, to let me know what salaries you can afford to give, and if I accede to your wishes, what business will be allotted me. This is a very material consideration, and I entreat you will be as explicit as possible. I have performed in the York theatre the entire range of principal low comedy, and am well studied. Have the goodness to inform me, if at any part of the season any of the established London performers are to be engaged.[8]

Noting that "on an average" only one actor in a hundred ever came to Drury Lane or Covent Garden (London's minor theaters were not nearly so desirable), Rede declared that this was not a matter of regret, since "many provincial situations are preferable to London ones; the favourite of the Bath, Dublin, Edinburgh, and Glasgow Theatres may, with reasonable prudence, realize from four to five hundred pounds per annum; and an income equal to that has been amassed on the York circuit. An engagement of twelve guineas per week at a royal theatre amounts, with the deductions made during Lent, Passion Week, and the usual vacation, to something less than five hundred pounds a year."[9] In Rede's opinion "no actor or actress should come to London except under an engagement, and not then if they hold comfortable country situations, unless, indeed, they see the field open for them."[10]

A "comfortable country situation" in a good provincial company was a far cry from the conditions in which many young actors had to work. To secure a berth in a circuit in which the performers moved at fixed seasons from one familiar town to the next, and in which salaries, though small, were regularly paid and employment relatively secure, was one thing; but to join an itinerant, often badly and irresponsibly managed "sharing" troupe, as so many actors did for want of a better job, was to court poverty and starvation. These troupes, constantly dissolving and forming again in different combinations, led an irregular and highly uncertain life. When under financial difficulties some of the old circuits began to break up, and small towns were thus deprived of their annual stock company visit, such troupes increased in number. John Coleman remembered, about 1846, tramping around small Scottish towns with a poor company in which shares sometimes came to half a crown a night, sometimes a shilling, sometimes nothing at all. Transferring from the theater at Greenock to Helensburgh, Coleman and his companions were rowed across the Clyde in a drenching rainstorm, so famished that they fell eagerly upon a field of turnips when they landed. Then came a long hike to Helensburgh. "The horrors of that tramp over moor and fell I can never forget. Cold, hungry, badly shod, thinly clad, drenched with rain, snow, and hail, we limped into Helensburgh more dead than alive." Finding nowhere to sleep, they had to accept the charity of gypsies.[11] About 1880 Robert Courtneidge joined a sharing company touring small towns in Yorkshire, mostly with old melodramas. In Barnsley he did not eat for two days and slept in an old barn. In Hoyland he too had to resort to field turnips. The theater and the circumstances of rehearsal in Hoyland were typical of the conditions to which these itinerant groups were accustomed — one could say inured:

It [the theater] was an unsteady erection of wood covered with canvas, patched and torn in many places. A number of rough wooden benches were lined up facing a little stage, with lamps for footlights. There was a curtain, raised and lowered by a rope at the side, on which was daubed something resembling a landscape. The rehearsal did not take long. We all had some knowledge of the plays and it was sufficient to say: "You come on here and say so and so," and then "I reply so and so, and we 'pong' away until, etc. etc." The art of ponging, I must explain, is the ability to go upon the stage with only a slight knowledge of the structure and characters of a play and improvise the dialogue, fitting it to the situations agreed upon. Practice soon sharpens the wits and makes one an adept in improvization. The actor moulds his part as he goes along and frequently finds a keener pleasure than when speaking the words of an author.[12]

After a fortnight in Hoyland, business had so fallen off from the opening share of one shilling and sixpence each that the company had to
disband. When Courtneidge finally secured a regular job as a low comedian at Bury, his salary of twenty-five shillings a week seemed untold
riches. Even in more settled companies conditions could be far from
satisfactory. Russell Craufurd in 1874 answered an advertisement for a
young man to join a Lancashire company, accepted the manager's offer,
despite the very low salary, and traveled north:

I found the theatre, interviewed my manager, who seemed to take more interest
in the fact that I had quite a collection of wigs and "props" than anything else,
and was given a small part to study for the next night. He did not seem to attach
much importance to rehearsals, but said I could run through the lines with him in
the morning. The play was *The Home Wreck*. I got through somehow. The
company appeared very careless, and I gathered from certain uncomplimentary
remarks made in the dressing-room that salaries were somewhat in arrear. Oh,
that dressing-room! It was under the stage, a mere cellar with an earthen floor, a
rude shelf fixed round, two or three bottomless chairs, and lighted by a few
guttering tallow candles stuck in bottles.[13]

The main problem encountered by the penurious actor in his first job,
whether in a stock or itinerant company — apart from the serious matter
of paying for food and lodging — was providing himself with a sufficient
variety of costumes to meet the requirements of his parts in both stock
and new plays. Through most of the nineteenth century it was not the
practice of country managements to provide a wardrobe for their actors,
although the better ones could help out on occasion. Thus a new actor
had to find his own costumes, wigs, and often his properties (like
swords) as well. Leman Rede pointed out that a player could lose parts in
a good company if he could not dress them properly. His list of the basic
dresses needed for the whole range of stock characters is pages long. "For
those Thespians who study economy in their purchases," he advised,
"the tribe of Israel should be resorted to," since "the descendants of
Moses are notorious as vendors of theatrical wardrobes."[14] Charles
Mathews, Sr., wrote from Dublin in 1794 that "I can make my cash hold
out very well, but am in want of many stage properties, particularly for
tragedy: buskins, russet boots, Spanish hat, sword, ruff, & c."[15] Over the
next hundred years the problems and the possible solutions remained the
same. On the point of setting out to his first engagement at Barrow-in-
Furness in 1881, John Martin-Harvey was advised to invest in the kind of
wardrobe "considered indispensable to start on my career, viz: a pair of

red worsted tights, a pair of black velveteen shoes, a sword hanger, in which to carry my father's old volunteer sabre, a frock coat of uncertain period, which could, therefore, with the addition of gold braid, be turned into a military tunic, and several black American cloth 'tops' by the addition of which a pair of Wellingtons could be lengthened into ordinary riding boots, bucket-tops, Cavalier, or even Elizabethan turret-tops."[16] With considerably less money than Martin-Harvey, Russell Craufurd, acting in a low company at Portsmouth in the seventies, noted to what varied uses the essential items of a theatrical wardrobe could be put, and what makeshifts were necessary to hide its deficiencies:

I found it was customary in a stock company to start the season with white tights, which could be dyed lavender, red, and, finally, black. What curious expedients we were sometimes put to. I have known a dress coat handed from one to another in the wings several times during a performance. It was a current idea that white cotton stockings assumed the appearance of silk from the front by making a heavy line of white chalk on the shin bone. A white tie was easily made from a strip of notepaper, and even a shirt front could be managed from highly glazed notepaper. White cotton gloves were *de rigueur* in place of the more expensive kid ones.[17]

Robert Courtneidge, struggling to survive at Barnsley, remembered the inventiveness of a fellow actor, a real artist of makeup and costume:

If he wanted a wig, he would manufacture it out of an old stocking, stitching whatever shade and mass of crape hair he required upon this foundation. Paper, white and brown, served him for many purposes. If he had to wear a dress-suit, a sheet of white cardboard made him a shirt-front, cuffs, and a collar. On these were painted studs, and to the collar was attached a paper tie. Pins, needles, and thread transformed his own seedy black coat and vest into a fashionable appearance, and if a silk hat was wanted he would make the top with brown paper, blacked and varnished. This he slipped over his weather-beaten bowler, which was carefully touched-up around the rims to match. For a sporting character, Reg. walked on stage in improvised gaiters of brown paper, glued on to a piece of calico, a paper vest backed with the same cheap material, on which he had stamped a spotted pattern, with a cardboard collar, a stock, and a flower in his buttonhole made of coloured paper. If spats were needed, he covered the tops of his boots with a thick white paste. His ingenuity was endless, affording us constant amusement, but from the front he was the best-dressed man in the company.[18]

Whether he began at the bottom of the theatrical ladder or at a higher rung, the workload for the young actor was extremely heavy; standards, of course, were more exacting the higher he climbed. Until the days of the long run in London or of the touring company formed for the production of one play and disbanded after the tour ended, the stock company was organized on true repertory principles. In many small companies the bill would change nightly as long as they stayed in the same place. In the larger centers three or four changes a week could be expected, and the arrival of a visiting star with his own repertory could mean a week or two of nightly changes. The entertainment offered consisted of two, three, and sometimes four pieces an evening, so that it was not merely a question of an actor playing one part. The smaller and more makeshift the company, the more doubling and trebling of roles resulted, with a consequent increase of labor for the player. After he had been doing this for several years, one of two things happened. If he remained near the bottom of the ladder, as so many did, he became familiar with an enormous number of parts and could draw on his experience, thus reducing his effort. If he graduated to better companies and reached the position of leading actor, he played fewer parts and, as befitting his status, appeared in fewer pieces.

At the start, however, the amount of work was staggering, especially in companies above the itinerant level where scripts had to be studied and memorized. Leman Rede estimated that "a country actor in a small company, and aspiring to a first-rate situation, will invariably have to study about *five hundred lines per diem* . . . . this will occupy the possessor of a good memory for six hours — his duties at the theatre embrace four hours in the morning for rehearsal, and about five at night; here are sixteen hours devoted to labour alone, to say nothing of the time required to study the character, after the mere attainment of the words."[19] This estimate of sixteen hours a day labor for the novice was confirmed by John Coleman, looking back to the forties and fifties. "Four and even as many as six hours were daily devoted to study, four at least to rehearsals, and five to the nightly performance."[20] Lester Wallack recalled playing alternate nights in Southampton and Winchester in 1844, the company traveling between the two theaters in a small omnibus, lit inside by a single lantern:

We acted in three plays a night in those days, and had to write out our own parts too. We were not provided with books, and studied by the light of this lantern, arriving at our own destination awfully tired in the middle of the night, or perhaps early in the morning. Sometimes we had but one rehearsal, and sometimes two, seldom more; and to this early discipline I owe the retentive powers of memory which have been of such wonderful assistance to me ever since.[21]

The number of parts an actor had to play under this system was very large, and rehearsals comparatively few: there was simply not enough time. In his first professional engagement on the York circuit in 1826, Samuel Phelps is reported to have played six parts in *Macbeth*: a Witch, Duncan, Ross, the First Murderer, an Apparition, and a Messenger. Sixty years later the situation was much the same. In 1889, George Arliss, who had answered an advertisement in the *Stage*, arrived in Doncaster to join the Irish Repertoire Company at twenty-five shillings a week. He was met at the station by the stage manager and handed six long parts in Irish dramas and two farce parts, all to be played the following week at Rotherham. "I put my back into it, sat up of course nearly all night every night, studying, and I think I spoke most of the lines."[22] In the summer of 1861 Squire Bancroft played forty new roles in thirty-six nights at Cork, "so had little time for anything but work, long hours of the night being often devoted to copying out my part from a well-thumbed book which had to be passed to another member of the little company, while the days were spent in study and rehearsal; for the performance was changed, or partly so, nearly every evening."[23] After this Bancroft played thirty leading parts new to him, together with many familiar ones, in a six-week summer season at Devonport. Altogether, in four years and four months of acting in the country before he went to London, he played 346 different parts. This incredible figure was exceeded by Henry Irving, who played 428 parts in his first thirty months on stage in the 1850s. Such work was not only exhausting from the point of view of time and effort spent in study, rehearsal, and performance, but it could also be physically most demanding. Acting utility roles in Aberdeen in the eighties, Robert Courtneidge supplemented his small salary with five shillings a week for playing the long-suffering "swell" in the comic scenes of Christmas pantomime:

For this I had to jump through traps, be smothered in flour, half-drowned with water, and knocked on the head by the clown, policeman, and supers. It was hard and often painful work, for the Aberdeen lads were strong, and enjoyed hitting me. There were many angry scenes at the sides as I came off after a particularly heavy drubbing, but I bore all gladly for the sake of the money it brought me.[24]

The necessary grinding labor of an actor's early days in the theater, combined with the inevitable separation from the community imposed by his vocation and his constant traveling, meant that what rare time he had was spent with his fellows. Actors lived together in boarding houses catering only to theatricals, worked together, and socialized together after the performance, frequently not even talking to anybody unconnected with the theater. Such a life could be pleasant in its leisure moments, but it imposed its own peculiar strains and tensions. Cyril Maude, who was born into a prosperous middle-class family with aristocratic connections and intended for the army or the church, but went on the stage in 1883, said of his tour with a small "fit-up" company playing mostly in town halls that "the lives of us young people on tour were lonely and demoralising. We hardly ever met any people of our own class outside the members of the company, and I remember with shame and indignation being usually classed in the little towns we visited as 'them theatricals'; and when we applied for rooms we sometimes had the front door slammed in our faces!"[25] In some northern industrial towns actresses could receive very rough treatment from mill workers if found alone and unprotected, an extreme example of the considerable moral hostility toward the acting profession almost universally found outside the larger and more sophisticated cities. Moments of relaxation and ease, when they came, were eagerly seized — too eagerly, in many cases. Robert Courtneidge paints a picture of the social pleasures awaiting the actor after the play:

What a delight it was to the young actor to sit with pipe and glass in a cosy room hearkening to the elders of his calling pouring out a flood of anecdotes; listening to their criticism, their jokes, and oftentimes their songs and recitations. For a youth it was an easy apprenticeship to drunken habits, and I embraced it readily, going home in the early morning with a fuddled brain, waking to reproach and the determination to "forswear sack and live cleanly," and then again at night yielding to the temptation. How often I lingered at the stage-door, hesitating between duty and inclination. On one side a lamp-lit cheerless room, with a meagre fire; on the table bread and cheese and, near at hand, my bed, my books. Around the walls, black-edged funeral cards, grim photographs and family groups, distressing in their ugliness. Duty urged me to go home to study, but on the other hand there was a bright parlour, cheerful with glowing fire, laughter, good fellowship, wit and humour, and on the table, glasses filled with pleasant liquor. An arm is placed round my shoulder — "Coming, Bob?" — and I would weakly give way to inclination, comforting myself that I was a quick study and by early rising I could easily be perfect for rehearsal.[26]

Very soon after this, Courtneidge by a strong effort of will pulled himself out of the drifting life of seedy dissipation into which such habits were inexorably drawing him, but many actors did not, and many — like George Frederick Cooke, Edmund Kean, and Charles Dillon — had brilliant stage careers cut short by drink. In justification, one could suggest that "if the actor unduly prolonged the notes of good fellowship much might be forgiven to one whose life was precarious, and whose pleasures, apart from his work, were but few."[27]

The pattern of the small touring company and its round of little towns remained constant all through the Victorian period, but higher up in the theatrical scale significant organizational changes were altering the actor's traditional means of entering upon his career. The decline of Covent Garden and Drury Lane from their old position as the ultimate goals of the ambitious actor and their replacement by a variety of West End theaters has already been referred to. With the arrival after 1850 of the long run in London and the rapid development of good railway communications, it became possible to send out to the provinces whole companies touring the latest long-running West End hit.[28] Formerly the visiting star would play a short season with the local stock company on his own tour of the provinces, but now the stock company itself was superfluous; provincial theaters ceased to be locally owned, many falling into the hands of big organizations that used them as mere staging posts for their West End–originated tours. By the 1870s the old circuits and stock companies were rapidly vanishing, and the usual route of the aspirant to acting fame — from small country theater to stock company of high standing to London — was fast becoming impossible.

By the late seventies an argument was already raging over the acting merit of the old stock companies compared to that of the new groups put together for a long run or for the extended tour of a single play. A classic defense of the stock company experience was advanced by Percy Fitzgerald:

This experience, though acquired in a hurried and perfunctory fashion, is of enormous value in the way of training. The player is thus introduced to every shade and form of character, and can practice himself in all the methods of expression. Such will prompt or inspire a performer of even indifferent abilities. He is forced, almost in spite of himself, to find proper expression for modes of thought, humours, and the like. When he finds himself in possession of some new part, the old experience will supply him with devices or suggestions. It is only in this way that the actor will acquire the incomparable and invaluable gift of *breadth*, which is the sole and perhaps exclusive property of the actors of "the old school." . . . .[29]

"They are always 'ready,'" W. Davenport Adams noted of stock company actors; "there is scarcely a part in the legitimate or romantic drama in which they have not figured, and which they cannot undertake 'at the shortest notice.'"[30] Opponents claimed that these actors had too much work to do and too short a time to do it in, being thus unable to rise above respectable mediocrity. Both dramatists and the public, they said, were better served by the careful casting, the adequate rehearsal period, and the more finished production given to the touring or long-running play. The debate between the two schools was heated and protracted, extending well into the twentieth century.

Whatever the merits of the argument — and actors who knew both systems invariably argued in favor of the old one — the problem remained of how the actor was to obtain his training (or self-schooling) and experience now that country stock companies hardly existed. The number of old actors giving lessons in elocution and stage deportment increased, but few were really useful or could help their pupils after lessons were over. Such instruction had always been given, and some teachers were very good and very influential. Marie Wilton "worked hard every day in a little quiet room at the back of the house we lodged in" taking lessons in elocution from her mother,[31] but this was standard practice in theatrical families and could hardly be considered teaching in the formal sense. Representative of the best sort of teacher taking paying pupils was Leigh Murray, an accomplished comedian and *jeune premier* whom ill health forced into early retirement. In 1864 he gave lessons to John Hare, accompanied him to Liverpool afterward, and secured him an engagement with the stock company at the Prince of Wales's there. A few months later Hare was a notable member of the Bancrofts' new company in London. In 1867 Frank Archer went from taking fencing lessons with an old soldier to instruction in elocution from Murray, who then found him a job with the Savilles at the Theatre Royal, Nottingham. Russell Craufurd took lessons in 1874 from Walter Lacy, who had acted with Madame Vestris and Charles Kean. John Ryder, a leading actor with Macready, was also a celebrated teacher; he gave elocution lessons to the young Martin-Harvey in 1881. However, teachers of this caliber were few and far between; more characteristic of the general quality was Martin-Harvey's second teacher, whom he found by answering an advertisement in the *Daily Telegraph* — typical of hundreds like it — that said, "Stage aspirants taught the whole art of acting including make-up. £2 2s. Engagements guaranteed." The "learning" process consisted of playing opposite an "inoffensive little man," in a sordid little room, in the ancient melodrama *A Tale of Mystery*. The "guaranteed engagement" meant looking through the pages of the *Era* for theatrical vacancies.[32]

Instruction of this latter kind was next to useless, but there were few alternatives. Some young men and women were fortunate enough to walk straight into good engagements with little or no experience behind them, and no training. In 1874 the dramatist W. G. Wills asked Norman Forbes-Robertson, then an art student, to take a part in a new play of his at the Princess's, *Mary, Queen o' Scots*. Weedon Grossmith, an unsuccessful society painter, was sitting on the top of a coach at the 1885 Eton-Harrow match when he was asked by a friend to play comic parts on an American tour at fifteen pounds a week; he had never acted before. These were the days when fashionable young men and women felt urged to go on stage; the tendency of the modern drama toward drawing-room plays with fashionable young men and women for characters encouraged this desire. Society's impulse toward the stage as a career, or at least a fashionable plaything, followed the precedent set by the beautiful Lillie Langtry, the daughter of the Dean of Jersey and wife of a wealthy Irishman, who in 1882 went from her role as a prominent society hostess to a three-month engagement with the Bancrofts at a very large salary; her debut created an enormous social sensation and drew packed houses.

Good fortune and social status were given singly or in combination to relatively few young hopefuls, however, and they had to consider more practical courses of action. A part with a touring company might be obtained, but one part played over a long tour did not enlarge the actor's horizons. The West End was still difficult to break into, and the long run again prevented a variety of experience. H. J. Byron, who favored the new touring combinations because, he claimed, they presented better acting to the public than the old stock companies, was against them from the point of view of the beginning actor:

If a person wishes to accustom himself to the boards and to test his own fitness, playing one or two very short parts, possibly of a few lines, for a year or two with a "travelling" company can be of no use, and is only a waste of time. . . . London for a start is of course out of the question. There are some instances of well-dressed, good-looking young men who have had no experience whatever, strolling through unemotional characters without giving any particular offence, but from whom it is hopeless to expect anything better without larger opportunities for practice; and London audiences expect their actors to come before them "ready-made." [33]

George Alexander questioned the value to the actor of trying to reproduce on tour what he had seen in the West End:

A play is a success in London. So soon as it has reached its fiftieth or hundredth representation, a touring company is organised. Young inexperienced actors and actresses come to see it a few times, learn the words like parrots, are engaged, and make the character they have to assume as close a copy of the original as they possibly can. Instead of being an education, the engagement is a positive draw-back to them.[34]

Complaining that it took him ten years to break into the West End despite being well known in the provinces, George Arliss protested against the West End manager's lack of interest in searching out good young actors:

When he was casting a play he never looked beyond the four-mile radius. I don't think a manager would even have taken a cab and driver to a suburban theatre in order to see or discover new talent. The man who broke into the West End did it either through his own tremendous exertions or else through the efforts of some "friend at Court." A West End manager never knew anything about an actor until he was thrown in his lap.[35]

However, Arliss discovered when he finally reached the West End in 1899 that "I had a considerable advantage over most of those actors who, by influence or by choice, had started their career in the West End of London and who at the end of ten years had not played more than a score of parts at the most."[36]

Several solutions were proposed to the problem of how to bring up the late-Victorian actor to the stage, but only one proved effective; indeed, it was the only one that saw the practical light of day. George Alexander suggested a system of theatrical apprenticeship in which the actor would study at a school of dramatic art, undergo examinations, and if successul be apprenticed for a fixed term to a manager at a small but increasing salary. B. W. Findon scorned the modern young actor who "rises late; saunters down to his club, and devotes the most precious moments of his life to the consumption of mild cigarettes and seltzers and whiskies," and who ranks "luxurious clubs and fashionable 'at homes' among the neces-saries of life."[37] Instead, he recommended that the amateur dramatic society be the future School of Dramatic Art. Anyone wishing to become a professional actor would have to join such a society. All amateur societies would be regulated by the professional theater, which would also offer lessons in elocution, fencing, and other subjects. The best amateurs would give four performances annually in the West End, and from these the professionals would recruit their fresh talent. The idea of some kind of school was very much in the air, and it was often proposed that it be attached to a new National Theater, an institution that all through the Victorian period was so strongly urged upon an uninterested public and reluctant government. Finally, however, in 1904 Herbert Beerbohm Tree founded the Royal Academy of Dramatic Art at his own theater, His Majesty's; two years later the Central School was started by Elsie Fogerty.

Thus at the end of the nineteenth century the actor was much more restricted in opportunity than at the beginning. The old system of advancement through a traditional and well-ordered hierarchy of theaters had been destroyed forever; his career was much more dependent upon chance and luck than it ever had been before. However, even when the initial obstacles had been overcome, a theatrical career was the most uncertain of occupations, for both the new and experienced actor. This, after a lifetime in the theater, Robert Courtneidge well knew, and his words make a fitting if melancholy conclusion to the exploration of a subject so passionately important to thousands of young men and women of the nineteenth century:

It is obvious, then, that the theatrical calling is only a seasonal occupation, subject to many hazards that no prudence can avert, but which very seriously affect the actor's income. For the great majority of those employed on the stage it is a life of struggle and disappointment, with unprovided old age in the distance. To a lesser number it is a fairly comfortable living; to a comparative few it brings a handsome income. Except with a tiny number, the conditions are never stable. Those who stand on firm ground one day may find a quicksand underfoot the next.[38]

There Began to Be a
Great Talking about
the Fine Arts

George P. Landow

There began to be a great talking about the Fine Arts. It was a tempting time for ambitious ignorance. If the knowing had failed to instruct, why should not others try their hand? There was little difficulty in setting about it. Every quack was an example; — abuse all the old and the regular bred of the faculty. Do as a celebrated one did; — rub a good itching disorder into the backs of people, and tell them boldly that's the way to get health and a sound taste. . . . If possible, be "a graduate," and be sure to repeat the title upon every occasion.[1]

The writer is the Reverend John Eagles of *Blackwood's*, and that troublesome graduate, of course, is John Ruskin, the giant of Victorian art criticism whose long shadow cast many such competitors into the shade. Eagles's attack upon the author of *Modern Painters* furnishes a convenient point of departure for a brief exploratory voyage through Victorian art criticism, reminding us, first of all, of its essentially polemical nature and, second, of the central importance of both Ruskin and periodical reviewing.

Their importance derives from the increasing democratization of the art public in Victorian England. As the conservative *Blackwood's* pointed out in 1862, "Patronage is now not solely in the sovereignty of the state or in the power of the church, but in the hands of the people. Palaces and churches in these days call for fewer pictures than the private dwellings of merchants and manufacturers."[2] This movement of patronage downward in the social scale had major effects upon the nature of the painter's audience, his relation to it, and the kind of art he consequently produced. Although the relation of the artist to patron did not change either as rapidly or as decisively as did that of the English author to his public, one can nonetheless note obvious parallels between the situation in each art. Shortly after the middle of the eighteenth century Dr. Johnson had announced the decline of the literary patron, whom he had defined for Lord Chesterfield as "one who looks with unconcern on a Man struggling for life in the Water and when he has reached ground encumbers him with help." Although chapbooks and broadsides had existed to supply ephemeral reading matter for the lower and middle classes for more than a century, serious literature generally required a generous sponsor to defer the cost of publication. One of the most important changes in the relation of the writer to his public is thus signaled when writers, like Dr. Johnson himself, publish works by subscription, for this mode of printing and distribution divides the power of a single wealthy, usually aristocratic patron among several hundred sponsors.

A far more drastic enlargement of the reading public occurs in the next century: repeal of repressive taxation on periodicals allowed the rapid growth of magazines and newspapers, while the growth of large lending libraries, such as Mudie's, effectively subsidized publication of novels and other literature. Students of the Victorian age increasingly call it a second English Renaissance — and with reason, for during these years the movement down the social scale of financial and political power was accompanied by a rapid expansion of the English reading public, which by the second half of the century already included many members of the working class; this greatly enlarged audience, in turn, called forth and magnificently sustained the golden age of the English novel.

One may doubt to what extent the situation in Victorian art can resemble that in literature, because the nature of painting makes it so difficult for a work to reach a large number of people. In particular, since oil painting is a medium which produces a single work at a time, a work in an edition of one, it cannot ever be quite as popular as a novel which can be printed in an edition of thousands or even tens of thousands. Nonetheless, despite these essential difficulties, similar changes in the relation of artist to audience did take place. First of all, as *Blackwood's* emphasized, most Victorian commissions came not from church, state, or aristocracy but from merchants and manufacturers. But to attract this new, expanding group of potential buyers the artist had to make them aware of his works, and this he could only do by exhibiting them in public. Such public display of paintings in turn produces periodical criticism: periodical art reviews require periodic exhibitions, a practice which begins in England with the first annual summer show of the Royal Academy in 1769.[3] Throughout most of the nineteenth century this exhibition remained the major event of the art world, for if an artist wished to establish his reputation and command good prices for his creations, he usually had to make his mark at this show.

Furthermore, he could secure both his reputation and his financial position by gaining election to the Royal Academy, first as an associate and then as a full member of that powerful body. But because the art world was far less centralized in England than it was in France, where access to the salons was a matter of financial survival, painters, such as Hunt and Rossetti, could make their way outside of the Academy. Artists, for instance, could make use of exhibitions in Manchester, Liverpool, and other cities of the industrial north, while in London they could send pictures to the various watercolor societies, the British Institution (until 1867), the Society of Female Artists, and, later in the century, private galleries, such as the Grosvenor, which became increasingly important as ways to reach the public. To the dismay of many artistically and politically conservative critics, the new middle-class patron, who was apt to be independent-minded and unwilling to follow the lead of the art establishment, greatly weakened the authority of the Royal Academy. As F. G. Stephens, an original member of the Pre-Raphaelite Brotherhood turned art critic, pointed out in 1871, "The so-called middle-class of England has been that which has done the most for English art. While its social superiors *'praised'* Pietro Perugino, neglected Turner, let Wilson starve, and gave as much for a Gaspar Poussin as for a Raphael; the merchant princes bought of Turner, William Hunt, Holman Hunt, and Rossetti."[4]

In addition to attracting individual patrons at the Royal Academy or similar shows, the artist could exhibit major works, either by himself or with the assistance of a dealer. By charging the public for admission to such a private show the painter effectively transferred his financial dependence from a single buyer to a large number of people. During the course of the nineteenth century one can occasionally observe painters, both English and foreign, thus exhibiting their works in London, but the great master of this technique for reaching the middle-class public was

Holman Hunt, who after 1860 chose to show all his major productions in this manner.[5] In part because these exhibitions remained relatively uncommon — to make a success of them the artist had already to have achieved his reputation — they had the further advantage of securing major periodical reviews, which provided necessary publicity. The final adjustment of the art world to a mass audience occurred in the late decades of the century when the museum movement acknowledged that the lower classes also form part of the artist's public.[6]

In addition to these changes in exhibition practice, there are other indications that painting was acquiring far larger audiences than ever before. For example, the practice of making engraved reproductions of important contemporary paintings, such as Hunt's *Light of the World*, simultaneously provided an important source of income to many Victorian artists while making available to the middle and lower classes works which they could not otherwise have afforded.[7] Finally, for those artists who did not wish to restrict themselves to the more prestigious medium of oil painting, there was the opportunity to work in book and periodical illustration — an area in which the artist could match the writer as both acquired a mass audience.[8]

Conservative critics, such as those of *Blackwood's* and the *Art-Journal*, found such changes in the nature of patronage particularly disturbing. Rather than recognizing Victorian opportunities for a new art, they saw only the democratic destruction of what they took to be aristocratic culture. To begin with, the very practice of exhibiting one's paintings to attract patronage was dangerous, for as Frederic Harrison explained in 1888, "An Exhibition is necessarily more or less a competition, and a competition where for the most part the conspicuous alone catches the public eye. *Il faut sauter aux yeux*, and that in the eyes of the silly, the careless, the vulgar, in order to be popular."[9] The need thus to command public attention, according to *Blackwood's*, made "the arts pander to sensation, and like popular politics, obtain applause by realising through low expedients the greatest happiness of the greatest number."[10]

Furthermore, as Atkinson of *Blackwood's* observed in 1862, changes in patronage necessarily produced important changes in the kinds of work artists painted, for now "small cabinet pictures of homely subjects"[11] had become the general rule, while commissions for monumental art, history painting, and what the critics took to be other aristocratic forms became increasingly rare — so rare, in fact, that when Parliament decided to decorate the new House, it had difficulty in finding men who could properly execute these commissions. As Atkinson complained, "Art, in common with other products of genius, has had to descend from her high pedestal, and become popular in sympathy and secular in spirit. Thus the people, both for evil and for good, have, throughout Europe, grown into a power, and pictures, accordingly, are made to pander to the wants of a dominant democracy. Painters paint down to the level of the multitude." Again in 1865, Atkinson lamented that "in these days too little of ideal beauty, too little of scholarly culture, too little of gentlemanly refinement" can survive.[12] For almost three decades one can observe Atkinson of *Blackwood's*, who is typical of many conservative critics, express his dismay at the effect of democracy upon the arts. It was not only the prevalence of homely portraiture and domestic scenes which troubled him, but also the fact that realistic styles, including the Pre-Raphaelite, had triumphed. "Imagination," he complained, "has wellnigh been driven away from her favourite haunts, and . . . the domain of art is now delivered over to the dominion of the senses."[13]

Critics thus fought the battles of realism versus the neoclassical ideal and genre versus heroic art over and over, because their conceptions of painting were so closely related to their political beliefs, and, more important, to their political fears, particularly to their fear of democratic revolutions. Those on the other side were equally insistent that it was all for the good that the times triumphed. William Michael Rossetti, left wing in both political and religious beliefs, thus argued against allegorical art, because "the tendencies of the age are — we will not say material, but eminently positive," and practical men in the age of Victoria dislike older symbolism and iconography which does not speak to them: "The motto of the practical man, 'Facts and Figures,' may be made to serve his turn as well for pictures as for blue-books; but he is as far from understanding the 'figures' to mean a *figurative rendering* in the one as *figures of speech* in the other."[14] It is no coincidence that Rossetti should have chosen as his representative man the reader of parliamentary blue-books, the weapons of the Benthamite political reformer, while Atkinson should have attacked that reformer's credo of the greatest happiness for the greatest number.

One can thus perceive the urgency and the undercurrents in these critical battles, for both Ruskin and the periodical reviewers saw themselves fighting for the allegiance of the new audience for art. Samuel

Carter Hall's *Art-Journal*, "the very voice of the Victorian art establishment,"[15] nailed its colors to the mast early in the battle, proclaiming in 1845: "Conservative by education, habit, and principle, we shrink from the idea of aiding the adversaries of any established institution."[16] Apparently, to weaken the Royal Academy was to weaken the power of conservatism, and to weaken the power of conservatism was to bring on the revolution. Such political elements in Victorian art politics do much to explain why Ruskin and the Pre-Raphaelites were attacked with such vigor: they threatened not only vested interests in the art world but also Order itself. Atkinson thus appropriately repeated attacks made a half century earlier upon the Lake poets, who were also thought politically and socially dangerous, when he lambasted Pre-Raphaelitism as mere "Cockney caprice."[17] Similarly, this defender of the old order hated and feared Ruskin as one who had created "civil war of opposing parties [who] threaten the empire of Art with hopeless anarchy."[18] One of the severest criticisms such conservative spokesmen could make is that a work was vulgar, by which they meant not only that it was without taste, but — returning to the root word — that it spoke too much to the people and for them. Holman Hunt's works frequently met with such criticism, and less understandably the 1856 *Art-Journal* commented of Millais's superb *Autumn Leaves* that it contained "a significant vulgarism," because "the principal figure looks out of the picture at the spectator."[19] With somewhat more justice the 1858 issue of this magazine commented of Frith's *Derby Day* (plate 8), which it admitted was "the picture of the season," that "the tone of the subject is essentially vulgar and no supremacy of execution can redeem it."[20]

One can surmise that many conservative critics, such as Eagles and Atkinson, found the claims of Ruskin and the rising school of young painters particularly upsetting, since they themselves had led a sort of revolution in taste. For example, John Eagles, the friend of W. J. Muller and Francis Danby, had been progressive when he espoused the cause of poetic landscape, thus doing his part to attack the practical — if not the theoretical — primacy of history painting. Considered from a sociological point of view, Eagles's writings, particularly the essays published as *The Sketcher*, stated the claims of the cultured upper-middle-class gentleman to a learned, relatively informal art appropriate to his taste and position in life.[21] The battle — for the conservatives tended to see the history of art in terms of conflict — had just been won when they found themselves under attack, not from above but from below. However much they may have urged others that the older order changes, giving place to the new, when an order new to them appeared, they loudly proclaimed that it wasn't time.

In such a battle for the minds of the Victorian audience, newspaper and magazine reviews played a major part. There were many other kinds of art writing published in Victorian England, including histories of technique by Sir Charles Eastlake, president of the Royal Academy;[22] studies of iconography, such as those by Anna Jameson, Lord Lindsay, and Ruskin himself;[23] treatises on aesthetic and critical theory, such as those by Ruskin and his followers;[24] and studies of individual artists, both ancient and modern.[25] But the magazines and newspapers reached a wider general audience — the *Art-Journal* claiming a monthly circulation of 25,000 in 1851.[26] As this conservative organ asserted in 1861, "The power of the British Press has been as great as that of the Royal Academy, and it has been much more abused."[27] It directly linked this abuse by the British press to the presence of a new, uninformed audience, for "writing upon a subject the alphabet of which was unknown to general readers, an unintelligible jargon was substituted for knowledge, and the amount of technical slang was taken as the standard of critical acumen."[28] During the course of the century art criticism had changed, but empty phrases still characterized its method. "Formerly critics shook their heads at pictures — some critics can do nothing else so vigourously — and pronounced the 'carnations diluted,' or the 'empasto destitute of force'; that the handling wanted breadth, or that the *chiaroscuro* was imperfect," and people were expected to wonder at such knowledge and such skill. Now critics tell us, the *Art-Journal* complained, that "the 'pose' is 'too pronounced,' or 'not pronounced' enough; the colour is not 'articulated.'"[29] In other words, critics had exchanged the catchwords of the aristocratic connoisseur for a pretended knowledge that was to impress the new middle-class audience. One knows of the journal's long continued hostility to Ruskin, and since these descriptions sound so like *Blackwood's* many attacks on him, it is surprising to come upon its admission that "thanks to the labour of a few, some change for the better is perceptible; and although blind admiration of Ruskin is no part of our creed, he has been a vigorous pioneer in that improvement."[30] Admitting that Ruskin's "dogmatism is oftener right than wrong," this old foe went on to grant that his "knowledge has crushed polyglots of words thrown at him by sentence-making opponents," some of whom, one must point out, were employed by the *Art-Journal* itself.

As annoying as such technical jargon may have been, it did at least serve on occasion to point out something about the picture as a work of visual art, and such attention is comparatively rare in Victorian art reviewing. How then did the critic proceed, and what were his criteria? As Helene Roberts has pointed out, "of 500 or so paintings amassed on the walls, reviewers would briefly notice perhaps 150, often mentioning several works by a single artist in one sentence, and concentrate their attention on 20 or 30 works."[31] Occasionally critics employed the kind of scurrilous invective with which Eagles greeted Turner's later works, but in general they contented themselves with a brief description of the painting, concentrating upon an explanation of its subject. The 1847 *Illustrated London News* thus characteristically commented of Thomas Webster's "most admirable picture," *A Village Choir*, that the artist has "painted a church destitute of an organ; and, for the bass, has sought out all the deep solemn mouths, and, for the tenor, the loud singing mouths, of the country bumpkins. In looking at this picture one is apt to style one's ears like Hogarth's 'Enraged Musician.' Some of the faces are full of character, and there is a touching little picture in the foreground of the choir — an orphan girl singing from the fullness of her heart and voice, as if, like Sir Philip Sidney's shepherd boy, she never would grow old. One cannot comment too highly," the reviewer concludes, upon "the extreme care with which every part is painted — care well bestowed when such a picture as this is the result."[32] Aside from the writer's condescension toward the lower classes of rural England, what is most remarkable about this favorable review of Webster's painting is that it has nothing to say about it as a work of visual art. One reads of "the extreme care with which every part is painted," but one does not know precisely what this indicates. The reviewer's emphasis, as is so frequently the case throughout the century, falls upon the painting's subject. Similarly, when almost three decades later a reviewer for the same newspaper noticed Frank Holl's *Her Firstborn* at the 1876 exhibition, he commented only that "four girls are bearing a tiny coffin slung in a white cloth, followed by the father looking dazed with grief, and the young mother bowed forward with more poignant anguish. The colouring partakes of the mournfulness of the theme, but we have had solider painting from the young artist."[33] When the writer for the same periodical noticed Hubert Von Herkomer's *The First-Born*, he remarks only that "a workman's wife, carrying her baby, [is] coming to meet her husband as he is returning home. The scene is probably laid in the neighbourhood of Bushey: and whilst the sentiment of the picture recalls Fred. Walker, the colour, strong and bright, is altogether that of Herkomer himself."[34] One is perhaps surprised to discover no mention of the sweeping sky which dominates Herkomer's composition, but in fact except for the mention that his colors are bright and that Holl has painted better (by which the reviewer apparently means he has finished more highly), there is no attention paid to these elements. Painting, in other words, becomes reduced to subject.

Except when a reviewer is attacking something he takes to be a great flaw or dangerous excess, he is unlikely to say anything about what happens visually in a painting. If one wished to formulate a rule, one might state that it is generally only in hostile reviews, such as those which greeted Pre-Raphaelite painting, that one can learn what a picture looked like to its contemporary audience. Thus, when we read of Brett's *Pearly Summer* that "the glassy calm of the sea has been very carefully studied, but, as so often happens, his pictures seem to have no focus & very little, if any, cadence in lights and colours,"[35] we can conclude that the painter's attempt to create a new kind of sea painting, abandoning conventional points of interest and a foreground, has jarred upon the reviewer's eye. Moreover, we also learn that Brett's attempt to manipulate color and light in a particularly complex way has also struck the critic as peculiar.

Although contemporary reviews admittedly have little to tell us directly about the visual elements in the paintings they notice, they nonetheless provide much useful information for students of art and historians of taste. In addition to giving an idea of what the Victorian public read about the arts, these periodical writings indicate broad trends that affect the taste of artist and audience alike. Frequent complaints about the prevalence of portraiture, for example, indicate the relative importance of this genre at Royal Academy exhibitions, while other remarks also suggest the relative importance of landscape, history painting, and scenes of domestic life. The opening sections of the annual reviews usually contain such comments on the century's changing views of realism, Pre-Raphaelitism, symbolism, and other major issues, and occasionally a writer will use an individual work as a stepping-off place for such theoretical criticism. For example, when praising Edward Poynter's *Return of the Prodigal Son* in 1869, the critic for the *Illustrated London News* took the opportunity to attack Holman Hunt and his defenders, among whom one can number Ruskin, Stephens, and W. M. Rossetti. According to the reviewer, "some highly respectable persons are very likely, by plausible theories and partisan propagandists, brought to believe that this promising young painter nor any master, ancient or modern, has any right whatever to deal with this often-painted episode before us, without having previously informed himself of the precise shape, measurement, pattern, and material, if not also the market price of the textile fabric made up into *abbah*, the under garments, and the *potah*, or continuation, if any, worn by the excellent parent of the Gospel narrative, on the particular day of his hopeful younger son's return."[36] Thus, having effectively parodied Hunt's realistic methods, the critic can claim that a more idealized style makes the point of the parable with equal force.

Perhaps the most important use of such periodical notices is as a depository of valuable, if incomplete, records of particular subjects and themes. When dealing with a painter like Holman Hunt, who placed a great deal of importance upon original subject, it is useful to discover notices that show his *Awakening Conscience* (plate 12), was preceded by two similarly titled pictures.[37] Occasionally the reviewer himself will do the art historian's task, pointing out possible analogues and influences. Thus, after praising Poynter's version of the prodigal son theme, the reviewer remarks that William Gale and W. F. Poole exhibited similar subjects the same year; and turning to the notices of the 1861 exhibition we discover ourselves that J. C. Horsley had painted a well-received painting on the same theme.

Reviews thus furnish particularly valuable assistance when we try to gauge the popularity and influence of Millais. After the young member of the Pre-Raphaelite Brotherhood painted his interpretation of Tennyson's "Mariana" in 1851, he was followed by one R. S. Cahill four years later, about whose efforts the *Art-Journal* only remarked: "Mariana is one of the hacknied subjects of which we now see yearly. When one artist . . . opens a new vein, it is not only soon exhausted by others who do not read for themselves, but it continues to be reproduced long after it has ceased to interest."[38] Three years later in 1858, this periodical again complained that if one painter "is original by accident, all the others follow in Indian file. One paints Evangeline, the Lady of Shallott, or some other conception of equal pungency, when, lo! there is a creation of fifty Evangelines and Ladies of Shallott; and so it is with every vein of thought." [39] These comments upon the way lesser painters reacted to the demands of the Victorian art market are perhaps nowhere better demonstrated than in the *Art-Journal's* own notice of a Miss A. Burgess, who in 1860 exhibited not only yet another Mariana and an Evangeline but also a picture of children freeing a bird from a cage, which she entitled *The Order of Release*, thus alluding wittily to another of Millais's important works. [40]

Although these periodical reviews and related criticism serve as a depository of information valuable to the modern student of Victorian art and culture, one must admit that as art criticism they are not very good. Not only do many of these art writers find it difficult to relate what occurs visually in a painting, but they all too frequently find themselves puzzled by pictorial symbolism as well. For formal and iconographical criticism one must go to the writings of John Ruskin, Victorian England's great critic of art and society. Ruskin's primacy as *the* art critic of the Victorian years, one must emphasize, is not the result of adulatory modern scholarship or a small band of contemporary disciples. As a good Victorian, I must cite my own experience of conversion, admitting that even long after I had begun to work on this great master of nineteenth-century prose, I remained a bit skeptical about the almost incredible importance modern students of the period have claimed for him. Only after reading through hundreds of periodical essays and reviews did I realize that after mid-century it is almost impossible to turn to writings on the arts without finding a mention of Ruskin, borrowing from him, or allusion to his works. For the art critics, as for a large portion of the public, Ruskin remained the one important voice. He had a great many disciples, few of whom accepted all his criteria and judgements, but all of whom made it their business to promulgate Ruskinian notions of painting, literature, sculpture, architecture, or the decorative arts. For example, F. G. Stephens and W. M. Rossetti, both original members of the Pre-Raphaelite Brotherhood, draw heavily upon one side of Ruskin's art theories when they campaign for a realistic style in figure and landscape painting; while Robert St. John Tyrwhitt explicitly draws upon another when he attempts to popularize the master's iconographic and mythological readings of art.[41] The aesthetician Eneas Sweetland Dallas exemplifies yet another strain in Ruskin when he builds upon his theories of imagination and unconscious creative processes.

To the question, why Ruskin had such great influence, one must reply that he was the right man at the right time, not only because he had such valuable knowledge and feeling for art, but also because his conception of the art critic as a combination of sage, satirist, and prophet exactly suited the needs of his audience. As an astute American admirer perceived in 1857, Ruskin's situation at mid-century in relation to painting was exactly analogous to that in poetry of Wordsworth and Coleridge fifty years before. Whereas the poets had composed their own critical defenses, Turner needed someone else to defend, popularize, and interpret the revolution he had achieved in Romantic landscape painting: "Turner will reach the general mind through the mediation of Ruskin, who stands and struggles among the Art critics of the period a veritable champion of England. Amid these twaddlers he presents the formidable front of a man with meaning, confident of his cause, and devoted to it with all his faculty. Like one of Cromwell's troopers, he brings heart and conscience to his work, which is a modern crusade, a medley of fighting, preaching, and poetry. Strong in conviction and feeling, he is fearless of tradition."[42]

This apt image of Ruskin as Cromwellian campaigner does much to explain contemporary reactions to him. To the rising middle class, many of whom were evangelicals both within and without the established church, Ruskin's use of argument, method, and tone derived from the Puritan heritage of preaching and biblical interpretation made a great deal of sense; for such procedure simultaneously justified the importance of art in a manner they could appreciate while it made painting and architecture seem very much a part of their conception of things. Ruskin, in other words, is the great master of Victorian relevance. But relevance, like beauty, is very much in the eye of the beholder, and it is the great task of liberal education to make us able to perceive it. Ruskin had the capacity to demonstrate the relevance of Turner and Tintoretto to the lives of the Liverpool artisan and the Manchester manufacturer. His defiance of tradition and recognized authority, which so infuriated conservative critics,[43] struck just the right note for an audience in the midst of asserting its own power and place in English society.

Ruskin's first task as a polemical critic was to defend and explain artists who were unfairly attacked, little known, or underrated, and here his writings on Turner, the Pre-Raphaelites, and the great buildings of Venice come to mind. Second, he created a critical theory upon which to base his individual judgments by transferring romantic notions of poetry, particularly those of Wordsworth's prefaces, to painting and architecture, thereby originating a romantic theory of the sister arts which emphasized sincerity, originality, intensity, truth to nature and experience, and visionary imagination.[44] He could thus discard traditional neoclassical conceptions of painting, which had as their center a theory of intellectualized imitation, by simply abandoning the idea of imitation. Ruskin makes one of his major contributions to art theory when he points out that art does not imitate the natural world but makes statements about it. According to him painting uses structures of proportional relationships between colors and forms to convey man's phenomenological experience of the external world.[45] Hostile to any crude didacticism, he can yet demonstrate the value of art as a means of important truths about the human environment. Characteristically, he offers a theory of instinctive beauty, which he derives from the fact that man is created in his Maker's image, to argue that the mere contemplation of beauty in nature and art is a spiritual, spiritualizing act. In addition to setting forth his aesthetic and critical theories, which provide his audience with an entirely new way of looking at the arts, Ruskin is a superb practical critic whose analyses of composition, color, form, and tone serve to enable his readers to see painting more clearly and with new delight. Ruskin, who is one of the great defenders and explicators of realism, was also one of few Victorian critics who understood the iconography and symbolical modes of earlier art and architecture. Thus this great formalist critic is also one of the greatest interpretive critics as well. Similarly he is also one of the originators of modern myth criticism, such as we see in the works of Frye,[46] and he is the first English art critic to place individual works, both ancient and modern, in their social, political, economic, and intellectual contexts. As Arnold Hauser reminds us:

He was indubitably the first to interpret the decline of art and taste as the sign of a general cultural crisis, and to express the basic, and even today not sufficiently appreciated, principle that conditions under which men live must first be changed, if their sense of beauty and their comprehension of art are to be awakened. . . . Ruskin was also the first person in England to emphasize the fact that art is a public concern and its cultivation one of the most important tasks of the state, in other words, that it represents a social necessity and that no nation can neglect it without endangering its intellectual existence. He was, finally, the first to proclaim the gospel that art is not the privilege of artists, connoisseurs and the educated classes, but is part of every man's inheritance and estate. . . . His influence was extraordinary, almost beyond description. . . . The purposeful-ness and solidity of modern architecture and industrial art are very largely the result of Ruskin's endeavours and doctrines.[47]

At the heart of all these wonderfully diverse aspects of the Ruskinian enterprise was his central task of making his contemporaries see. To do so he relies upon his unique gifts as a man of many styles and many visions. He urgently wants us to open our eyes and see, perceive all those beauties of an infinitely various nature which we have never before even noticed. In other words, he wishes to vivify our sight, thus making us more alive and more able to delight in the life that surrounds us. Here he makes particularly effective use of his talent for close observation, send-ing us to nature and art with both new vision and new appetite. For example, when Ruskin is teaching his reader what shadows look like in water, in all kinds of water, he tells us:

It is always to be remembered that, strictly speaking, only light objects are reflected, and that the darker ones are seen only in proportion to the number of rays of light that they can send; so that a dark object comparatively loses its power to affect the surface of water, and the water in the space of a dark reflection is seen partially with the image of the object, and partially transparent. It will be found on observation that under a bank, suppose with dark trees above showing spaces of bright sky, the bright sky is reflected distinctly, and the bottom of the water is in those places not seen; but in the dark spaces of reflection we see the bottom of the water, and the colour of that bottom and of the water itself mingles with and modifies that of the colour of the trees casting the dark reflection.[48]

The loving observation in these passages, which places Ruskin among an honored group of nineteenth-century naturalists and nature writers,[49] educates our eyes, enabling us to see without conventional schemata.[50] They serve the additional rhetorical purpose of convincing us that Ruskin deserves our attention and forbearance, for by thus continually demonstrating his awesome knowledge of the visual world he wins us to his side. Even his apparently outlandish and paradoxical judgments begin to seem worthy of consideration when they come from a man who can see so much. The outraged writers in *Blackwood's* and other periodi-cals can charge him with all kinds of inconsistencies, ignorance, and even charlatanism, yet such obvious knowledge and love of nature always serves to make us, as it made his Victorian audience, give him a hearing. As he begins to assemble example after example of visual truth, drawn from both nature and art, we become increasingly willing to assume the position of scholars in vision, and his frequently schoolmasterish tone — "It is always to be remembered" and "It will be found on observation" — is accepted, because he is, after all, our teacher.

Far more characteristic of Ruskin's methods, however, are those passages which not only inform us about visual fact but which place us in a position to confront it imaginatively. Ruskin's word painting, his primary educative and satirical technique in the early works, takes three forms, each more complex and more powerful than the last. First of all, he employs what we may term an additive style, in which he describes a series of visual details one after another.[51] Second, he creates a dramatized scene which he sets before us, focusing our attention on a single element which moves through the space he has conjured up with language. For example, when writing about rain clouds, Ruskin explains how they first form and then move in relation to the earth below, after which, like the evangelical preacher and the romantic poet, he cites his own experience:

I remember once, when in crossing the Tête Noire, I had turned up the valley towards Trient, I noticed a rain-cloud forming on the Glacier de Trient. With a west wind, it proceeded towards the Col de Balme, being followed by a prolonged wreath of vapour, always forming exactly at the same spot over the glacier. This long, serpent-like line of cloud went on at a great rate till it reached the valley leading down from the Col de Balme, under the slate rocks of the Croix de Fer. There it turned sharp round, and came down this valley, at right angles to its former progress, and finally directly contrary to it, till it came down within five hundred feet of the village, where it disappeared; the line behind always advancing, and always disappearing, at the same spot. This continued for half an hour, the long line describing the curve of a horse-shoe; always coming into existence and always vanishing at exactly the same places; traversing the space between with enormous swiftness. This cloud, ten miles off, would have looked like a perfectly motionless wreath, in the form of a horse-shoe, hanging over the hills.[52]

Ruskin thus sets us before his Alpine scene, permitting us to observe the movement of a single element within it. After he has concluded his examination of the moving cloud, he moves us farther away, and tells us what it would look like — how we would experience it — from a different point of view.

In such a passage of description, Ruskin proceeds by placing us before a scene, making us spectators of an event. In his third and most elaborate form of word painting, in contrast, he sets us within the scene and makes us participants. He here fulfills his own descriptions of imaginative art. Several places in *Modern Painters* explain that both the novice and the painter without imagination must content themselves with a topographical art of visual fact. "The aim of the great inventive landscape painter," on the other hand, "must be to give the far higher and deeper truth of mental vision, rather than that of the physical facts, and to reach a representation which . . . shall yet be capable of producing on the far-away beholder's mind precisely the impression which the reality would have produced."[53] As he himself explains, in this higher form of art "the artist not only *places* the spectator, but . . . makes him a sharer in his own strong feelings and quick thoughts."[54] The great imaginative artist, in other words, grants us the privilege of momentarily seeing with his eyes and imaginative vision: we experience his phenomenological relation to the world. Ruskin achieves this goal in language by employing what we may anachronistically term a cinematic prose; that is, he first places himself and his reader firmly in position, after which he generates a complete landscape by moving this center of perception, or seeing eye, in one of two ways. He may move us progressively deeper into the landscape in a manner that anticipates cinematic use of the zoom lens, or he may move us laterally while remaining at a fixed distance from the subject — a technique which similarly anticipates cinematic panning. By thus first positioning his center of observation and then directing its attention with patterned movement Ruskin manages to do what is almost impossible — create a coherent visual space with language. Such a procedure, which he employs both when describing works of art and the nature they depict, appears, for instance, in his brilliant description of La Riccia in the first volume of *Modern Painters* and in many crucial passages in *The Stones of Venice*, including his magnificent tour of Saint Marks, his narration of the approach to Torcello, and his aerial view of the Mediterranean Sea.

Such beautiful passages of language are not mere embellishments of his main argument, nor are they self-indulgent displays of virtuosity. They are not even tactics which he employs to smooth over the rough spots in his argument. Such writing in fact is central to Ruskin's conception of himself as critic. First of all, these descriptions are basic to his conception of himself as one who teaches others to see, since he relies upon such cinematic prose to educate his audience's vision, teaching its members to note shapes, tone, colors, and visible fact they have often confronted but failed to observe. Second, such writing again serves to establish what the older rhetoricians termed the speaker's *ethos*. The main problem for the Victorian sage is to convince others that he is worthwhile listening to, that he is a man whose arguments however strange they may at first appear are the products of a sincere, honest, and above all, *reliable* mind. Thus, one of the first tasks of any speaker or writer is to establish himself before his audience as a believable, even authoritative voice; and this Ruskin easily accomplishes by demonstrating that he has seen and seen more than the critics who oppose him. His critics are blind, and he has vision. These passages of highly wrought prose, one must further emphasize, always take their place as part of a larger structure of argument. They serve, in fact, as a major part of Ruskin's complex rhythm of satire and romantic vision, something made abundantly clear in his discussion of Claude's *Il Mulino*, which begins with a description of the painting so beloved of critics hostile to Turner:

> The foreground is a piece of very lovely and perfect forest scenery, with a dance of peasants by a brook-side; quite enough subject to form, in the hands of a master, an impressive and complete picture. On the other side of the brook, however, we have a piece of pastoral life; a man with some bulls and goats tumbling headforemost into the water, owing to some sudden paralytic affection of all their legs. . . . When we look farther into the picture, our feelings receive a sudden and violent shock, by the unexpected appearance, amidst things pastoral and musical, of the military; a number of Roman soldiers riding in on hobby-horses, with a leader on foot, apparently encouraging them to make an immediate and decisive charge on the musicians. Beyond the soldiers is a circular temple, in exceedingly bad repair; and close beside it, built against its very walls, a neat water-mill in full work. By the mill flows a large river with a weir all across it. The weir has not been made for the mill (for that receives its water from the hills by a trough carried over the temple), but it is particularly ugly and monotonous in its line of fall, and the water below forms a dead-looking pond, on which some people are fishing in punts. The banks of this river resemble in contour the later geological formations around London, constituted chiefly of broken pots and oyster-shells. At an inconvenient distance from the water-side stands a city, composed of twenty-five round towers and a pyramid. Beyond the city is a handsome bridge; beyond the bridge, part of the Campagna, . . . [and] the chain of the Alps; on the left, the cascades of Tivoli.[55]

Ruskin presents the painting by Claude as a three-dimensional, rationally organized space, first sketching in the foreground and then moving deeper into the imaginative world of the canvas. Again, he characteristically sets the observing eye with care and then proceeds to move it deeper into the picture space. His earnest tone gradually reduces the painting to mockery, for at each pause he lets us observe a detail which reveals severe lack of either observation or coherent, imaginative organization. First of all, we perceive (through Ruskin's eyes) the primary motif of the peasant dance, after which we come upon an unnecessary bit of pastoral, which, we are led to believe, has been painted with such lack of vitality that the animals have sudden paralytic afflictions. Then we perceive the soldiers, and looking beyond them, we encounter the irrationally and unimaginatively organized cityscape. Ruskin turns his attacking criticism up another notch, employing satiric analogies — the riverbanks look like garbage dumps along the Thames — and a bald, flat tone reduces the city to absurdity, a mere construction of child's blocks. He concludes his satiric foray through the picture by directing our attention at the distant landscape it contains.

At this point, he turns away from the Claude to address his audience, employing one of the most powerful weapons in the arsenal of the Victorian sage — redefinition. Having conducted his tour through the canvas, discovering its flaws, he now draws a first conclusion: "This is, I believe, a fair example of what is commonly called an 'ideal' landscape; *i.e.*, a group of the artist's studies from Nature, individually spoiled, selected with such opposition of character as may insure their neutralizing each other's effect, and united with sufficient unnaturalness and violence of association to insure their producing a general sensation of the impossible." [56] This satiric redefinition strikes to the heart of the neoclassical style, destroying its claims to be a higher or imaginative form of art. Had Ruskin begun in such a blunt manner, he would have lost our sympathy, for taken in isolation such a description of the ideal strikes one as little more than invective. But when we come upon this polemical definition after making our tour through the painting, we are at least willing to admit that it applies to our recent experience.

His satiric description and redefinition merely serves as Ruskin's opening salvo, for he now turns to the details of the work in question. Since he is trying to make us feel that the high art of the connoisseurs and periodical critics is as unimaginative as it is untruthful, he next examines a potentially sublime element in the picture. Asserting that "perhaps there is no more impressive scene on earth than the solitary extent of the Campagna of Rome under evening light," Ruskin sets the reader within the sublime landscape of this Italian wasteland:

Let the reader imagine himself for a moment withdrawn from the sounds and motion of the living world, and sent forth alone into this wold and wasted plain. The earth yields and crumbles beneath his foot, tread he never so lightly, for its substance is white, hollow, and carious, like the dusty wreck of the bones of men. The long knotted grass waves and tosses feebly in the evening wind, and the shadows of its motion shake feverishly along the banks of ruin that lift themselves to the sunlight. Hillocks of mouldering earth heave around him, as if the dead beneath were struggling in their sleep; scattered blocks of black stone, four-square, remnants of mighty edifices, not one left upon another, lie upon them to keep them down. A dull purple poisonous haze stretches level along the desert, veiling its spectral wrecks of massy ruins, on whose rents the red light rests, like a dying fire on defiled altars. The blue ridge of the Alban Mount lifts itself against a solemn space of green, clear, quiet sky. Watch-towers of dark clouds stand steadfastly along the promontories of the Apennines. From the plain to the mountains, the shattered aqueducts, pier beyond pier, melt into the darkness, like shadowy and countless troops of funeral mourners, passing from a nation's grave.[57]

Ruskin readies us for our excursion into this gothic wasteland by reminding us that he is going to withdraw us from the "sounds and motion" of the living world, immersing us in a world of the Burkean sublime, the sublime of deprivation and darkness. We then become aware of the sight and feel of the white pumice that we find ourselves standing upon, after which Ruskin directs us to look up — and we perceive feebly moving grass and ruins upon which the light strikes. Next, we turn about and encounter the more distant hillocks upon which lie the stones of more ruins. Looking through the purple haze that stretches across the desert, we see, first, the blue ridge of the Alban Mount and, next, the line of crumbling aqueducts which lead our eyes into darkness. Ruskin here draws upon his characteristic technique of word painting to place us within a landscape of death, a landscape which embodies the passing of Rome, and as such it doubly comments upon the Claudean ideal: for this verbal landscape not only reveals what Claude has omitted from his painting, but it also suggests that the Roman source of that ideal is irrecoverably dead and gone. We find ourselves in a vast gothic graveyard, and however much the description may owe to both Mrs. Radcliffe and Burke, Ruskin has made it comment upon an entire civilization and an entire art.

Having thus offered his own experience of the Campagna to his reader, the author of *Modern Painters* then follows it with a satiric recipe for producing the Claudean ideal. "Let us, with Claude," Ruskin tells the reader, "make a few 'ideal' alterations in this landscape. First, we will reduce the multidinous precipices of the Apennines to four sugar-loaves.

Secondly, we will remove the Alban Mount, and put a large dust-heap in its stead. Next we will knock down the greater part of the aqueducts, and leave only an arch or two, that their infinity of length may no longer be painful from its monotony. . . . Finally, we will get rid of the unpleasant ruins in the foreground."[58] By this point, it should be obvious that Ruskin has successfully made his primary point — namely, that the neoclassical ideal in landscape is both less truthful and less imaginative than that of Turner and the moderns. Ruskin convinces us of his position by means of a superbly controlled alternation of vision and satire, preparing us for his polemic at each step of the way by allowing us to borrow his eyes and see. His skill at presenting us with his experience of landscape and landscape art continually makes us feel that his critical opponents and the painters he attacks both work from theory, from recipes, rather than from vision. *Modern Painters, The Stones of Venice, Praeterita*, and many of Ruskin's other works progress by means of a series of such passages of visual and visionary experience. Careless readers have occasionally accused him of lack of organization, but in fact he, like Tennyson, develops a literary structure that can accommodate and build upon such intense moments of perception.

Thus far we have observed Ruskin employing his various modes of word painting to educate our eyes about both nature and those who have attempted to paint her. His emphasis here is upon reproducing visual experience in words, and his successful re-creation of his own experiences before art and nature fulfills his own definitions of imaginative art. His second major use of such word painting in his art criticism — to interpret the meaning of a work of art — differs, in that although he still re-creates the experience he also explains and interprets that experience to us. Of course, even in his most apparently pure word painting, his literary allusions, mythological references, and analogies do not permit his descriptions to remain entirely on a visual level; nonetheless, the kind of descriptions at which we have looked thus far places chief importance upon conveying a visual experience of place and object. With his more explicitly interpretative passages, in contrast, he matches each experience of appearance with an experience of meaning. Perhaps the finest example of such interpretative method — both because it lies so close to the center of his thought and because it had such an effect upon the Pre-Raphaelites — occurs in his reading of Tintoretto's Scuola di San Rocco *Annunciation* in his chapter on the penetrative imagination. After briefly describing the gentle vision of Fra Angelico, he prepares us for the different imaginative world of Tintoretto:

> Severe would be the shock and painful the contrast, if we could pass in an instant from that pure vision [of Fra Angelico] to the wild thought of Tintoret. For not in meek reception of the adoring messenger, but startled by the rush of his horizontal and rattling wings, the Virgin sits, not in the quiet loggia, not by the green pasture of the restored soul, but houseless, under the shelter of a palace vestibule ruined and abandoned, with the noise of the axe and the hammer in her ears, and the tumult of a city round about her desolation. The spectator turns away at first, revolted, from the central object of the picture forced painfully and coarsely foward, a mass of shattered brickwork, with the plaster mildewed away from it, and the mortar mouldering from its seams.[59]

Re-creating the picture and the spectator's experience of it, Ruskin goes on to point out that at first these ruins and the carpenter's tools beneath them appear to do little more than give the painter a means of alluding to the occupation of Joseph. But then, observing important elements in the picture's composition, he leads us to its meaning. When the spectator "looks at the composition of the picture," Ruskin tells us, "he will find the whole symmetry of it depending on a narrow line of light, the edge of a carpenter's square, which connects these unused tools with an object at the top of the brickwork, a white stone, four square, the corner-stone of the old edifice."[60] Such visual elements lead to imaginative, symbolical ones, for this annunciation, Ruskin finds, deploys the traditional iconography of typological, or figural, symbolism; that is, the means by which Christians read the Old Testament in terms of foreshadowings of Christ. Thus "the ruined house is the Jewish dispensation; that obscurely arising in the dawning of the sky is the Christian; but the corner-stone of the old building remains, though the builders' tools lie idle beside it, and the stone which the builders refused is become the Headstone of the Corner."[61] Citing Psalm 118, Ruskin provides us with both the text and its traditional symbolic reading. Most important, he uses his capacity for word painting, iconographical interpretation, and compositional analysis to provide us with the experience of one who gradually realizes the meaning of a work of art. In other words, as part of his rhetoric of vision, he does not simply tell us what the picture means. Rather he furnishes us with the experience of perceiving that meaning — thus again fulfilling his own definitions of imaginative art.

Ruskin repeats these procedures many times in the course of his art and social criticism. Since he firmly believes that imaginative art can take form in either realistic or symbolic modes, or in those which combine the two, he himself often conducts his argument by means of wonderfully effective allegories or, as he chose to call them, symbolical grotesques.[62] Another major use of his complex rhetoric of vision and satire appears in his skillful interpretations of paintings, buildings, and myths as emblems of a nation's or a culture's world view. (This last technique, or aspect, of the Ruskinian method is that on which Pater draws so heavily in *The Renaissance* and his other writings on the arts.) But all of Ruskin's many maneuvers succeed in educating us to see art with fresher, more delighted eyes. As a defender of Ruskin wrote in 1863, "It may be asked when this educating function of the art critic is to cease. It is like asking when schoolmasters are to cease. . . . [The critic] will have to train the public in those eternal truths which are the beginning of criticism. He and his successors will have to repeat them over and over again so long as civilization shall endure."[63]

Architecture, History, and the Spirit of the Age

Phoebe B. Stanton

M ore than in any other period, knowledge of the past exerted an influence on the nineteenth century. In the arts this phenomenon may best be observed in architecture.[1]

Slowly, from the seventeenth century onward, historical writing had increased in quantity and evolved in its form and techniques. From the massive collections of fact assembled in England by men such as Dugdale, author and editor of the *Monasticon Anglicanum* (1655–1677), and in France by the Benedictines of St. Maur, who had chronicled the history of their order, the art of historical writing and the skills of scholarship had grown. As the eighteenth century opened, preparation was complete for the appearance of history as a discipline which would inevitably attract the intellectual leadership of the Enlightenment. Voltaire was, for example, to see it as a "witness not a flatterer." The subjects history could properly consider came to include the whole of the way of life and, ultimately, the feeling of a people.

Histories of every kind were available as the nineteenth century began. In the arts Winckelmann and Lessing had been at work. Antiquaries and topographers had recorded not only the history of medieval monuments but their appearance. Systematic chronological accounts of the history of literature had begun in Germany with the Schlegels. Recovery and assessment of earlier historical writers and their books had become a fascinating study in itself.

After 1800 the view of man's past continued to expand. Archaeological research burgeoned; the history of pre-antique societies became a specialty. More than any other studies, those of the Middle Ages and the Reformation were to have an impact on the practice of the arts and particularly on architecture. Medieval history could be related to the development of the nation-states of northern Europe, where buildings and whole cities which that age had left behind could be studied at first hand. Medieval life was thought to have been devout, prosperous, unified in its institutions and its spirit — vague attributes but ones which were all important to the romantics and to those uneasy about the dislocations and lack of unity which appeared to mar the quality of life in the nineteenth century.

Renascences were not new. Men as different as Charlemagne, the patrons of the Italian Renaissance, and the political leaders of the French Revolution had pursued the hope that recovery of antiquity would enhance and rectify their present. But these and other examples of the influence of historical knowledge and perspective on the arts and social behavior differed in character, magnitude, and result from the effect that knowledge of history was to have on the nineteenth century.

The early years of the nineteenth century were so charged with event and change that it was not strange that in 1807 Hegel should have announced "It is surely not difficult to see that our time is a time of birth and transition to a new period."[2] Coleridge as well as numerous anonymous pamphleteers intoned the lesson that a new "age" had come and that it would and must possess characteristics of its own.

A feeling of obligation, unique among societies which had revered the past, was to dominate this one. Examination of previous ages tended to present an overview of them from which a simplified version of their complexities emerged. Each seemed to have possessed its characteristic features, its style in the arts and in government. If, indeed, the opening of the nineteenth century introduced a new and possibly a great age, and everyone was reasonably sure that it had, then it was incumbent upon its inhabitants to produce their own equivalent of the fresh and original expressions which it appeared other ages had in their time acquired. No age was an "age" without these manifestations; they were felt to be an inevitable result of living and a demonstration of "greatness." No other period had appraised its aspirations and its future achievements in this way. The nineteenth century came to regard itself as history in the process of being made. The arrival of originality was awaited. Continuity with the past, especially with the immediate past, was discounted.

Reactions to the burden of history varied. Carlyle lamented that philosophers and historians had "no love and no hatred" but stood "among us not to do nor to create anything, but as sort of Logic Mills to grind out the true causes and effects of all that is done and created." He concluded by saying that "by arguing on the force of circumstance we have argued away all force from ourselves and stand leashed together uniform in dress and movement like the rowers in some boundless galley." [3]

Others perceived change as an inexorable process; periods of wholeness would be followed by confusion and transition. Attempts to alter this rhythm would be useless, indeed destructive. The hope or attempt to restore what was passed was wasteful. Such were the views of the followers of Saint-Simon, among whom John Stuart Mill was numbered. In 1831 he commented on a remarkable trait manifest in his contemporaries. "The idea of comparing one's own age with former ages," he said, "or with our notion of those which are yet to come, had occurred to philosophers; but it never before was itself the dominant idea of any age." [4]

A conviction that the nineteenth century would attain its majority only when it had created artistic styles and institutions which were patently its own, desperation about the inexorable continuity of history, conviction that change would come despite admiration for one or another past society, and enthusiastic comparisons between past and present were, in part, reactions to the growth of historical knowledge.

Such investment of feeling and sense of purpose bred ardent but subjective loyalties. Inordinate admiration for medieval art and society provoked an equally violent rejection of the Reformation. It was interpreted as an episode which had brought both an end to medieval England and the onset of modern times with its many woes. The justice of such a view is not at question here. The fact that it was held by men as diverse as William Cobbett and A. W. N. Pugin is fundamental to the rise of the most prevalent and the strangest of the nineteenth-century revivals, that of Gothic.

Support for this idea was to come from another quarter. The Catholic historians of Germany restored the art of ecclesiastical history and the history of dogma, reasserting, as they did so, the role of the church in the creation of a common spiritual life. It is interesting to note that in the early days of the Catholic Revival in England pilgrimages to Germany to talk with Johann von Döllinger (1799–1890), the great Catholic historian, were almost as frequent as journeys to Chartres to see the cathedral.

So it was that the will to reform, the expectation and demand for what was new and contradictory of the immediate past, the desire to minimize the influence of its ideas and reach deep into history in search of inspiration, were joined.

When the century opened, the reigning and creative architectural taste was one derived from classical and Renaissance precedents. As the decades unfolded the authority of this first "revival" waned as it was challenged by others. Among them the Gothic Revival came to represent an avant-garde preference closely associated with romanticism. It in its turn was to yield to a variety of styles in a cycle of eclecticism which occurred with the assistance of historical erudition of various sorts.

Within neoclassicism a remarkable body of architectural and aesthetic theory had developed in the eighteenth century. It was destined to survive long after the style which had occasioned it had been relegated, in the nineteenth century, to a secondary and defensive position. The doctrines of this neoclassical architectural revolution were the sources of the ideas which were used to defend the architecture of Hegel's new age. It is my view that the association of virtue, social responsibility, and reforms of society through the arts which had in the eighteenth century been the property of neoclassical architects and writers was, in the nineteenth century, transplanted to the Gothic Revival. Virtue simply changed its costume. Despite their protests nineteenth-century theorists were never to be free of their immediate forebears.

The ways in which this union of earlier theory and nineteenth-century eclecticism was accomplished, the reasons that made the associations of the two possible, and evidence that both did indeed occur may be specifically illustrated.

The architects, critics, and architectural theorists who worked in the first half of the nineteenth century had been trained in the school of these earlier men. Prepared though they were to accept Gothic on faith, because they preferred it for aesthetic and social reasons and because it differed totally from neoclassical building, they felt compelled to supply a rational explanation of its forms, features, and historical development. In this way they acted not as medieval men but as heirs of the late eighteenth century and as historians of a style.

Gothic, unlike the classical style which had an impressive pedigree of authorities who went back to Vitruvius, was not accompanied by a theoretical system. It was this which Pugin, for example, set out to supply in his remarkable *True Principles of Pointed or Christian Architecture*, published in 1841. The originality of this book has long been an accepted premise in histories of the Gothic Revival and of the evolution of the modern movement in architecture. It is now time to revise that estimate. Pugin had been preceded by authors whose work he could easily have known. Attribution of some of his major ideas to them and establishment of lines which connect him with methods of thought traditional in refined architectural theory serve, simultaneously, to make him more credible and more logical than he otherwise appears. It will also illustrate the extent to which Hegel's new age was the product of that which had gone before it. Finally it will allow us to separate out the elements of Pugin's thought which were original and so Victorian.

The high quality of early nineteenth-century commentary on architecture is nowhere better represented than in the writing of Francis Palgrave (1788–1861), who in 1821 and 1822 contributed remarkable articles on medieval building to the *Quarterly Review*.[5] His learning was perfectly balanced by his perception of the aesthetic properties of Gothic.

At the time he wrote these articles — which were in the form of reviews of books, one of them a pioneering work by Pugin's father — he had not yet assumed the name of Palgrave. In 1823 when he married Elizabeth, daughter of the botanist and antiquary Dawson Turner (1775–1858), the former Meyer Cohen became a convert to Christianity and replaced Cohen with Palgrave, the maiden name of Mrs. Dawson Turner. After 1823 as Francis Palgrave and after 1832 as Sir Francis he was to establish himself as a major historian and archivist. His *Rise and Progress of the English Commonwealth* (1832) marked the beginning of his mature career.

In 1822 Palgrave was thirty-four and, it may be assumed, his acumen about architecture and its history had been acquired from earlier writers and from Dawson Turner, who had in 1820 begun serious antiquarian and topographical architectural studies. Remarkable though they were, neither Turner nor Palgrave were capable of summoning the brilliance of observation implicit in Palgrave's essays. The latter will illustrate the firm foundation in architecture, its history and appraisal of its character, which eighteenth-century authors had provided for the Gothic.

Palgrave was no casual enthusiast given to praise for Gothic architecture. He understood precisely what he was examining. He sought to define the purposes which were realized through the exploitation of structures. His knowledge of medieval architecture was accurate. He arrived at his definition of Gothic through comparison of it with the architecture of the Greeks, an appropriate historical procedure.

The Greek temple, he said, can be "compared to a single crystal," all the parts of which are perfectly related to one another and to their number. "The component parts have settled themselves into a shape of perfect harmony" which cannot be altered in proportion or detail without disturbance of the whole. It is too delicate to survive the transplantation of its parts or the addition of the whole or any part, such as a portico, to another building. Columns may not be "raised in stories," wings should not be added to the temple form. The Greek architect possessed "few elements," needed no variety; "he was required to perfect rather than to invent . . . a perfect solution had been given."

The Gothic mason confronted another task; the cathedral he set out to create "is to be considered rather as a forethought than as a finished specimen," for its aims could never be achieved by "human power." The imagination must bridge the gap between "forethought" and reality. Mysterious because "recession from shadow to shadow" causes it to appear "larger than its actual dimensions," Gothic "appeals to the imagination."

Palgrave then defined certain differences between the character of the details in early and late Gothic as he noted that "daylight is courted by the Gothic architect . . . Gothic architecture seeks to exclude the sight of middle earth. Its genius delights . . . in piles which expand and close round the spectator, leaving him naught to contemplate but themselves and the sky and the clouds"

Provocative though these observations are, they are surpassed by the summary of Palgrave's findings:

Gothic architecture is an organic whole, bearing within it a living vegetating germ. Its parts and lines are linked and united, they spring and grow out of each other. Its essence is the curve, which, in the physical world, is the token of life or organized matter, just as the straight line indicates death or inorganized matter. It is a combination of arches whose circles may be infinitely folded, multiplied and embraced. Hence the parts of a Gothic building may be expanded indefinitely without destroying its unity. However multiplied and combined, they still retain their relative bearing; however repeated, they never encumber each other. All the arched openings, the tall mullioned windows, the recessed doors are essential parts; they do not pierce the walls of the structure, on the contrary, they bind them together . . . Gravitation, which could bring the stone to the ground, is the power which fixes it in the archivolt. . . . The history of the style accounts for its propriety, its chiefest merit.

From this Palgrave moved easily to the conclusion that "In a Gothic Church no idea can possibly arise, save that of Christianity and of the rites of Christianity." Some, he said, recommended the introduction of "*pure* Grecian style for the purposes both of ecclesiastical and civil architecture," an idea he could not commend. Not even the finest architects could "naturalize the architecture of ancient Greece in modern England. The Grecian temple will not submit to be transported to our atmosphere," he says, and then, in a neat description provides an image of a Greek Revival building which resembles the ones A. W. Pugin was to present in the famous illustrations to *Contrasts* and in his *True Principles*: "plate glass windows glaring through the intercolumnations, and chimney pots arranged above the pediments, are just as appropriate as English nouns and verbs in a Greek hexameter."

These few quotations can only introduce the riches of Palgrave's essay. He had read the late medieval author Durandus, whose *Rationale Divinorum Officiorum* he cites as an authority for expenditure on ornament and for the use of traditional plans, and the *Origines Ecclesiasticae*, by Joseph Bingham, an eighteenth-century divine who had recommended faithful adherence to past liturgical practice in the use of the church interior.

Sculpture, painting, and other embellishments should never appear to be "strangers and brought in merely for show." They should seem "required by the predetermined plans of the architect . . . they should never be treated as other than ancillary to the architecture." This is, of course, another way of stating what Pugin was to say memorably in *True Principles*: "all ornament should consist of enrichment of the essential construction of the building."

Modern churches, according to Palgrave, suffered from lack of elevation; spires were essential. He found the church at Theale, Berkshire, which had been designed by Edward Garbett and built at the expense of Mrs. Sheppard, sister to Doctor Routh, president of Magdalen, who supervised its design and construction, and St. Luke's Chelsea by James Savage ample proof of his belief in Gothic as expressive of the national character, Christian and practical.

The acceptance of Gothic as a style for secular and ecclesiastical architecture had begun long before 1822, the year of Palgrave's statement. His recommendation of Gothic thus comes as no surprise. But the intricacy of his argument, the way in which he considers every point which would be marshaled a decade later by Pugin, the ecclesiologists, and John Ruskin pushes the date of the appearance of the mature theory of the Gothic Revival back into the early years of the nineteenth century. The quotations from Durandus are also startling; references to him by George R. Lewis in his *Illustrations of Kilpeck Church, Herefordshire*, published in 1842, and by Pugin in the same year and the translation of the *Rationale* by John Mason Neale and Benjamin Webb in 1843 have seemed to express the height of Victorian enthusiasm for symbolism.

In the 1840s John Ruskin began his career as a commentator on the arts and an arbiter of taste. His first major book on architecture, *The Seven Lamps of Architecture*, appeared in 1849. In it he united moral and ethical and aesthetic observations on architecture in a way which held appeal for his contemporaries. The *Seven Lamps* was a decisive work for both its author and the taste of those who read it.

Because Ruskin asserted he owed Pugin no debt in the formulation of the architectural thought set down in both *Seven Lamps* and *The Stones of Venice*, emphasis has been placed on the probability that such a debt did, indeed, exist. Pugin was so redoubtable a figure and his books were so remarkable that, distasteful though Ruskin may have found his religious convictions, he could not have been overlooked.

This search for the immediate forebears of Ruskin's thought has tended to preoccupy historians, who have logically assumed they need look no further than Pugin, Robert Willis, whose *Remarks on the Architecture of the Middle Ages* was published in 1835, and Lord Lindsay's *Sketches of the History of Christian Art*, in three volumes, which had appeared in 1847.

Another source may, it appears, have intervened. Claude-Nicolas Ledoux (1735–1806) had enjoyed a considerable reputation in France and abroad prior to 1789; his works had included buildings for the government of France; he had prepared drawings which were sent to St. Petersburg for the perusal of the czar. In 1793 he was imprisoned and threatened with execution. Released, he busied himself with speculative designs to embellish the rising regime of Napoleon and the preparation of a book, *L'Architecture considérée sous le rapport de l'Art, des Moeurs et de la*

Legislation, which contained a long text and plates illustrative of his theories. His plans for an ideal city, which this book contained, established him in the history of utopian thought on cities; his remarkable architectural designs placed him, equally, among the leaders of the proto-moderns who presaged the arrival of modern architecture.

Ledoux had issued his book in 1804 at his own expense, for no publisher was willing to underwrite so aberrant a work. Not until 1847, long after Ledoux was dead, were the third of the plates which Ledoux had prepared, but had been financially unable to publish, issued by Daniel Ramée as a supplement to *L'Architecture*. The existence of the book was, therefore, recalled.

I propose that to Ruskin, who was in 1848 involved in the preparation of a book on architecture in which feeling and religious and aesthetic values would be woven together, the title of Ledoux's book could well have proved attractive. The French text would have been no obstacle, for in the first volume of *Modern Painters* Ruskin had in 1843 used French and referred to conversations in French in which he had participated.

Ledoux's tone is enthusiastic: "Architecture is to stone masonry what poetry is to letters . . . One cannot talk about it without being carried away," an assertion warranted to attract Ruskin. But it is the essay "The Lamp of Power," one of the finest in *The Seven Lamps*, which most clearly suggests the influence of Ledoux, who had commented at length on the nature and aesthetic potentialities of walls, the very subject of Ruskin's discourse on power. "We think —" said Ledoux, "and experience has convinced us — that shadows that lie cleanly upon bare expanses of wall are the only ones that can be used successfully in long perspectives, where the nature of the building does not permit the use of colonnades across the front." And this is Ruskin in division VIII: "And it is a noble thing for men to do this [the creation of great wall areas] with their cut stone or moulded clay, and to make the face of a wall look infinite, and its edge . . . like an horizon: or even if less than this be reached, it is still delightful to mark the play of . . . light on its broad surface, and to see by how many artifices and gradations of tinting and shadow, time and storm will set their wild signatures upon it . . ." This is Ledoux again: "Under the touch of art, the stone will awaken new feelings, will develop its own expressiveness . . . The problem lies also in the carefully planned use of the commonest materials . . . When the surfaces are large enough to engage the mind, when the color of the stone bears comparison to the finest marble, when the viewer's eye is warmed by these inanimate surfaces, when the whole, by the freedom of its composition develops unexpected effects — then it is that architecture must be free of excess, economy being the first law of art, which allows only what is absolutely necessary." These phrases even resemble those in which Ruskin enveloped his ideas.

There are other telling comparisons; indeed the possibilities are only touched upon here. Ledoux had more to offer: "If you want to become an architect, begin by being a painter. What a variety of shapes you will find spread upon the still surface of a wall, though its pictorial eloquence may leave the apathetic multitude unmoved! High courses of stonework deeply grooved, walls rough-hewn or rusticated, pebbles sticking out, stones piled up artlessly — such elements are often enough to produce striking effects." This was a relationship which Ruskin, too, observed: "A wall surface is to an architect simply what a white canvas is to a painter, with this difference, that the wall has already a sublimity in its height, substance, and other characters already considered, on which it is more dangerous to break than to touch the canvas surface." He goes on to state that a "broad, freshly laid surface of gesso" is fairer than many pictures he has seen painted and a great wall fairer than the "features" it is made to carry.

Ruskin had some reason to be angry when he was described as a follower of Pugin, but he and Pugin were both intellectual offspring of the earlier nineteenth-century and late eighteenth-century theorists. The latter were the only sources from which might be drawn aesthetic doctrine to explain Gothic architecture and social arguments which made decision among the various architectural styles possible. To architects and critics trained in the earlier school the practice and assessment of design without rules — or principles, as Pugin called them — was an impossibility. Palgrave, in fact, used that telltale word *propriety* when he recommended Gothic: "The history of the style accounts for its propriety, its chiefest merit. Gothic architecture, whatever its primitive elements may have been, was created in the northern parts of Europe; it was there adapted to the wants of a more inclement sky."

Most of all, however, the eighteenth-century theorists offered a set of standards which could be used to supply the reasons for otherwise unreasonable preferences for one or another historic style. The shimmering world of multiple choices the historians proffered was too challenging to be comfortable. So it came about that some early Victorians escaped from their "boundless galley."

The history of art was, in the 1840s, undergoing a transformation as radical as the changes which dominated architecture. Alexander Lindsay, who was later the twenty-fifth Earl of Crawford, announced the theoretical premises which would underlie his other works when in 1847 he published *Progression by Antagonism: A Theory, Involving Considerations Touching the Present Position, Duties and Destiny of Great Britain.* A strange, almost hermetic work in which the "analogy between the Individual and the Universal Man will be found to supply the key to the history of the world, and enable us to determine the point on which we stand in it and the dignity of our position to argue from the past to the future, and to ascertain the duties of the present," *Progression by Antagonism* was a prime example of the will to conquer and organize the vast world of the past which had been exposed.

Lindsay's *Sketches of the History of Christian Art* (1847) in three volumes was in press, a remarkable combination of facts held together by his conviction that Christian art had and would in future produce perfection because it was, quite simply, Christian. The arts at their best were "a shadow on earth of the mysterious Trinity." It should, in passing, be noted that in addition to this idiosyncratic structural skeleton Lindsay contributed materially both to connoisseurship and explanations of the characteristics of and changes in styles and the definitions of national schools in painting.

Discussion of the art of the period from "the French Revolution and the Second Regeneration of Catholic Christianity — otherwise, from the commencement of the Nineteenth Century — to a period as yet undetermined" was to appear in subsequent volumes which were never published. For the historian of nineteenth-century art and ideas this is a disappointment, for Lindsay had hoped to consider the various "revivals" according to the nation in which they occurred. Germany, Italy, and France would have been followed by Great Britain, for which he held the highest hopes. The British revival pledged, he said, "a distinctly new style of architecture, expressive of the epoch in human progression of which Great Britain is the representative, as well as of a Sculpture and Painting founded, not in servile imitation, but on sound principles and the inspiration of Genius."

Lord Lindsay's elaborate system of progression was, to the history of art as he organized it, an equivalent of Palgrave's "propriety," Pugin's "principles," and Ruskin's various *Lamps*. All were attempts to induce order and to relate art to its time. The conviction that a "new style of architecture, expressive of the epoch" would emerge also, oddly, belongs to the decade of the forties for then, briefly, the demand for meticulous accuracy in the reproduction of Gothic held sway, its case argued by Pugin and the Ecclesiological Society. This earlier eclecticism tended to equate archaeologically exact borrowing with "propriety," "principles," and usefulness and function. To these shibboleths Lord Lindsay added his explanatory system which included a belief in Hegel's "new period."

These convictions were to survive but briefly. Pugin had always found replication of Gothic difficult to practice because of the parsimony of his patrons, the inadequacy of workmen, and the demands of his own talent for freedom to improvise. The authorities of the Ecclesiological Society were to continue to insist that Gothic be reproduced precisely and churches be used as they had been in the past. As a result of their intransigence, the style they supported aged as rapidly as their doctrines; after 1850 its influence was confined to churches, and the arguments of those who supported it became, if not obsolete, of tertiary importance among the ideas on the arts and their practice and purposes.

It was these early Victorian ideas and idealists to whom Henry Van Brunt alluded wistfully when, in 1886, he looked back over the track which architecture had traveled. "The Gothic Revival," he said, "is the only instance in history of a moral revolution in art." [6]

Early nineteenth-century theorists, practitioners, and critics in architecture had, thanks to the brilliance of their immediate forebears, begun their work in possession of a variety of vigorous suppositions. Definitions of aesthetic excellence in architecture had been established by those who had collated neoclassical theory. After Laugier, Jacques-Blondel, Ledoux, J.–N.–L. Durand and others had written, it became impossible for any earnest and informed architect to work without self-criticism founded on their standards. The notion that responsible design could work a "moral revolution" had acquired a place among the reigning doctrines. Historians had provided and were continuing to provide quantities of accurate information about earlier arts and the societies which had created them.

Among these three resources the identification of Gothic with the "moral revolution" was to prove the least durable. Through the 1840s it was under constant attack; by the end of the decade its more rigorous manifestations had all but disappeared. Pugin was to die in 1852 a disappointed man, though in his own late works he had brilliantly demonstrated the way to unite Gothic inspiration and personal style.

The future was to be the province of another combination of the ideas which had been inherited. James Fergusson in *An Historical Inquiry into the True Principles of Beauty in Art* (1849) sought to define the sources of excellence, and in doing so he discounted "edifices which are merely monuments of our servility and ignorance till we have filled the land with dried specimens of past civilizations, as if to tell posterity that we had no art of our own and dared not think for ourselves." [7] Fergusson also perceived that the buildings produced by engineers bespoke his times.

In *The Grammar of Ornament* (1856) Owen Jones opened with a list of the principles which had governed fine ornament in the past and, one presumes, should do so in future, and then published a remarkable series of plates illustrative of historic ornament and closed with a series of new designs illustrative of the application of his "principles."

This change in thought which occurred in the late 1840s separates early and later Victorian architectural works and thought. The aspiration to restore a past and idealized art petered out, but the principles of design, the feeling of obligation to create a style for the new "age" remained. These were solid inheritances from the eighteenth-century theorists and the historians who had assembled the knowledge of the past, creating a panorama in which generalized patterns of cause and effect and characteristics of societies and whole ages could be detected by those in search of an explanation for their own times.

In many ways Pugin's Gothic Revival, though a challenge, had been the easier course to pursue. Without a fixed goal but imbued, first, with as remarkable a set of rules and observations on architecture as an art as had ever been assembled, and, second, with the idea that architecture, ethics, and historical change were, somehow, one, the "age" set forth on its wanderings. Its whole story cannot now be written because the journey has not yet ended.

Narrative Painting

Melvin Waldfogel

Some forty years ago Sacheverell Sitwell wrote a book entitled *Narrative Pictures*. While it begins with Hogarth and ends in the present, the bulk of the book deals with the Victorian period. The emphasis leaves no doubt that a primary aim was to restore Victorian painting to its proper place historically and aesthetically and to do so by gaining a sympathetic hearing for the most reviled branch of Victorian painting, namely the narrative picture. Sitwell opens his book by frankly stating the habitual criticism of Victorian painting: "It has been said too often of British painting that its inspiration lies always in literature. As painters, our artists are no better than illustrators of poetry or fiction . . . It has seemed better therefore not to deny allegations but to collect together as much evidence as possible in support of them." [1] In his opening broadside Sitwell has assured his readers that the "narrative picture" is a uniquely British expression, and they need feel no diffidence about it. He goes on to predict that his survey of *Narrative Pictures* will uncover aesthetic merits which have hitherto been forgotten or not yet discovered: "it is likely to reveal a good many excellent and unknown things to some of which . . . the term of lesser or minor masterpiece must surely be accorded . . ." [2] Whether his hypothesis is sound or his arguments are persuasive is beside the point. The name of Sitwell was enough to give them weight, and coinciding as his book did with the landmark studies of G. M. Young, it contributed massively to the sympathetic reappraisal of Victorian art. [3]

Sitwell defines narrative painting as the depiction of an action but embroidered by clues and hints which reveal to us the "before and after" of the story. In other works, we are given some intimation of what caused the action in the picture, and what the consequences will probably be. He cites as an ideal example Martineau's *Last Day in the Old Home* (plate 2), which is a sermon on the evils of drink and gambling, on the one hand; and the goodness of woman contrasted with the foolishness of man, on the other. Our first impression that this is an example of upward mobility and that the family is preparing to move to fancier digs is contradicted by a series of clues which would have been immediately apparent to a Victorian audience.

The old family seat, Hardham Court (its name is on the catalogue lying on the floor), is about to be sold up to pay for gambling debts of the heir to the estate, here seen raising a glass of champagne, his other arm on the shoulder of his son, who is already being taught by his father to gamble and drink. In the man's hand is a racing notebook, with racehorses on its cover, and a picture of a racehorse stands against the cupboard on the left. The wife, who has been weeping, holds out an appealing, restraining hand, while her mother-in-law, weeping bitterly, hands over her keys and last few possessions to the agent, who takes them with all the tact he can muster. The little girl looks at her sympathetically.

Through the door, the auctioneer's men may be seen removing *objets d'art* in readiness for the sale. They have already been through the room in which the scene is set, for everything bears a lot ticket.[4]

From the point of view of modern sensibility, the objection to the *Last Day in the Old Home* is not to the story itself, which is indeed tragic and to which we would respond appropriately in another medium, but the way in which it is told. We have been taught that a picture must be apprehended on impact, so to speak, through an immediate response to the mechanism of its form; and, to the contrary, if it is designed to be comprehended by a process of reading or assembling details, clues and hints, it is a bad picture. The old theory of *ut pictura poesis* which states that a picture is painted poetry, and which was already polemical in the eighteenth century, had been thoroughly discredited when Sitwell wrote *Narrative Pictures* in 1937, even though it was universally recognized that *ut pictura poesis* had been the express intent of the old masters.[5] What Sitwell was contending with in his plea for narrative pictures was a formalist view of art which had been disseminated in England as early as the 1860s — by Swinburne, Pater, and Whistler, and later by Oscar Wilde, Clive Bell, and Roger Fry, and which derived its authority from the greatest critic of the nineteenth century, the French poet Charles Baudelaire. Baudelaire was clearly on the side of apprehension, that is, of responding intuitively and immediately to the forms of a picture. In an essay in defense of his friend Delacroix, written in 1863, he argues that a "picture by Delacroix will already have quickened you with a thrill of supernatural pleasure even if it be situated too far away for you to be able to judge of its linear graces or the more or less dramatic quality of its subject. You feel as though a magical atmosphere has advanced towards you and already envelopes you . . ." [6] In the face of such authoritative and continued opposition, how are we to explain the growing addiction to Victorian painting? And by what mysterious process have Victorian painters, whose works have been written off as "kitsch" by modern critics, regained a serious and devoted audience?

First, nostalgia for the past, particularly the near past, has played a major part in the restoration of Victorian painting. One of the curious features of historical revivalism in our own age is a penchant for contiguity, that is, for the near past: for a decade or two or at most a half century earlier — for the sixties, the fifties or the thirties or twenties — for periods which fall within remembrance of the living old and sometimes the young. Ours is the first age to envisage the future, and we are repelled by what we see. We are drawn to the Victorian age by its seeming security and self-assurance, which is probably more myth than reality, although there can be no doubt that in some respects Victorians were more secure than we are. We seek warmth and shelter in their overdecorated and confining parlors, with their stuffed chairs, their bric-a-brac, and their potted ferns, and yearn to share in the affection and tender sentiments of the Victorian family, as it is depicted in the painting of the period.

Second, we have come to recognize that the narrative element was an important component in the works even of advanced artists of the nineteenth century and continues to be important in our own century, although with less emphasis or employment of what Sitwell calls the "before and after." Several of Degas's paintings are based on the literary theories of the realist writers with whom he was closely associated — Duranty, Zola, and Edmond de Goncourt — and in a few cases appear to narrate specific scenes from their novels.[7] Even Manet's great *Olympia*, which used to be interpreted as an exercise in tonal contrasts, conveys a very specific content, embedded in the objects, which must be read in much the same way as an English narrative picture. From iconographical studies undertaken by Sandblad and Reff we know that Olympia is the grand courtesan and that her brash presence was probably intended to *épater la bourgeoisie*.[8] It is also likely that Manet meant to raise some middle-class hackles since it would obviously react with shock in public to what it countenanced privately. In our own century surrealism and expressionism have often used the narrative mode.

And third, the proliferation of art styles and conflicting theories in our own day have reduced to absurdity the contention that true art is governed by universal rules. We have come to understand that rules of art are as time-bound as the styles they validate and grow like styles out of the needs of a given era.

In spite of our remove of some forty years from Sitwell's book and the tempering of opposition to narrative painting in the meantime, it is still with some diffidence that one approaches the subject of Victorian painting. It has become conventional to start with an apology or a defense, as Sitwell did, and this appraisal is no exception. First of all, the narrative picture was only one aspect of Victorian painting. History and landscape continued to be painted, although the former with less enthusiasm and support than in France or Germany. J. M. W. Turner, the greatest landscapist of the period whom we tend to locate in the Regency when he achieved his reputation, lived far enough into the Victorian period to visit the Crystal Palace and witness the shock of Pre-Raphaelitism. While his landscapes appear to belong to a later age, their titles and particularly the poetry he composed clearly reveal a penchant for Victorian sentiment.[9] *The Slave Ship*, accompanied to exhibition by verses from his own epic, "The Fallacies of Hope," is a case in point. Constable died in 1837, the year of Victoria's accession, but his mode of landscape painting survived him, not only in French Impressionism but at home in the works of countless anonymous amateurs, and in a number of artists of reputation: William Collins (the father of Wilkie of *Moonstone* fame) and David Cox, to name but one of the accomplished watercolorists who continued in the vein of Constable. Even the Impressionist-like seascapes of Henry Moore with their broad expanses of uniform water in intense blues partake of an unbroken landscape tradition which derives from Constable and Turner.[10]

No Impressionist revolution was needed to convert English painters to brilliant colorism. Not even the Royal Academy could dampen the English enthusiasm for color, perhaps in part because two of its early and very distinguished presidents, Reynolds and Lawrence, were so partial to strong, rich hues. Rich colorism was not limited to a few great or experimental artists, as was the case in France, but was equally characteristic of the narrative picture, addressed to an academy audience and destined for a middle-class interior. Paradoxically, Ruskin, whose views on form strike us as conservative today, found French painting unappealing because of its muddy darkness.[11]

The audience for narrative paintings was extremely large: Queen Victoria and Albert purchased them, as did many aristocrats; Ruskin approved of them; and they were admired and enjoyed uncritically by virtually the entire middle class. That they were popular, and at the same time taken seriously, we know from the frequency with which they were reproduced in large-circulation journals like the *Illustrated London News*, from its inception in 1842 to the end of the century. The Royal Academy's acceptance of narrative pictures for the annual exhibitions, even though they depart almost completely from academic precepts, is also indicative of their popularity and importance. Unlike academies on the continent, the Royal Academy received no financial support from the Crown or Parliament. All its expenses, including the salaries of officials and teachers, were paid from monies earned through the sale of catalogues and admission tickets at the annual exhibitions.[12] And I think it safe to assume that the narrative picture was largely responsible for the ample attendance and the consequent solvency of the academy. On the few occasions when guardrails had to be installed to protect pictures from admiring throngs, the works were narrative pictures: once for David Wilkie and six times for Frith later in the century. From the evidence it is clear that narrative pictures fulfilled the social and psychological needs and expectations of Victorian society.

Those needs and expectations were determined equally by contemporary conditions and the past. Beginning in the early eighteenth century with Hogarth, English painters had evinced a strong narrative bias not only by painting works which are expressly anecdotal but by enlivening portraits with an air of incident.[13] Even after the founding of the Royal Academy in 1768, artists of greater pretension and status than Hogarth lent a narrative flavor to their portraits. Both Reynolds's and Romney's individual and group portraits of Georgian aristocrats might be mistaken for genre or narrative pictures if the titles did not inform otherwise.[14]

The tendency toward narrative, particularly in its more sentimental form, was undoubtedly stimulated by the literature of the period. Hogarth's moral tableaux have their counterpart in the novels of Richardson, and in both we find an espousement of middle-class values. It is significant to note that early in the eighteenth century both artists and writers were already cognizant of a middle-class audience. This new audience bought the novels which mirrored its world and the prints of Hogarth but it was not until the advent of the nineteenth century that the middle class was to emerge importantly as collectors of painting. The international renown of the English sentimental novel, which by far surpassed that of painting, may also have impelled a narrative tendency in painting. By the end of the century, sentimental genre and narrative paintings were appearing with increasing frequency. The dependence of narrative painting on the prime literary expression of the middle class, namely the novel, is further borne out by the many Victorian paintings which take their subjects from novels of their own and the preceding century.

We are accustomed to seeing the Victorian period as sharply delineated from what immediately preceded it, namely the Regency, and as a result are inclined to impute to it — mystically — a conscious reversal of Regency values, almost from the moment of Victoria's accession in 1837; but in truth the reversal had been under way for some time. The Regency court, we know, was dissolute; but society as a whole was not. George IV and his brothers conducted themselves scandalously. The estranged wife of George IV, Queen Caroline, was actually tried by Parliament for licentious conduct.[15] But at the same time those virtues which we associate with Victorianism were on the ascendant. In 1818 the bowdlerized Shakespeare appeared. Thomas Bowdler, the publisher of *The Family Shakespeare* — the title under which it actually appeared — explained that "those words and expressions which cannot with propriety be read aloud in a family are omitted." His expurgated version of Gibbon's *Decline and Fall of the Roman Empire* followed in 1826. The evangelical movement, which had its inception in the late eighteenth century, also gained momentum rapidly and attracted a great many aristocratic adherents. The intent of evangelicalism was to encourage the application of Christianity to life and, in the words of Wilberforce, its founder, to curb "the decline of religion, manners and morals." A leading church historian has stated that "more than any other single factor, the Evangelical Movement . . . transformed the whole character of English society and imparted to the Victorian Age that moral earnestness which was its distinguishing characteristic."[16]

During the Regency painting also began to ascend the same road toward earnestness and probity. David Wilkie, who is generally recognized as the originator of the Victorian narrative picture, enjoyed accolades with the first picture he exhibited at the academy in 1806 (*The Village Politicians*). His *Distraining for Rent* (plate 3), in which a family's furnishings are being seized for nonpayment of rent, already has the sentimental appeal of Victorian melodrama and is highly suggestive of an evolved Victorian product like Martineau's *Last Day in the Old Home*. The narrative picture with the child as performer also made its appearance during the Regency, as did the animal as a vehicle for pathos. Both animals and children were to become stock characters in Victorian narrative painting.

Changing patterns of patronage also worked both directly and indirectly to stimulate the production of narrative painting.[17] Until the end of the eighteenth century collecting art was the prerogative of the aristocracy and their purchases were almost exclusively old masters from the continent. Mainly portraits — of faces, animals, and country houses — were commissioned from native artists. When the opportunity arose — the grand tour was such an opportunity — even portraits were done abroad. At the end of the century, however, in part as an expression of growing national pride and in part because the establishment of the Royal Academy signalized a coming of age artistically, there was a modest gravitation toward British art.

In the 1760s Lord Shelburne commissioned paintings from leading English landscape painters with the intent of laying the foundation of a school of British landscape. The planned foundation, unfortunately, never materialized. Sir John Leicester amassed a very important collection of British paintings, beginning about 1802, although there is evidence to suggest that the collection might have been begun as early as 1786. Others like Sir George Beaumont,[18] William Beckford, and the Earl of Egremont[19] were not only collectors of contemporary British art but patrons and friends of individual artists: Beaumont to Constable and Wilkie, Beckford to John Robert Cozens, and Egremont to Turner. Except for Wilkie we shall find few narrative pictures even in these collections.

The "rule of taste" continued to prevail in aristocratic collections, which meant that native artists were acceptable only if they worked in an old masterly manner. Sir George Beaumont's relationship with Constable is a case in point: he was more sympathetic toward Constable personally than toward his works, which he felt lacked the felicitous darks of the old masters and therefore lacked harmony.

Sir George was also among the aristocratic subscribers to the British Institution for Promoting the Fine Arts, which was established in 1805. Its primary objective was "to encourage and reward artists of the United Kingdom" through the inducement of prizes and exhibition opportunities, and through the formation of a "public gallery of the works of British artists, with a few select speciments of each school." In 1813 the British Institution sponsored an exhibition of Sir Joshua Reynolds's works, the first such one-man retrospective ever held in England. The exhibition of 1814 comprised works of four other eighteenth-century artists: Hogarth, Wilson, Gainsborough, and Zoffany. Between 1813 and 1823, in all 526 works by deceased British painters were shown, which goes a long way toward explaining the prevalence of works by the same artists in aristocratic collections of the Victorian period. What all this demonstrates is *not* an efflorescence of narrative painting but a quest for what Sitwell called "our native predilection in painting" which the Victorian era was soon to discover in the narrative picture.

With the appearance of a new kind of collector on the art scene in the early nineteenth century, the affluent merchant or industrialist, the future of narrative painting was assured. The new collectors were men like Joseph Gillot, whose factory in Birmingham for the manufacture of patented steel pen points employed more than a thousand workers; Robert Vernon, who had amassed a fortune supplying horses to the army during the Napoleonic Wars; and John Sheepshanks, who was the son of a Yorkshire cloth manufacturer.[20] Typically they felt pride in British civilization; in parliamentary government, which was unique in the world for equitable and stable rule; in the bounties of empire and industry, which promised utopian results; and in the improved moral tone of the age in which they lived. Their preference for contemporary English painting, and especially the narrative picture, was a natural extension of their social and other cultural beliefs; even their pragmatism directed them toward an art product where authenticity was never in doubt.

We know a great deal about English collections at mid-century from a guidebook which appeared in 1857, Dr. Gustave Waagen's *Cabinets and Galleries of Art in Great Britain*. Dr. Waagen was the eminent director of the Royal Picture Gallery in Berlin. His guidebook provides a work-by-work account of *all* the major and most of the minor collections, and in its thoroughness and specificity admirably demonstrates why the

Germans are prone to call art history *Kunstwissenschaft*. While Waagen's sympathies were clearly on the side of the old masters, he did take cognizance of several collections of English paintings by living artists. They were located, almost without exception, in new industrial centers like Manchester and Birmingham. Their owners' names were embellished by no aristocratic titles; instead they were suffixed by the simple honorific "esquire." Disraeli describes just such a collector in his novel *Coningsby*, written in 1844:

The walls of [his] dining room were covered with pictures of great merit; all of the modern school. Mr. Millbank understood no other, he was wont to say, and he found that many of his friends, who did, bought a great many pleasing pictures that were copies, and many originals that were very displeasing. He loved a fine free landscape by Lee, that gave him the broad plains, the green lanes, and running streams of his own land; a group of animals by Landseer, as full of speech and sentiment as if they were designed by Aesop; above all, he delighted in the household humor and homely pathos of Wilkie . . .[21]

It requires no effort on our part to visualize such a collector because a painting survives which might have served to illustrate the passage above. It is a portrait of John Sheepshanks (plate 4). Like Disraeli's Millbank, Sheepshanks appears to have "delighted in the household humor and homely pathos of Wilkie," although in this case the work was actually painted by Mulready.

The Sheepshanks portrait tells us much about the sitter personally and Victorian attitudes in general. Pictures and other objects of his collector's mania clutter much of the available space. On the bookshelves to the rear of the room but spilling over to the floor and the mantel are some of the rare books he began his collection with; on the left some of the 300 prints and drawings which he was to give to the nation in 1857. The few paintings which are in evidence hang in a way to suggest that wall space was at a premium in Sheepshanks's home. We know that he owned at least 233 paintings from the bequest of 1857.

The fact that he is portrayed with a servant rather than members of his family and that her demeanor verges on the familiar may strike the viewer as odd, but both conditions — his singleness and the servant's familiarity — are biographically correct. His friends considered him eccentric because he indulged his servants and fed them extravagantly while limiting his own personal expenses to about two pounds a year, which included omnibus rides.

Nor is it an accident that the overall feeling of the picture is domestic: a fire burns on the hearth, the room is an amiable clutter of his prized possessions, and the interruption by the servant is a particularly felicitous touch, enhancing the air of domesticity. In Walter Houghton's words, home "was both a shelter *from* the anxieties of modern life, a place of peace where the desires of the heart might be realized (if not in fact, in imagination), and a shelter *for* those moral and spiritual values which the commercial spirit and the critical spirit were threatening to destroy, and therefore also a sacred place, a temple." [22] Houghton was commenting on an oft-quoted passage from Ruskin's "Of Queen's Gardens," which deserves restatement:

This is the true nature of home — it is the place of Peace; the shelter, not only from all injury, but from all terror, doubt, and division. In so far as it is not this, it is not a home; so far as the anxieties of the outer life penetrate into it, and the inconsistently-minded, unknown, unloved, or hostile society of the outer world is allowed . . . to cross the threshold, it ceases to be a home; it is only a part of that outer world which you have roofed over, and lighted fire in. But so far as it is a sacred place, a vestal temple, a temple of the hearth watched over by Household Gods . . . it vindicates the name, and fulfills the praise, of home. [23]

The felicities of home and family, as expatiated by Ruskin, were recurring themes in Victorian painting, and their function was a serious one: the reinforcement and exemplification of accepted and requisite social values. As images they could even serve to deflect or mitigate the blow of war. *A Letter from Papa* (plate 5) was painted in 1855, during the Crimean War, and so the viewer was probably expected to infer that papa was off in Crimea, fighting the Queen's war. In narrative painting war is almost always viewed as it relates to the family. The soldier is seen *not* in battle but as a convalescent, returning home to recover from his wounds in the bosom of his family. In Millais's *Peace Concluded* (plate 6) brave papa, who has been wounded in Crimea, is surrounded by a grateful and adoring family. Like medals their adoration attests to his valiant service. That he need not return to the war we know from the announcement of peace in the newspaper. The Victorian soldier's gravitation toward home and family is in sharp contrast to an earlier and surely more realistic account of his conduct: in Dighton's *Men of War, Bound for the Fort of Pleasure* (plate 7), as the title unnecessarily tells us, their gratifications are of a lower and more natural order. Perhaps, if they catch some unmentionable disease, they will return to their families for convalescence.

Judged by their paintings, Victorians appear to have ascribed curative powers to the family. In a typical work painted in 1862 a convalescent is

being brought back to health by a combination of sea air and the solic-
itude of her family.[24] Even a great genre machine like Frith's *Derby Day*
(plate 8), which charms us at first glance by its festiveness and good-
natured jocularity, and sustains our interest through its multiplication of
incidents, is a kind of human comedy, built around family units. According to Frith, the "Principal Incident" in the picture is acted out by the
acrobat at the center and his hungry son whose performance has been
interrupted by the sight of a picnic hamper. Behind the acrobat-father is a
beggar woman with a child on her arm and another child who plays the
tambourine. On the far right, a fortune-teller tries to attract the attention
of the lady in the carriage, who seems more concerned with her husband
whose attention has been drawn to the pretty flower girl. On the far left
the young countryman in the smock is being restrained by his wife from
participating in the shell game, operated by the sharper behind the table.
Familial relationships are conspicuous here as in all of Frith's great
panoramas of contemporary life.

However, in an evangelical age given to churchgoing, prayer at home,
and sabbatarian discipline, a darker, more sermonistic approach was
equally prevalent in depictions of the family, as warning and object lesson. A frequent theme is the dissolution of the home or family, or the
undercutting of accepted standards of morality. Two of the paintings
discussed earlier, Wilkie's *Distraining for Rent* (plate 3) and Martineau's
Last Day in the Old Home (plate 2), depict families on the point of losing
their possessions or their homes, and in danger therefore of losing their
status and stability, and an even more precious Victorian commodity,
their respectability.[25] Frith also painted a series of five works in which the
gambling mania of a young aristocrat brings his family to destitution and
the gentleman to suicide. In the last scene of *The Road to Ruin* (plate 9),
the desperate man is shown alone in a garret, bolting the door and
meaningfully eyeing the pistol on the table. In Augustus Egg's *Past and
Present* essentially the same result is achieved, but more economically, in
three rather than five panels, and with a woman rather than a man as the
principal culprit; in this case the family is brought to ruin by the indiscre-
tions of the wife. Scene 1: The discovery of her infidelity (plate 10). The
picture is rife with symbols. It will suffice here to identify just two, the
flimsy house of cards the children are building, a portent of what is to
come, and the apple with its association of Eve and the fall from grace.
Scene 3: The mother, nursing her illegitimate child, seeks shelter under

the Adelphi Arches along the Thames. A fuller explanation is given in a quotation which appeared in the catalogue when the painting was exhibited at the Royal Academy in 1858: "Aug. 4: Have just heard that B. has been dead more than a fortnight; so his poor children have now lost both parents. I hear She was last seen on Friday, near the Strand, evidently without a place to lay her head — What a fall hers has been!"

Not surprisingly, the social situation of the Victorian woman was more fragile and circumscribed that that of the man. Again, if we judge by literature or painting, infidelity or the loss of virginity deprived her of all middle-class privileges and relegated her to a role outside of polite society. In Egg's *Past and Present* the fault lies clearly with the woman. But Victorians also recognized that in an age as unstable as theirs, circumstances might also be to blame. Elmore's *On the Brink* (plate 11), shows us a distraught woman being propositioned by a man. She has lost her money at the gaming tables in the background and is contemplating suicide when approached by the seducer, or perhaps a procurer. The viewer is asked to decide which is the more awful fate, suicide or prostitution. But it seems to me that at the same time the artist is perhaps intimating that, because she is, or has been, a lady, some ulterior and higher motive brought her to the gaming tables.

The fragility of virtue was adumbrated in a review of *Nameless and Friendless* in the *Art-Journal* in 1857: "A poor girl has painted a picture, which she offers for sale to a dealer, who, from the speaking expression of his features, is disposed to deprecate the work. It is a wet, dismal day, and she has walked far to dispose of it, and now awaits in trembling the decision of the man who is become rich by the labours of others." One wonders, can she maintain her respectability in the face of penuriousness, or will she succumb to the wiles of the leering men on the left? The work was painted by a women, Emily Mary Osborn, about whom little is known.[26] While there were many women artists, some even exhibiting at the academy, relatively few became or remained professional, which is explained in part by a comment which Christopher Wood made in his recent article on the Hayllar sisters.[27] Edith abandoned painting on entering a more noble profession — matrimony; however, her sister Jessica, a cripple like the heroine of Mrs. Craik's *Olive* and thus unsuited for marriage, was able to pursue a professional career.

Whether redemption was possible for the fallen woman, I'm not sure, but I would like to believe that Victorians thought it was. For the prostitute, restoration was possible through the Magdalen Hospital, although more likely it provided temporary refuge rather than restoration. The penitent had to undergo the humiliation of a head-shaving which must have deterred all but the most destitute. This seeming digression on redemption and prostitution is not introduced to titillate, but really is functional to my hypothesis because it leads directly to one of the most celebrated pictorial sagas of the fallen women of the Victorian period, William Holman Hunt's *Awakening Conscience* (plate 12). By what process her redemption was to come, I'm not sure, but Ruskin apparently believed it possible; at least that is my reading of his analysis which was published in a letter to the *Times* in 1854. But before we move to Ruskin's comments, a word of caution is in order.

The modern viewer unfamiliar with the rules of Victorian middle-class society and unaccustomed to reading a painting as often as not arrives at a conclusion that is 180 degrees off course. As we saw, the *Last Day in the Old Home* looks at first glance like a jolly celebration induced perhaps by fond memories of the old homestead, when in reality the home is being sold to pay the gambling debts of the young father. To the modern viewer, who is constantly exhorted by family experts to display affection to his or her spouse lest the children grow up to be emotionally stunted, the *Awakening Conscience* is a picture of consummate marital bliss. But not to a Victorian, who would have understood that such indecorous conduct — a woman sitting on a man's lap in such a new and tawdry setting — signified something other than a marriage relationship. With Ruskin as guide through the symbolic intricacies of the *Awakening Conscience*, the intended and intrinsic meanings become patently clear:

I suppose no one possessing the slightest knowledge of expression could remain untouched by the countenance of the lost girl, rent from its beauty into sudden horror; the lips half open, indistinct in their purple quivering, the teeth set hard, the eyes filled with the fearful light of futurity and with tears of ancient days . . . There is not a single object in all that room, common, modern, vulgar . . . but it becomes tragical, if rightly read. That furniture, so carefully painted, even to the last vein of rosewood — is there nothing to be learnt from that terrible lustre of it, from its fatal newness; nothing there has the old thoughts of home upon it . . . nay, the very hem of the poor girl's dress, at which the painter has laboured so closely, thread by thread, has a story in it, if we think how soon its pure whiteness may be soiled with dust and rain, her outcast feet failing in the street . . .[28]

But the important thing is that her conscience has been awakened. Recognition of the perilous state of one's soul is assuredly the first step toward redemption. The proper object of love between the sexes was marriage, and Victorians were understandably perturbed by anything which might impede marriage. A recurring theme in literature is the daughter of a genteel but impoverished family who is forced to seek employment as a governess or teacher. As a result her prospects for marriage are dimmed and her virtue perhaps threatened by a lustful employer. The same theme occurs in painting, although with less frequency. The best known example is Redgrave's *The Poor Governess* or *Teacher* (1844).[29] A spate of paintings on encumbered or impeded marriages appeared in the 1850s and 1860s. Arthur Hughes's *The Long Engagement* (1859) is self-explanatory.[30] The couple grows older but is no closer to marriage because his salary as a country curate is inadequate. In Calderon's *Broken Vows* (1856) a young woman has discovered her fiancé dallying with a flirtatious and presumably unvirtuous woman.[31] From her expression, and the clues dispersed through the picture, we know that "broken vows" signify a broken engagement.

It would be easy to multiply our examples, and in the light of the present feminist movement, interesting to analyze the role of women in Victorian narrative paintings more closely; but, unfortunately, space does not permit an extended discussion of female emancipation. Instead I would like to touch on two other themes which moved Victorians deeply.

One was the theme of emigration — of two sorts or at two different levels. First, there was emigration from Ireland to England,[32] and second, the departure from England of gentlefolk bound for the colonies and dominions, which immediately recalls the wonderfully moving and poignant *Last of England* (plate 13) by Ford Madox Brown. The couple stands at the stern of the ship, watching the land recede, but their faces are clouded by remembrance of the past and anxieties about the journey and their future. Heightening the poignancy is the child she shelters under her cloak. If we look sharply, we can see its hand clasped in hers.

Emigration was a reminder of the vagaries of nature or of commerce which could dispossess individuals and families and drive them from their homes to an uncertain fate abroad. Periodic depressions like the great panic of 1857 which swept through Europe as a whole gave direct impetus to emigration. Between 1853 and 1880 Britain sent out some two and a half million emigrants; most, but of course not all, left under duress. The couple in Madox Brown's *Last of England* is known to be the sculptor Woolner and his wife, who left England in 1852 for Australia.

The last theme which I intend to touch on as evidence of the seriousness of Victorian narrative painting is religion, more specifically the problem of religious doubt. The progress of science, and above all the credibility of its positivist methodology, inevitably gave rise to religious scepticism. As I suggested earlier, Victorian morality — in fact its whole system of values — was rooted in evangelical belief; conversely then, whatever threatened belief threatened to undermine the moral order which governed Victorian life. Darwin's *Origin of Species* struck like a thunderbolt when it appeared in 1859; but, while it was the most calamitous blow, it was hardly the first. Fundamentalism — that is, a literal reading of the Bible — had already been impugned by a new and more critical approach to biblical study, originating in Germany in the 1830's with the publication of David Strauss's *Life of Christ*. In the forties the flames of controversy were fanned even higher by the works of other German scholars. Ludwig Feuerbach's *The Nature of Christianity* was published in England in 1853, translated by George Eliot. Assaults on church doctrines and traditional practices also aroused uncertainty. Many Victorians were made uneasy by the zealous efforts of young reformers — I am referring to the Oxford movement — to bring the established Church closer to Rome, and were stunned by the conversion of Newman to Catholicism in 1845. Tennyson attempted to allay such doubts in *In Memoriam*, published in 1850:

> Our little systems have their day;
> They have their day and cease to be:
> They are but broken lights of thee,
> And thou, O Lord, art more than they.

That the poem was admired for its religious content we know from a variety of sources but perhaps the most telling comment is Queen Victoria's heartfelt tribute to Tennyson: "Next to the Bible, *In Memoriam* is my comfort." [33]

Artists also proffered religious advice and counsel. In 1851, a year after Tennyson's *In Memoriam* was published, the Pre-Raphaelite painter Holman Hunt exhibited his *Hireling Shepherd* (plate 14) at the academy. According to his own explanation, the picture alludes to "muddleheaded pastors who, instead of performing their services for their flock, which is in constant peril, discuss vain questions of no value to any human soul." The muddleheaded pastor is represented by the shepherd who, in his ignorance, has mistaken a death's-head moth for a foreboding of evil. To alleviate his anxiety he asks the advice of the fulsome young woman, but since her qualities are more corporeal than spiritual, she only serves (as Hunt puts it) to distract his faithfulness. She continues to feed her lambs with sour apples, and his sheep have got into the corn. Victorian painting can sometimes be very heady stuff. One wonders whether Hunt's censure was directed at the partisans of the new biblical criticism or the Oxford movement. More topical, and closer to *In Memoriam* in its message, is Henry Bowler's painting entitled *The Doubt: "Can These Dry Bones Live?"* (plate 15). Its date is 1856. The title comes from Ezekiel: "The hand of the Lord . . . set me down in the midst of the valley which was full of bones . . . And he said unto me, Son of man, can these bones live?" The young woman asks the same question — perhaps not consciously — as she takes in both the newly dug grave and the bones and skull unearthed in excavating it. The answer to her doubts is explicitly provided within the picture: a new shoot springs forth from a horse chestnut; a butterfly, representing resurrection or renewed life, sits on the skull; and on a tombstone the word *Resurgam* (or resurrection) literally spells out the answer.

I don't mean to give the impression that Victorian narrative pictures were always serious and full of moral earnestness, for often they were not. Nor am I trying to impart that their lessons are necessarily instructive for us. But what becomes apparent as one looks at the whole sweep of Victorian narrative paintings — whether one succumbs to them aesthetically or not — is how important and integral their role was to Victorian life. John Ruskin and William Morris both looked back reverentially to the Middle Ages and lamented the inability of their own time to assimilate its spirit. But what they failed to perceive is that for the Victorian era — like the Middle Ages — the book of life was writ in works of art. For better or for worse, the aesthetes closed that book.

Plate 1. Joseph Paxton, Crystal Palace, London, 1851 (colored lithograph from *Dickinson's Comprehensive Pictures of the Great Exhibition of 1851*, London, 1854). Photo: John Webb, Cheam, Surrey.

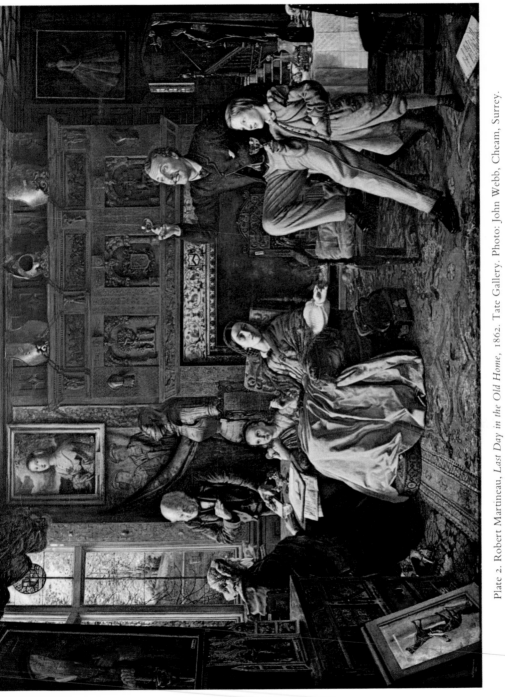

Plate 2. Robert Martineau, *Last Day in the Old Home*, 1862. Tate Gallery. Photo: John Webb, Cheam, Surrey.

Plate 3. David Wilkie, *Distraining for Rent*, 1818. Photo: William Gabler, Minneapolis.

Plate 4. William Mulready, *John Sheepshanks and His Maid*, before 1857.
Courtesy of Victoria and Albert Museum.

Plate 5. Frederick Goodall, *A Letter from Papa*, 1855. Tunbridge Wells Museum.
Photo: Michael Wheeler, Tunbridge Wells.

Plate 6. John Everett Millais, *Peace Concluded*, 1856.
Courtesy of the Minneapolis Institute of Arts.

Plate 7. Robert Dighton, *Men of War, Bound for the Fort of Pleasure*,
c. 1800. Sacheverell Sitwell. Photo: British Museum.

Plate 8. William Powell Frith, *Derby Day*, 1856–58. Tate Gallery. Photo: John Webb, Cheam, Surrey.

Plate 9. William Powell Frith, *The Road to Ruin*, v, 1887.
Courtesy of Marborough Fine Art (London) Ltd.

Plate 10. Augustus Egg, *Past and Present*, 1, 1858. Tate Gallery. Photo: John Webb, Cheam, Surrey.

Plate 11. Alfred Elmore, *On the Brink*, exh. 1865. Mrs. A. N. L. Munby.
Photo: Fitzwilliam Museum, Cambridge.

As he that taketh away a garment in cold weather, so is he that singeth songs to an heavy heart.

Plate 12. W. Holman Hunt, *Awakening Conscience*, 1853. Trustees of Sir Colin and Lady Anderson. Photo: Tate Gallery.

Plate 13. Ford Madox Brown, *Last of England*, 1852. Courtesy of
City Museum and Art Gallery, Birmingham.

Plate 14. W. Holman Hunt, *Hireling Shepherd*, 1851. Courtesy of
City of Manchester Art Galleries.

Plate 15. Henry Bowler, *The Doubt: Can These Dry Bones Live?*
1856. Tate Gallery. Photo: John Webb, Cheam, Surrey.

Plate 16. John Everett Millais, *Portrait of John Ruskin*, 1854.
Mrs. Patrick Gibson. Photo: Royal Academy of Arts, London.

Plate 17. John Ruskin, *Aiguilles of Chamonix*, 1849. Courtesy of
Fitzwilliam Museum, Cambridge.

Victorian Architecture:
An Introduction to
the Illustrations

Melvin Waldfogel

To a generation like my own conditioned to believe in function-alism and the future, Victorian buildings seemed more "grammars of ornament" than architecture in the true sense. The *horror vacui* of the Victorian facade, expressed through myriad excrescences, struck us not only as unfitting but as immoral and unclean, and suggested to us further that Victorians as a lot, with their penchant for darkness rather than light and muddiness rather than clarity, were psychologically flawed. It was alright for men of the Middle Ages or the Renaissance or even for eighteenth-century Palladians to build as they did, since the mysteries of industrial technology had not yet been revealed to them; but to continue to err when the truth was emblazoned on the iron members of the Crystal Palace and London railway stations was to place oneself beyond the pale of redemption. From the witness accounts of Gustave Doré (*London*, 1870s) and Charles Booth (*Life and Labour of the People of London*, 1891–1903), we knew the social consequences of such wrongheadedness and wondered why the Victorians, otherwise guided by reasoned liberalism, chose their architecture so irrationally.

Aesthetics and morality make strange bedfellows and are rarely seen as compatible when viewed from a distance as short as a generation, let alone a century or two. Until the onset of the modern movement, at the turn of the century, it was universally held that architecture was an associative art and could as a result strengthen moral fiber by example, i.e., by stylistic reference to an earlier, grander, and more salutary age. Revivalism had been rife in Western culture since the Renaissance, but only in the Victorian age did it become both systematic and encyclopedic. Accordingly, the history of nineteenth-century architecture is a succession of styles, perhaps more mélange than succession. But of all the styles emulated it was the medieval which was thought to have the greatest moral and social efficacy — Pugin, Ruskin, and Morris, the greatest minds in theory and practice, were all fervent medievalists — which goes a long way toward explaining why so many of the examples in the illustrations that follow display medieval elements, even when the function of the building is as prosaic as a warehouse.

In *The Spirit of the Age*, written in 1831, John Stuart Mill remarked on rapidity of change as characteristic of modern life and as differentiating his own period from what had immediately preceded it, the Middle Ages. Was Mill's knowledge of history so vague and approximate that he could only divide the whole spectrum of time into two broad bands, the modern and the medieval? Not at all. Rather, what he meant to signify was that a way of life dominated by the aristocracy and preindustrial technology had come precipitously to an end, thrusting man into a new world as abruptly and with as little protective raiment as the original parents when they were expelled from Eden. The shock of change and destabilizing newness was softened by evangelicalism and philanthropy, by bluster and the belief in progress, and by the bounties and benefits of empire — and in architecture by revivalism. Even had they heard them, Victorians would have lent no credence to foreigners like the German architect Karl Friedrich Schinkel, who, following his visit to England in 1830, was full of enthusiasm for the new, undecorated structures erected to house industry; nor would they have listened to the French Romantics from the 1830s on and later the Positivists, who subscribed to "*il faut être de son temps.*" Ruskin's prescription, we know, was: "We want no new style of architecture." He was offended by the Crystal Palace, which he lampooned mercilessly, yet at the same time he decried the ornamentation of railway architecture as inappropriate and a needless expense.

Our own feelings toward technology are less mixed than the Victorians', and if anything we are less optimistic about its prospects. What formerly we condemned as hypocrisy — their habit of veneering railway stations or even machines with ornamentation extracted from hallowed styles — can be appreciated now for what it was: an effort to soften the blow of the new industrialism and to assure themselves that old values had not been entirely forsaken.

The illustrations that follow show that Victorians excelled in their choice of building fabric, in adapting old styles to new needs, and in the quality of workmanship, evident in their drawings, which are as beautiful as they are painstaking. The project for an elevated railway by Clephan and Curtis, to be propelled by pneumatic power, is logically set against a Renaissance facade with its pronounced horizontals echoing the movement of the train. In the warehouse by R. W. Edis the Gothic verticality of the facade and the linkage of three windows within a pointed arch are consonant with the movement of goods in and out of the building by a crane.

Additionally, the illustrations were selected to show representative works by the leading architects, a broad range of styles, and the wide variety of building types treated as architecture. Rather than arrange them chronologically or stylistically, I have chosen to divide them by function or type — with the exception of the first section — on the assumption that such an arrangement would better acquaint the reader with the broad goals of Victorian architecture, from the modest shop front by Philip Webb to the mill for Titus Salt, and from housing for humble workers to the grandiose resort hotel and the estate in the country. The first section contrasts the reality of Victorian London with Pugin's projection of an ideal city, in the only style he considered suitable, namely the Gothic, and also contrasts styles used for prominent or public buildings in London — the Renaissance palazzo style of Charles Barry's Reform Club with the Gothic chosen by G. E. Street for his entry in the competition for the Law Courts.

The reader interested in the details and niceties of style and in the development of Victorian architecture should turn to Henry-Russell Hitchcock's *Early Victorian Architecture in Britain* (New Haven, 1954), Robert Furneaux Jordan's *Victorian Architecture* (Harmondsworth, 1966), Mark Girouard's *The Victorian Country House* (Oxford, 1971), J. Mordaunt Crook's *Victorian Architecture: A Visual Anthology* (New York, 1971, reprint), and Nikolaus Pevsner's *High Victorian Design* (London, 1951).

City Contrasts

Plate 18. Henry Ashton, Apartment Houses in Victoria Street between Carlisle Place and Howick Place, London, 1852–54 (*Illustrated London News*, 18 Nov. 1854). Photo: William Gabler, Minneapolis.

Plate 19. A. N. W. Pugin, An English Town of 1440. (A. N. W. Pugin, *Contrasts*, 2nd ed., 1841). Photo: British Library.

Plate 20. Charles Barry, The Reform Club, London, 1838–40.
Photo: A. F. Kersting, London.

Plate 21. G. E. Street, The Law Courts, London. Elevation, The Strand Front,
1866. Photo: Royal Institute of British Architects.

Plate 22. G. E. Street, The Law Courts, London. The Strand Front, 1874–78.
Photo: A. F. Kersting, London.

Commerce

Plate 23. Lockwood and Mawson, Titus Salt's Mill at Shipley Glen, Saltaire, near Bradford, Yorkshire, completed 1853. Photo: City of Bradford.

Plate 24. R. W. Edis, Warehouses, Southwark Street, London, 1873
(*The Architect*, X [1873] 207b). Photo: Avery Library.

MISS BURDETT COUTTS'S NEW MARKET, BETHNAL GREEN.——Mr. H. A. Darbishire, Architect.

Plate 25. A. Darbyshire, Columbia Market, Bethnal Green, London, 1866–68
(*The Builder*, XXIV[1866]797). Photo: Avery Library.

Plate 26. Philip Webb, Shops, 90–91 Worship Street, Finsbury, London, 1862–63
(*The Builder*, XXI[1863]620). Photo: Avery Library.

The Church

Plate 27. A. N. W. Pugin, Rejected Proposal for St. George's, Southwark, 1839.
Photo: Royal Institute of British Architects.

Plate 28. A. N. W. Pugin, Frontispiece, *An Apology for the Revival of Christian
Architecture in England*, London, 1843. Photo: Avery Library.

Cathedral of St Finn Bar – Cork
W. Burgess, Architect.

Plate 29. William Burgess, St. Finbar Cathedral, Cork, Ireland, 1865–83
(*The Architect*, I [1869] 36b). Photo: Avery Library.

Art and Technology

Plate 30. Joseph Paxton, Crystal Palace, London, 1851 (*Dickinson's Comprehensive Pictures of the Great Exhibition of 1851*, London, 1854). Photo: John Webb, Cheam, Surrey.

Plate 31. B. W. H. Barlow, Train Shed, St. Pancras Station, London, 1863–67 (*The Building News* [1869]). Photo: Avery Library.

Plate 32. G. Gilbert Scott, St. Pancras Hotel, London, 1867–74.
Photo: A. F. Kersting, London.

Plate 33. Clephan and Curtis, A Scheme for a London Railway, c. 1850.
Photo: Royal Institute of British Architects.

A Place in the Country

Plate 34. Alfred Waterhouse, Eaton Hall, Cheshire, 1867–80.
Photo: National Monuments Record.

Plate 35. William Butterfield, St. Saviour's Vicarage, Coalpitheath,
Gloucestershire, 1844–55. Photo: National Monuments Record.

Plate 36. Cuthbert Broderick, Grand Hotel, Scarborough, 1863–67.
Photo: A. F. Kersting, London.

Plate 37. S. Sanders Teulon, Cottages for Crown Laborers, Windsor Great Park,
1853–54 (*The Builder*, XII[1854]99). Photo: Avery Library.

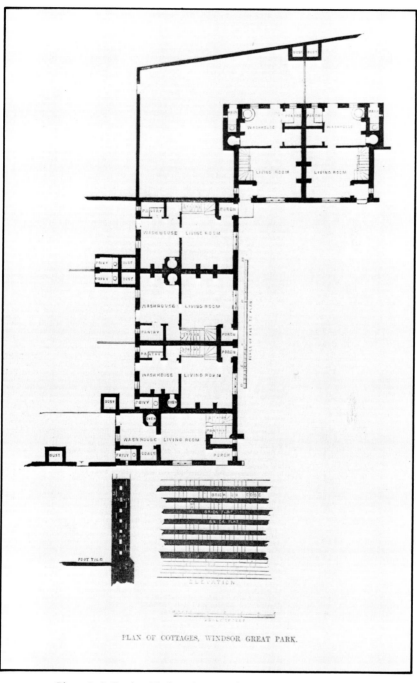

Plate 38. S. Sanders Teulon, Cottages for Crown Laborers, Plan
(*The Builder*, XII[1854]98). Photo: Avery Library.

Home in the City

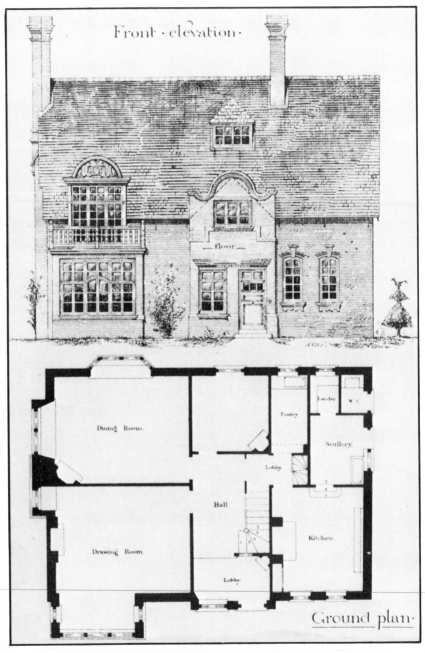

Plate 39. Norman Shaw, A Detached Villa, Bedford Park Estate, 1879
(*The Building News*, XXXVI [1879]421). Photo: Avery Library.

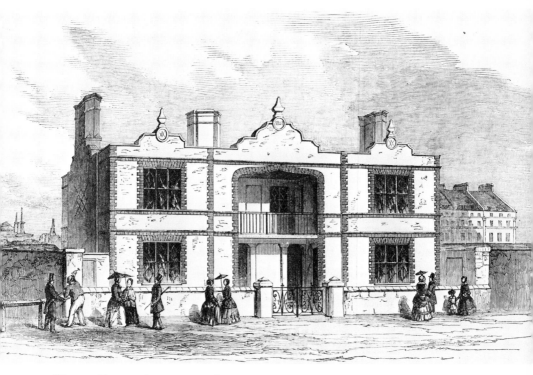

Plate 40. Henry Roberts, Prince Albert's Model Lodging House, Hyde Park, 1850–51
(*Illustrated London News*, 14 June 1854). Photo: William Gabler, Minneapolis.

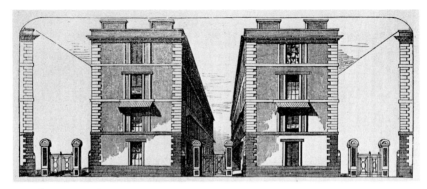

Plate 41. Workmen's Dwellings, Birkenhead, 1845–47 (*Companion to the British Almanac*, 1848). Photo: William Gabler, Minneapolis.

Plate 42. William Young, Project for Model Town Houses for the Middle Class, 1849 (*The Builder*, 1 Dec. 1849). Photo: Avery Library.

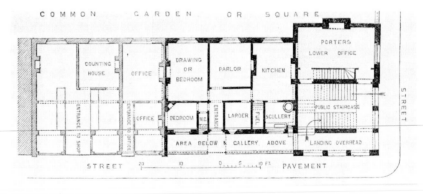

Plate 43. William Young, Project for Model Town Houses for the Middle Class, Plan.

Notes and Bibliography

Notes

Victorian England: The Self-Conscious Society
Jerome H. Buckley

1. Alfred Russel Wallace, *The Wonderful Century* (1898; New York: Dodd Mead, 1899), p. 380.

2. John Canaday, *New York Times*, July 28, 1974, sec. 2, p. 17.

3. See John Stuart Mill, "Civilization" (1836), *Dissertations and Discussions*, 4 vols. (London: Longmans, 1875), I, 181.

4. From a letter to Clough, in H. F. Lowry, ed., *The Letters of Matthew Arnold to Arthur Hugh Clough* (New York: Oxford University Press, 1932), p. 97.

5. Newman, "Secret Faults," *Parochial and Plain Sermons*, 8 vols. (London: Longmans, 1894), I, 42–43.

6. Charles Darwin, *The Origin of Species* (New York: Modern Library, n.d.), chap. IV, p. 65.

7. See R. D. Laing, *The Politics of Experience* (New York: Pantheon Books, 1967), and John Vernon's account of "schizophrenia in twentieth-century literature and culture," *The Garden and the Map* (Urbana: University of Illinois Press, 1973).

8. John Stuart Mill, *Utilitarianism, Liberty, and Representative Government* (London: Dent, 1910), pp. 73, 75, 31 (italics mine).

9. Hopkins, selection from a meditation, "On St. Ignatius's Spiritual Exercises," John Pick, ed., *A Hopkins Reader* (Garden City: Image Books, 1966), pp. 396–97.

10. Claude Colleer Abbott, ed., *Letters of Gerard Manley Hopkins to Robert Bridges* (London: Oxford University Press, 1935), p. 291 (Sept. 25, 1888) and p. 66 (Feb. 15, 1879).

11. Patricia Alleridge makes this point in her excellent catalogue, *The Late Richard Dadd, 1817–1886* (London: Tate Gallery, 1974), pp. 41–43.

12. Wordsworth, letter of May 1, 1805, Philip Wayne, ed., *Letters of William Wordsworth* (London: Oxford University Press, 1954), p. 72.

The Art of Victorian Literature
Robert Langbaum

1. For Wordsworth and Coleridge poetry operates by fusing subject and object. Coleridge wrote that "the mystery of genius in the Fine Arts" is "to elicit from, and to superinduce upon, the forms [of nature] themselves the moral reflexions to which they approximate, to make the external internal, the internal external, to make nature thought, and thought nature . . . the conscious is so impressed on the unconscious as to appear in it" ("On Poesy or Art," *Biographia Literaria*, ed. J. Shawcross, 2 vols., London: Oxford University Press, 1965, II, 258).

2. Robert Langbaum, *The Poetry of Experience: The Dramatic Monologue in Modern Literary Tradition*, new ed. (New York: Norton, 1971). See ch. I, "The Dramatic Lyric and the Lyrical Drama."

3. See Robert Langbaum, "The Victorian Idea of Culture," in *The Modern Spirit: Essays on the Continuity of Nineteenth- and Twentieth-Century Literature* (New York: Oxford University Press, 1970).

4. For a brilliant analysis of the Victorian sages' artfulness, see John Holloway, *The Victorian Sage* (New York: Norton, 1965). Holloway discusses the prose of Carlyle, Disraeli, George Eliot, Newman, Arnold, and Hardy, but unfortunately omits Ruskin and Pater. See also *The Art of Victorian Prose*, ed. George Levine and William Madden (New York: Oxford University Press, 1968).

5. My italics. W. C. DeVane, *A Browning Handbook*, 2nd ed. (New York: Appleton-Century-Crofts, 1955), p. 104.

6. *The Poems of Tennyson*, ed. Christopher Ricks (London: Longmans, 1969). The references are to part and line.

7. See Carol T. Christ's reading of this scene in *The Finer Optic: The Aesthetic of Particularity in Victorian Poetry* (New Haven: Yale University Press, 1975), pp. 27–29.

8. "The Novel in 'The Ring and the Book,'" *Notes on Novelists* (London: Dent, 1914).

9. Ed. John Paterson (Boston: Houghton Miffllin, Riverside Edition, 1968), pp. 150, 152–53.

10. Ed. Gordon S. Haight (Boston: Houghton Mifflin, Riverside Edition, 1956), p. 122.

11. Quoted in George H. Ford, *Double Measure: A Study of the Novels and Stories of D. H. Lawrence* (New York: Holt, Rinehart, and Winston, 1965), p. 20. "Before, you know," Lawrence continues, "with Fielding and the others, it [the action] had been outside. Now I wonder which is right?" The question explains Lawrence's own attempt to externalize the internal action through the use of animals and landscapes that symbolize psychic states (e.g., the arctic landscape that projects Gerald's psyche in *Women in Love*).

12. Dickens, wrote George Eliot, "is gifted with the utmost power of rendering the external traits of our town population; and if he could give us their psychological character — their conceptions of life, and their emotions — with the same truth as their idiom and manners, his books would be the greatest contribution Art has ever made to the awakening of social sympathies" ("The Natural History of German Life," *Essays*, Edinburgh and London: Blackwood, 1884, pp. 236–37). Henry James called Dickens "the greatest of superficial novelists": "it is one of the chief conditions of his genius not to see beneath the surface of things" (review of *Our Mutual Friend*, in *Views and Reviews*, Boston: Ball, 1908, p. 159).

13. *The English Novel: Form and Function* (New York: Harper and Row, Torchbook Edition, 1961), p. 131.

14. *English Novel*, p. 133.

15. Notre Dame: University of Notre Dame Press, 1968, pp. 119–20.

16. *The Living Novel* (New York: Reynal and Hitchcock, 1947), p. 88.

17. When we apply depth psychology to the Victorian novel, however, we restore the integrity of the plot as symbolic action. This corresponds to Lawrence's way of making a new symbolic externalization of the internal action, which is the next step in the development of the twentieth-century novel.

18. "The Comic World of Dickens," in Ian Watt, ed., *The Victorian Novel: Modern Essays in Criticism* (New York: Oxford University Press, 1971), p. 39.

19. *Study of Thomas Hardy*, in *Phoenix: The Posthumous Papers, 1936*, ed. E. D. McDonald (New York: Viking, Compass Edition, 1972), p. 420.

20. Robbe-Grillet insists, however, that his novels aim at "a total subjectivity"; for though they concentrate on objects, "it is a *man* who sees [the objects], who feels, who imagines, a man located in space and time, conditioned by his passions . . . And the book reports nothing but his experience" ("New Novel, New Man," *For a New Novel: Essays on Fiction*, tr. Richard Howard, New York: Grove, 1965, pp. 138–39). While it is true that the objects project a psychic condition, we are not always sure exactly where or when they are seen or by whom. The objects project the psychic condition of an unnamed, sometimes unknown narrator, who never or almost never says "I," who has no separate existence, who is swallowed up in the objects he perceives. The perceiver, in other words, does not have

the dialectical relation with the object that he has in the tradition of romantic-realist writing beginning with the dramatic lyric.

The Poetry of Thought
David J. DeLaura

1. From "The Rationale of Reward" (1825), cited by Lionel Stevenson, "The Key Poem of the Victorian Age," in Max F. Schulz, ed., *Essays in American and English Literature Presented to Bruce Robert McElderry, Jr.* (Athens, Ohio: Ohio University Press, 1967), pp. 261–62.

2. *Biographia Literaria*, ed. J. Shawcross (London: Oxford University Press, 1907), II, 19 (ch. XV); Mill's 1835 review of Tennyson, cited in *Tennyson: The Critical Heritage*, ed. John D. Jump (London: Routledge & Kegan Paul, 1967), p. 92 (hereafter cited as Jump).

3. The reputation of the metaphysical poets was best studied by Arthur H. Nethercot, notably in two articles: *Journal of English & Germanic Philology*, 23 (April 1924), 173–98, and *Studies in Philology*, 22 (Jan. 1925), 81–132. For the nineteenth century, see Joseph E. Duncan, *The Revival of Metaphysical Poetry* (Minneapolis: University of Minnesota Press, 1959), and Kathleen Tillotson, "Donne's Poetry in the Nineteenth Century," in *Mid-Victorian Studies* (London: Athlone Press, University of London, 1965), pp. 278–300.

4. *Biographia Literaria* (n. 2, above), I, 15 (ch. I).

5. "Thomas Gray" (1880), in *The Complete Prose Works of Matthew Arnold*, ed. R. H. Super (Ann Arbor: University of Michigan Press, 1960–), IX, 202 (hereafter cited as *CPW*).

6. *Selected Essays*, 3rd ed. (London: Faber & Faber, 1951), pp. 287–88.

7. Francis Jeffrey, 1814, cited in *Romantic Perspectives*, ed. Patricia Hodgart and Theodore Redpath (London: George G. Harrap, 1964), p. 30 (hereafter cited as Hodgart and Redpath); and 1802, cited in John O. Hayden, *The Romantic Reviewers, 1802–1824* (London: Routledge & Kegan Paul, 1969), p. 81 (hereafter cited as Hayden).

8. Hayden, p. 87; and see J. H. Merivale, cited in Hodgart and Redpath, p. 53.

9. *The Spirit of the Age* (1825), in *Complete Works*, ed. P. P. Howe (London: J. M. Dent, 1930–34), XI, 76.

10. An 1824 review of Shelley, in Theodore Redpath, *The Young Romantics and Critical Opinion, 1807–1824* (London: Harrap, 1973), pp. 388–91.

11. *Works*, XI, 76–77.

12. Jeffrey, 1822, in *Byron: The Critical Heritage*, ed. Andrew Rutherford (New York: Barnes & Noble, 1970), p. 233 (hereafter cited as Rutherford). For similar arguments by other critics, see pp. 219, 238. Contemporary reaction to *Cain* is generously presented in Truman Guy Steffan, *Lord Byron's "Cain"* (Austin: University of Texas Press, 1968), pp. 307–426.

13. See Newman Ivey White, *The Unextinguished Hearth: Shelley and His Contemporary Critics* (Durham, N.C.: Duke University Press, 1938), p. 18.

14. Cited in Jump, p. 135. W. M. Rossetti noted in 1850 that "all living poets" have the quality of "self-consciousness"; we now get "the belief of a poet as of a theologian or a moralist." Cited in *Matthew Arnold, The Poetry: The Critical Heritage*, ed. Carl Dawson (London: Routledge & Kegan Paul, 1973), p. 56 (hereafter cited as Dawson). See also W. J. Fox, 1830, in Jump, p. 25; and W. M. Rossetti, 1866, in *Swinburne: The Critical Heritage*, ed. Clyde K. Hyder (New York: Barnes & Noble, 1970), p. 84 (hereafter cited as Hyder). The opposite charge — that his poetry exhibited a "forcible divorce from thought" — prevailed in Keats criticism until about 1860. See the introduction and headnotes in *Keats: The Critical Heritage*, ed. G. M. Matthews (London: Routledge & Kegan Paul, 1971). Picking up themes first developed by Hazlitt and Macaulay, the reactionary W. J. Courthope continued, late in the century, to long for the "old" poetry founded on "positive acceptance and belief," and to deplore the "atmosphere of Doubt," "the method of introspection," and "the principle of analysis," first brought in by the romantic poets. See his numerous articles in the

Quarterly Review (now listed in the *Wellesley Index*) and his *The Liberal Movement in English Literature* (London: John Murray, 1885) — I have quoted here from p. 239. R. V. Johnson, "Pater and the Victorian Anti-Romantics," *Essays in Criticism*, 4 (Jan. 1954), 42–57, studied this reactionary mood in the *Quarterly* but did not know that his "critics" were mostly the singular Courthope. There is an excellent rebuttal of Courthope by Rowland Prothero, "Modern Poetry," *Edinburgh Review*, 163 (April 1886), 466–98.

15. See Hayden (1820), p. 196; Frederic Rogers, *British Critic*, 24 (1838), 285; *Keble's Lectures on Poetry, 1832–1841*, tr. E. K. Francis (Oxford: Clarendon Press, 1912), II, 201; Frederick Robertson (1852), *Lectures, Addresses, and Other Literary Remains* (London: Kegan Paul, Trübner, 1906), p. 88; Walter Bagehot (1859), in Jump, p. 217, and (1864), in *The Collected Works of Walter Bagehot*, ed. Norman St. John-Stevas (Cambridge, Mass.: Harvard University Press, 1965), II, 326–27; William Knight (1873), *Studies in Philosophy and Literature* (London: C. Kegan Paul, 1879), p. 269.

16. H. B. Forman (1868), cited in Dawson, p. 199.

17. See *Browning: The Critical Heritage*, ed. Boyd Litzinger and Donald Smalley (London: Routledge & Kegan Paul, 1970), pp. 109 (1845) and 122 (1847) (hereafter cited as Litzinger and Smalley).

18. See Litzinger and Smalley, 1868, p. 298; Alfred Austin (1868), in Dawson, pp. 202–203; Bagehot (1859), in Jump, p. 223.

19. The fact that the critics Arnold was implicitly answering in the preface of 1853 (e.g., Kingsley) asked for "modern" subject matter should *not* be confused with a call for everyday or domestic detail, such as could be found in Thackeray's novels. Despite the example of Tennyson's domestic idylls, poetry was still to be reserved for "heightened" and "idealized" effects. The question was raised by Bagehot in 1859; see Jump, pp. 222–23, 225.

20. John Sterling (1842), and J. W. Marston (1847), in Jump, pp. 120, 171.

21. For example, W. E. Aytoun (1849), in Dawson, p. 48.

22. Gladstone (1859), in Jump, p. 252; H. G. Hewlett (1874), in Dawson, p. 246; J. H. C. Fane (1869), in B. R. McElderry, "Victorian Evaluation of *The Ring and the Book*," *Research Studies of the State College of Washington*, 7 (June 1939), 89.

23. Charles Kingsley (1853), in Rutherford, p. 355, and (1854), in Dawson, p. 138.

24. These two themes are explored in DeLaura, "The Future of Poetry," forthcoming in a *Festschrift* for Charles Richard Sanders, ed. John Clubbe (Durham, N.C.: Duke University Press); the Stevenson article (n. 1, above) opened up some of these issues.

25. The *English Review*, 13 (March 1850), 207–13, enrolled Arnold and Clough in the "transcendental school" of Tennyson, Browning, and Mrs. Browning although "the hopeless despondency and vague dreaming" of the newcomers is seen as a new and disturbing note.

26. "The Hero as Poet," *On Heroes, Hero-Worship and the Heroic in History, The Works of Thomas Carlyle* (Centenary Edition), ed. H. D. Traill (New York: C. Scribner's Sons, 1897–1901), V, 83.

27. I have tried to explain this notion in my essay mentioned in n. 24, and more fully in "Arnold and Literary Criticism: Critical Ideas," forthcoming in *Matthew Arnold* (Writers and Their Backgrounds), ed. M. and K. Allott (London: Bell).

28. *The Writings of Arthur Hallam*, ed. T. H. Vail Motter (New York: Modern Language Association of America, 1943), pp. 187, 184. Robert Preyer treats this phase of Tennyson's career admirably in "Tennyson as an Oracular Poet," *Modern Philology*, 55 (May 1958), 239–51.

29. It should be noted that "Supposed Confessions" was not reprinted until 1884 and thus almost certainly remained unknown to the Arnold–Clough generation.

30. Jump, p. 26.

31. *Ibid.*, pp. 149, 151.

32. *Ibid.*, pp. 120, 123. "Locksley Hall," lines 119–28.

33. George Gilfillan, *Second Gallery of Literary Portraits* (1st ed., 1850), 2nd ed. (Edinburgh: James Hogg, 1852), p. 280. The succeeding quotations in the paragraph are from pp. 285, 292, 269.

34. In *Fraser's*, Sept. 1850; here cited from Jump, pp. 172–85.

35. The reviewer in the High Church *English Review* (Sept. 1850) was one of the few to score the dubiously orthodox theology; cited in *"In Memoriam": A Casebook*, ed. John Dixon Hunt (London: Macmillan, 1970), pp. 85–100. See also Edgar Finley Shannon, *Tennyson and the Reviewers* (1952; reprint ed., Hamden, Conn.: Archon Books, 1967), pp. 149–51. Gladstone, in 1859 (Jump, p. 248), offered a less blatant version of Kingsley's hope. He called on Tennyson to work toward the solution of the problem, "so fearful from its magnitude," how — in an age marked by "the progress of physical science and a vast commercial, mechanical, and industrial development" — "to harmonise this new draught of external power and activity with the old and more mellow wine of faith, self-devotion, loyalty, reverence, and discipline."

36. One of the best attempts to catch the tone of the 1840s — "the band of young truth-seekers," and their eventual "sceptical weariness" — occurs in John Tulloch's *Movements of Religious Thought in Britain During the Nineteenth Century* (New York: Charles Scribner's Sons, 1885), pp. 197–98, 255–56. Probably the best account of the effect of the French Revolution on English poetry is M. H. Abrams's "The Spirit of the Age," in *Romanticism Reconsidered*, ed. Northrop Frye (New York: Columbia University Press, 1963), pp. 26–72.

37. Goldwin Smith, *Lectures on Modern History* (Oxford & London: J. H. & Jas. Parker, 1861), p. 34.

38. *Amours de Voyage*, V, 101–103, in *The Poems of Arthur Hugh Clough*, ed. H. F. Lowry, A. L. P. Norrington, and F. L. Mulhauser (Oxford: Clarendon Press, 1951), p. 216.

39. Jean-Marie Carré, *Goethe en Angleterre* (Paris: Plon-Nourrit, 1920), pp. 225–47.

40. In the memoir attached to Alexander Smith's *Last Leaves: Sketches and Criticisms* (Edinburgh: P. Nimmo, 1868), p. lxv, Patrick Alexander uses *Faust* and *Hamlet* as his examples in offering the following rather tendentious definition of Spasmodic Poetry: "the Poetry of unrest and despair; of irregular struggle; of baffled effort, wild, bewildered, and mistaken — the Poetry, in one word, of *Scepticism*, not cool in the intellect, as Hume's, but raging, like mutiny of passion in the blood, with the whole perverted might of the heart and the moral emotions." Joseph J. Collins, "Tennyson and the Spasmodics," *Victorian Newsletter*, no. 43 (Spring 1973), pp. 24–28, argues that Tennyson was not influenced by Bailey and the other Spasmodics.

41. Arnold of course made Hamlet and Faust the archetypes of "modern" doubt and discouragement, in the 1853 preface (*CPW*, I, 1).

42. Kathleen Tillotson, in *Novels of the Eighteen-Forties* (London: Oxford University Press, 1954), pp. 115–39, discusses the rise of the topical novel and the new role of "thought" in fiction.

43. Clough's creation of "an intellectual man" was brought up by J. M. Robertson in a very penetrating essay of 1897; see Thorpe, p. 355. Maurice Beebe, in *Ivory Towers and Sacred Founts: The Artist as Hero from Goethe to Joyce* (New York: New York University Press, 1964), pp. 79–97, usefully discusses mid-century "artist" novels in England. Beebe understandably neglects the immediate intellectual and literary setting, which would well repay study. Behind several of the "art" novels of the period lies of course Goethe's *Meister*, often "moralized" in English; see Susanne Howe, *Wilhelm Meister and His English Kinsmen* (1930; reprint ed., New York: AMS Press, 1966). David Masson's splendid discussion of the "Art and Culture Novel" in *British Novelists and Their Styles* (Cambridge: Macmillan, 1859), pp. 265–302, deserves the closest scrutiny by any student of this "moment" in English cultural history. He distinguishes three classes of works which address, not the special claims of various parties, but the new and "deeper question of fundamental faith as against fundamental scepticism" (p. 266). *Copperfield* and *Pendennis* present secular heroes who struggle "through doubt and error towards certainty and truth," though the doubt is very "moderate" and the final faith only "tantamount" (pp. 266, 274). Kingsley's novels introduce a more specifically "Christian" demand for a new "faith metaphysical" (p. 276). The alternative to this "muscular Christianity" is "a contemporary school of 'nervous Paganism.'" (I judge that "nervous" is used here, not in the sense now most common,

"excitable, easily agitated, timid," but in the sense of "vigorous, powerful, forcible." The *OED* gives examples of this usage, to characterize literary style, by both Carlyle and Kingsley.) These new poets and novelists — and Masson seems to be thinking of the poetry of Clough (whom he succeeded at University College, London) and Matthew Arnold, and the fiction of Froude — occupy "a bleaker and more extreme standing-ground on the plain of speculation," and "are incessantly ruminating the same high problems of the metaphysical, without having the privilege of rest in the same solution" (p. 284). Masson, here and elsewhere (see n. 65. below), is himself plainly torn between the more conventional claims of a Kingsley and the new "bleak" school of speculation. (It may be noted that *Moby Dick* was published in 1851.) George Eliot seems to me a rather late example of a novelist who treats the themes of "1850," and in a not dissimilar spirit — especially in *Romola, Middlemarch,* and *Daniel Deronda.* David Carroll, the editor of *George Eliot: The Critical Heritage* (London: Routledge & Kegan Paul, 1971), points out (pp. 38–39) that even sympathetic reviewers, from Richard Simpson to Henry James, deplored a "growing earnestness, abstractness, and despondency" in her fiction, and judged that she "was a successful novelist despite her radical intellect to which she finally succumbed." James shrewdly suggested that her natural métier was "enthusiasm, sympathy, and faith," and wished she had "fallen upon an age of enthusiastic assent" (pp. 427–28). R. H. Hutton, in *Essays on Some of the Modern Guides to English Thought in Matters of Faith* (London: Macmillan, 1888) perhaps best conveys the view that George Eliot's "great speculative intellect" eventually stagnated in a deep "weariness" (pp. 153, 265).

44. William R. Brown, in "William James and the Language of Personal Literature," *Style,* 5 (Spring 1971), 151–63, suggests that "personal literature," in which a structure of ideas is deeply infused by the author's personality, includes both the meditative poem and the reflective essay. Close analysis of some of the key poems of 1850 would also show a connection with the Romantic "conversation poem" first developed by Coleridge. See M. H. Abrams, "Structure and Style in the Greater Romantic Lyric" (1965), reprinted in *Romanticism and Consciousness,* ed. Harold Bloom (New York: W. W. Norton, 1970), pp. 201–29.

45. *New Letters of Thomas Carlyle,* ed. Alexander Carlyle (London: John Lane, 1904), p. 59. For Arnold's similar view of F. W. Newman, see *The Letters of Matthew Arnold to Arthur Hugh Clough,* ed. Howard Foster Lowry (London: Oxford University Press, 1932), p. 115 (hereafter cited as *LC*).

46. Stevenson (n. 1, above), pp. 269–70, mentions a category of "reflective poems," among the few effective examples of which are *In Memoriam, Christmas-Eve and Easter-Day,* "Dipsychus," and "The Scholar-Gipsy," in which "there is sufficient tension between the philosophical argument and the author's emotional involvement to arouse even a modern reader's response." I do not understand exactly what a "tension" between argument and emotion might be; I should say that in these successful examples the emotion is *generated in* the dialectical struggle, fed by a sense of the argument's "existential" consequences.

47. A. W. Crawford, "Browning's 'Cleon,'" *Journal of English and Germanic Philology,* 26 (Oct. 1927), 485–90.

48. See lines 1–34 of "O Land of Empire, art and love!" in *Poems,* p. 64; first printed, 1951.

49. William Clyde DeVane, *A Browning Handbook,* 2nd ed. (New York: Appleton-Century-Crofts, 1955), p. 197.

50. *Studies in Poetry and Philosophy* (Boston: Houghton, Mifflin, 1889), pp. 269–70.

51. All my examples of negative terms are drawn from the reviews in Thorpe; obviously Clough's poetry presented the severest test to contemporary assumptions about disallowed subjects and modes.

52. *Writings of Arthur Hallam* (n. 28, above), p. 118; *CPW,* I, 1, 8. Arnold misrepresented Masson in the preface: see Michael Adams, "David Masson's Theory of the Imagination and Matthew Arnold's 1853 Preface," forthcoming in *Studies in Scottish Literature.*

53. I have given two citations actually used by critics of the day: the first by Palgrave in 1862 (Thorpe, p. 113), the other by Morley (Hyder, p. 29). See also the bilingual version of *Pascal's Pensées,* ed. H. F. Stewart (New York: Pantheon Books, 1950), pp. 21, 25, 173.

54. For example, as Humphry House perceptively put it, "the memorial purpose of [*In Memoriam*] and the speculative purpose each worked on the other from the beginning, because the friendship itself had so much of its peculiar value only in the context of speculation." *"In Memoriam": A Casebook* (n. 35, above), p. 170. And as Sidgwick put it, Clough does not have *too much thought* for good poetry: "He becomes unpoetical chiefly when he becomes less eagerly intellectual, when he lapses for a moment into mild optimism, or any form of languid contentment," that is, when "the depths of his mind" are *not* stirred. Thorpe, p. 272.

55. *Collected Works of Walter Bagehot* (n. 15, above), II, 322. Bagehot had been anticipated, and even more fully, by Arnold's prescription, expressed privately in 1852, that modern poetry should become "a complete magister vitae as the poetry of the ancients did: by including, as theirs did, religion with poetry, instead of existing as poetry only." *LC*, p. 124.

56. See Geoffrey H. Hartman's important, and relevant, essay, "Romanticism and 'Anti-Self-Consciousness'" (1962), in *Romanticism and Consciousness* (n. 44, above), pp. 46–56.

57. W. H. Smith, 1866, in Thorpe, p. 209.

58. *Ibid.*, p. 208.

59. 1869; Thorpe, pp. 247–48.

60. Best told in Wendell V. Harris, *Arthur Hugh Clough* (New York: Twayne, 1970), pp. 139–50; and see Alba H. Warren, Jr., *English Poetic Theory, 1825–1865* (1950; reprint ed., New York: Octagon Books, 1966), pp. 155–61.

61. *LC*, pp. 99, 63.

62. Despite unfortunate phrases like "the noble and profound application of ideas to life" (*CPW*, I, 211; see IX, 44). "The Function of Criticism" (1864) makes clear, as T. S. Eliot was to do, that the poet does not himself *generate* ideas. See the provocative article by Murray Krieger, "The Critical Legacy of Matthew Arnold: Or, The Strange Brotherhood of T. S. Eliot, I. A. Richards, and Northrop Frye," *Southern Review*, n.s. 5 (April 1969), 457–74.

63. Best explained in Kenneth Allott, "A Background for 'Empedocles on Etna,'" *Essays and Studies 1968*, ed. Simeon Potter (London: John Murray, 1968), pp. 80–100.

64. Tennyson's characteristic "modern" hero persists only through *Maud* (1855); the later poetry of Browning is overwhelmed by his strong didactic impulse and the "philosophical" insistences to which the critics had of course always objected. This turn to a kind of "naked" metaphysics, unmitigated by his earlier efforts at creating character and dramatic situation, was best studied in William C. DeVane, *Browning's Parleyings* (New Haven: Yale University Press, 1927), ch. 3.

65. On Shakespeare, see *British Quarterly Review* (Nov. 1852), reprinted in *Essays Biographical and Critical* (Cambridge & London: Macmillan, 1856), pp. 1–36; on Wordsworth, see *North British Review* (Aug. 1850), reprinted in *ibid.*, pp. 346–90. On Browning, see *British Quarterly Review*, 23 (Jan. 1856), 151–80; on Tennyson, *British Quarterly Review*, 21 (Jan. 1855), 163; on Clough, *Macmillan's Magazine* (Aug. 1862), reprinted in Thorpe, pp. 139–54. For the Browning and Tennyson references I am indebted to Michael W. Adams, "David Masson: A Study of His Literary Criticism," Ph.D. diss., University of Texas, 1973, p. 13. Of course Masson may amuse the modern reader (*BQR*, Nov. 1852), when he not only virtually identifies Shakespeare with his own "melancholy" Hamlet, but also reads him almost as a nineteenth-century Obermann or Scholar-Gipsy.

66. In *"In Memoriam": A Casebook* (n. 35, above), pp. 122–26.

67. 1866; Hyder, p. 29.

68. 1870; Rutherford, pp. 407–8.

69. One of the first and best attempts to describe the change was by J. R. Mozley, in "Modern English Poetry," *Quarterly Review*, 126 (April 1869), 328–59. After judiciously surveying the four poets of "1850" (adding Elizabeth Barrett Browning as a fifth), he calls, not very hopefully, for a new poet to present in permanent form "the picture and visible shape" of the more restless times that have followed 1848; against this desideratum he places "a school of poetry altogether novel" that takes "classical legends as its main theme"

and "only occasionally and in lyrical fashion glances from thence at the thoughts which are most prevalent among the inquirers and workers of the age." His examples are Morris and Swinburne.

70. Kermode, *Romantic Image* (London: Routledge & Kegan Paul, 1957), pp. 165–66; Abrams, *Victorian Studies*, 2 (Sept. 1958), 75–77. See also David Kalstone, *New York Times Book Review*, Sept. 17, 1972, p. 47.

71. A distinction made by Renford Bambrough, *Reason, Truth and God* (London: Methuen, 1969), p. 118.

The Warfare of Conscience with Theology
Josef L. Altholz

1. The first scholar to explicate this point was Howard R. Murphy, "The Ethical Revolt against Christian Orthodoxy in Early Victorian England," *American Historical Review*, 40 (July 1955), 800–817: "the Victorian religious crisis was produced by a fundamental conflict between certain cherished religious dogmas . . . and the meliorist ethical bias of the age" (pp. 800–801). See also James C. Livingston, *The Ethics of Belief* (AAR Studies in Religion no. 9; Missoula, 1975).

2. This phrase and certain other passages have been borrowed, with the permission of the Bobbs-Merrill Co., from the chapter "Science and Conscience" in Altholz, *The Churches in the Nineteenth Century* (Indianapolis, 1967).

3. See Frank M. Turner, "Rainfall, Plagues, and the Prince of Wales: A Chapter in the Conflict of Religion and Science," *Journal of British Studies*, 13 (May 1974), 46–65. For the pivotal role of the professions, see Harold Perkin, *The Origins of Modern English Society, 1780–1880* (London, 1969).

4. Thus Canon Liddon as late as 1889: "The trustworthiness of the Old Testament is, in fact, inseparable from the trustworthiness of our Lord Jesus Christ." Quoted in W. Neil, "The Criticism and Theological Use of the Bible, 1700–1950," in *The Cambridge History of the Bible: The West from the Reformation to the Present Day*, ed. S. L. Greenslade (Cambridge, 1963), p. 267.

5. Stanley to Hugh Pearson, Sept. 21, 1841, in Rowland E. Prothero and G. G. Bradley, *The Life and Correspondence of Arthur Penrhyn Stanley, Late Dean of Westminster*, 2 vols. (New York, 1894), I, 302.

6. Jowett to Stanley, Aug. 17, 1846, in Evelyn Abbott and Lewis Campbell, *The Life and Letters of Benjamin Jowett*, 2 vols. (New York, 1897), I, 150.

7. Quoted in Ernest G. Sandford, ed., *Memoirs of Archbishop Temple, by Seven Friends*, 2 vols. (London, 1906), I, 303.

8. A sermon in the 1830s, quoted in Standish Meacham, *Lord Bishop: The Life of Samuel Wilberforce* (Cambridge, Mass., 1970), p. 229. Also p. 225: "God intended revelation to train the heart, not to gratify the intellect." Significantly, Wilberforce published in 1861 a volume of sermons entitled *The Revelation of God the Probation of Man*. Goldwin Smith, a layman, responded with *The Suppression of Doubt Is Not Faith*.

9. Meacham, *Lord Bishop*, p. 228.

10. Newman to Malcolm McColl, Mar. 24, 1861, in Charles S. Dessain, ed., *The Letters and Diaries of John Henry Newman*, XIX (London, 1969), 488. Newman, with the detachment of a Roman Catholic, could observe that "The religion of England depends, humanly speaking, on belief in 'the Bible and the whole Bible,' etc., and on the observance of the Calvinistic Sabbath. Let the population begin to doubt in its inspiration and infallibility, where are they?"

11. Quoted in William Irvine, *Apes, Angels, and Victorians* (New York, 1955), p. 109.

12. These passages from "On Atonement and Satisfaction" are quoted in Geoffrey Faber, *Jowett, a Portrait with Background* (London, 1957), p. 219, and Abbott and Campbell, *Life of Jowett*, I, 234.

13. This point is made by Murphy, "The Ethical Revolt," p. 811. Another illustration of the state of mind which produced this revulsion is the case of Tennyson, who vividly remembered an aunt saying, "Alfred, Alfred, whenever I look at you I think of the words, 'Depart from me, ye cursed, into everlasting fire.'" A Catholic critic remarked, "It is the Calvinistic idea of God and hell which is at the bottom of it." Maisie Ward, *The Wilfrid Wards and the Transition* (London, 1934), I, 167–68.

14. Mill, *An Examination of Sir William Hamilton's Philosophy* (4th ed., London, 1872), p. 129. The reference was specifically to Mansel's philosophy, discussed later in this essay. Mill's phrase seems to echo James Anthony Froude in 1849: "oh, I would sooner perish for ever than stoop down before a Being who may have power to crush me, but whom my heart forbids me to reverence." Froude, *The Nemesis of Faith* (New York, 1879), p. 17.

15. A student of hymnology has pointed out that references to hell in revival hymns had almost disappeared by the 1870s; and the Congregationalist divine R. W. Dale said in 1874 that eternal punishment had been relegated to "the house of beliefs which we have not rejected, but which we are willing to forget." G. Kitson Clark, *An Expanding Society: Britain 1830–1900* (Cambridge, 1967), p. 104; H. G. Wood, *Belief and Unbelief since 1850* (Cambridge, 1955), p. 32.

16. "If the teaching of Christ is not in any one thing the teaching of God, it is in all things the teaching of men." H. L. Mansel, *The Limits of Religious Thought* (Oxford, 1858), p. 155. A good discussion of the Mansel controversy is R. V. Sampson, "The Limits of Religious Thought: The Theological Controversy," in *1859: Entering an Age of Crisis* (Bloomington, Ind., 1959), pp. 63–80.

17. George Rawlinson and J. W. Burgon, respectively, cited in Neil, "The Criticism and Theological Use of the Bible," pp. 260, 283.

18. At a meeting of the Society for Increasing Endowments of Small Livings in the Diocese of Oxford, Nov. 25, 1864; W. F. Monypenny and G. E. Buckle, *The Life of Bejamin Disraeli, Earl of Beaconsfield*, 6 vols. (London, 1910–20), IV, 374.

19. Accounts of this debate vary; the standard account, made famous in Leonard Huxley's life of his father, is taken from [Isabel Sidgwick], "A Grandmother's Tales," *Macmillan's Magazine*, 78 (Oct. 1898), 433. A minimizing account is given by Owen Chadwick, *The Victorian Church*, 2 vols. (London, 1966–70), II, 10–11.

20. "To the Reader," introductory note to *Essays and Reviews* (London, 1860).

21. Jowett, "On the Interpretation of Scripture," *Essays and Reviews*, p. 374.

22. The mock epitaph on Lord Westbury containing this phrase is attributed to Sir Philip Rose, but the phrase itself is said to have been coined by Charles Bowen, one of Jowett's favorite pupils. J. B. Atlay, *The Victorian Chancellors*, 2 vols. (London, 1906–8), II, 264.

23. The quotations are from the preface to part I and the "Concluding Remarks" of part II of Colenso, *The Pentateuch and Book of Joshua Critically Examined*, 2 vols. (New York, 1863), I, 8; II, 301–2.

24. *The Guardian* (1863), p. 302, cited in Bernard Reardon, *From Coleridge to Gore* (London, 1971), p. 343, n. 1.

25. *The Times* (London), Feb. 20, 1861.

26. "On the Interpretation of Scripture," p. 373.

27. Goldwin Smith: "a certain number of men may be growing up, not exactly in infidelity, but in the belief that Christianity is an open question." Earl of Selborne, *Memorials*, ed. Lady Sophia Palmer, 2 vols. (London, 1896), II, 64–65.

28. Huxley to Charles Kingsley, cited in Irvine, *Apes, Angels, and Victorians*, pp. 131, 129.

29. G. M. Young, *Victorian England: Portrait of an Age* (Garden City, N. Y., 1954), p. 277.

30. Wilde to Lord Alfred Douglas, *The Letters of Oscar Wilde*, ed. Rupert Hart-Davis (London, 1962), p. 468.

Thoughts on Social Change and Political Accommodation
John M. Robson

1. Edmund Burke, *Reflections on the Revolution in France*, in *Works* (London, 1803–27), V, 183–84.

2. There were of course negative or counter models (including many that had positive connotations for others). One negative model may be cited as a commonplace: China, past and present, was normally depicted as having a stagnant polity and society.

3. Burke, *An Appeal from the New to the Old Whigs*, in *Works*, VI, 217–18; James Mill, "Government," in *Essays* (London, [1825]), 31–32 (the penultimate paragraph in all editions).

Science by Candlelight
Leonard G. Wilson

1. Mary E. Lyell to William Hickling Prescott, February 6, 7, 1853. Prescott Mss., Massachusetts Historical Society.

2. Sir Arthur Elton, "Gas for Light and Heat," in Charles Singer *et al.*, *A History of Technology*, 5 vols. (London: Oxford University Press, 1954–58), IV, 258–75.

3. In 1897 Sir Archibald Geikie considered that Lyell's doctrine of uniformitarianism was "probably now held by few geologists in any country." Archibald Geikie, *The Founders of Geology* (London: Macmillan, 1897), p. 281.

4. Charles Lyell, *Principles of Geology*, 3 vols. (London: John Murray, 1830–33).

5. J. Joly, *Radioactivity and Geology: An Account of the Influence of Radioactive Energy on Terrestrial History* (London: Archibald Constable, 1909), pp. 211–51.

6. Anthony Hallam, *A Revolution in the Earth Sciences* (Oxford: Clarendon Press, 1973).

7. Leonard G. Wilson, "The Origins of Charles Lyell's Uniformitarianism," in Claude C. Albritton, Jr., ed., *Uniformity and Simplicity — A Symposium on the Principle of the Uniformity of Nature* (New York: Geological Society of America, special paper 89, 1967), pp. 35–62. Cf. Leonard G. Wilson, *Charles Lyell, the Years to 1841* (New Haven: Yale University Press, 1972), esp. pp. 183–293.

8. The state of scientific thought about Darwinism was surveyed very thoroughly by Kellogg in 1907; the situation remained essentially the same in 1910. See Vernon L. Kellogg, *Darwinism To-Day: A Discussion of Present-day Scientific Theories, Together with a Brief Account of the Principal Other Proposed Auxiliary and Alternative Theories of Species-forming* (New York: Henry Holt, 1907).

9. Julian Huxley, *Evolution: The Modern Synthesis*, 2nd ed. (London: George Allen & Unwin, 1963). The first edition of this book in 1942 signaled the new understanding of evolution resulting from the cumulative researches of the preceding two decades.

10. G. R. M. Garratt, "Telegraphy," in Singer, *A History of Technology*, IV, pp. 644–62.

11. L. Pearce Williams, *Michael Faraday: A Biography* (London: Chapman and Hall, 1965).

12. Sidney Spokes, *Gideon Algernon Mantell* (London: John Bale, Sons & Daniellson, 1927).

13. T. G. Bonney, "The Scientific Work of William Pengelly, F.R.S.," in Hester Pengelly, *A Memoir of William Pengelly of Torquay, F.R.S.* (London: John Murray, 1897), pp. 291–322.

14. E.g., H. W. Bates, *The Naturalist on the River Amazon*, 2 vols. (London, 1863); A. R. Wallace, *The Malay Archipelago*, 2 vols. (London, 1869).

15. Edmund Gosse, *The Life of Philip Henry Gosse, F.R.S.* (London: Kegan Paul, Trench, Trübner, 1890).

16. Gerald L. Geison, "Social and Institutional Factors in the Stagnancy of English Physiology," *Bulletin of the History of Medicine*, 46 (1972), 30–58.

17. D. A. Winstanley, *Early Victorian Cambridge* (Cambridge: Cambridge University

Press, 1940), pp. 259–63. Cf. W.R. Ward, *Victorian Oxford* (London: Frank Cass, 1965), pp. 158–60.

18. Gerald L. Geison, "Michael Foster and the Rise of the Cambridge School of Physiology, 1870–1900" (Ph.D. diss., Yale University, 1970).

19. D. M. Turner, *History of Science Teaching in England* (London: Chapman & Hall, 1927), pp. 135–36.

20. Robert G. Frank, Jr., "Science, Medicine, and the Universities of Early Modern England," *History of Science*, 11 (1973), 194–216, 239–69.

21. *Ibid.*, p. 197.

Going on Stage
Michael R. Booth

1. *The Road to the Stage* (London, 1827), p. 15.

2. Charles Kean resolutely persevered, however. After years in the provinces and America he amassed £ 20,000 and was able upon his return as a star to Drury Lane in 1838 to command £ 50 a night for forty-three nights.

3. *The Road to the Stage*, pp. 14–15.

4. Like many other young young men of the late eighteenth and nineteenth centuries, the stage-smitten Mathews had taken his first steps toward an acting career by paying to act a leading part at a private theater. Private theaters made money by charging, for a single performance, fees graded to the importance of the part and supplied everything needed for the production. In Mathews's case the part was Richmond in *Richard III* — Mathews prided himself on his fencing — and the fee was seven and a half guineas. Not surprisingly, private theaters were thought poorly of by the profession.

5. Wallack noted that "three pounds a week was a good salary in a country theatre, and five pounds was enormous. . . . I very much doubt if any leading actor at Bath, Bristol, Liverpool, or Manchester ever received more that ten pounds a week in those days." *Memories of Fifty Years* (New York, 1889), pp. 39–40.

6. "Utility," "walking gentleman," "low comedian," etc., are terms denoting particular lines of business into which the actors of a stock company were divided, and in which each one usually specialized to the exclusion of roles outside his line.

7. *Seymour Hicks* (London, 1910), p. 45.

8. Ann Mathews, *Memoirs of Charles Mathews, Comedian* (London, 1838–39), I, 345–46. Mathews eventually settled with Colman for £ 10 a week and a benefit.

9. *The Road to the Stage*, p. 8.

10. *Ibid.*, p. 65.

11. John Coleman, *Fifty Years of an Actor's Life* (London, 1904), I, 217.

12. Robert Courtneidge, *I Was an Actor Once* (London, n.d.), pp. 102–3. Such improvisation was more the rule than the exception in companies of this kind, which usually traveled without scripts.

13. *Ramblings of an Old Mummer* (London, 1909), p. 18. The same manager, according to Craufurd, would shout to his company every Saturday, "Now then, gentlemen, Saturday night; more guts and less art" (pp. 19–20).

14. *The Road to the Stage*, p. 106.

15. *Memoirs of Charles Mathews*, I, 95.

16. *The Autobiography of Sir John Martin-Harvey* (London, 1933), p. 35.

17. *Ramblings of an Old Mummer*, pp. 25–26.

18. *I Was an Actor Once*, pp. 90–91.

19. *The Road to the Stage*, p. ii. Until late in the century provincial actors usually did not have access to a complete script, unless they bought the play — if it had been printed — in an acting edition. They copied out, or were given, only their own parts and cues and thus had to discover as best they could what the play was about and how their own parts related

to others, from rehearsal and performance. For a new or unfamiliar play, this method posed particular problems of understanding.

20. *Fifty Years of an Actor's Life*, II, 693.

21. *Memories of Fifty Years*, p. 41.

22. *Up the Years from Bloomsbury* (New York, 1927), p. 77. Arliss remembered that "my advent was a Godsend to the leading man, because I had a top-hat. . . . My clothes were always at the disposal of any one they would fit. . . . There was only one officer's coat, and if you were the officer you had to wear it, regardless of the relative size of you and the coat" (p. 79).

23. Squire and Marie Bancroft, *Mr. and Mrs. Bancroft On and Off the Stage*, 4th ed. (London, 1888), I, 139.

24. *I Was an Actor Once*, p. 67.

25. *Behind the Scenes with Cyril Maude* (London, 1927), p. 64.

26. *I Was an Actor Once*, pp. 113–14.

27. *Ibid.*, pp. 114–15.

28. Additionally, highly respected managements would tour with a repertory of several plays, such as Irving's Lyceum company.

29. *Henry Irving* (London, 1893), p. 12.

30. " 'Stock' v. 'Star' Companies," *Theatre* (November 1878), p. 278.

31. *Mr. and Mrs. Bancroft On and Off the Stage*, I, 30.

32. *The Autobiography of Sir John Martin-Harvey*, pp. 44–45.

33. "Going on the Stage," *Theatre* (October 1879), p. 131.

34. "On Theatrical Apprenticeship," *Theatre* (January 1893), p. 54. This practice was often encouraged by stage managers because the provincial public, if they could not see the West End star himself (which they often did), could at least be satisfied with a close imitation. One also has to take into account the traditionalism of the Victorian actor and his instinctive emulation of the star — expecially if that star had played the same part as he was now playing.

35. *Up the Years from Bloomsbury*, pp. 171–72.

36. *Ibid.*, p. 178.

37. "The Amateur Club as a Stepping-Stone to the Stage," *The Theatre* (August 1890), pp. 190–91.

38. *I Was an Actor Once*, p. 253.

There Began to Be a Great Talking About the Fine Arts
George P. Landow

1. "The Fine Arts and Public Taste in 1853," *Blackwood's*, 74 (1853), 92. Ruskin's relationship with *Blackwood's* provides an instructive example of Victorian art politics. Eagles's anonymous reviews had attacked Turner with such scurrility that in 1836 Ruskin, while still a boy, had written a pamphlet in defense of that painter, but finally not published it at his request. When both Eagles and *The Times* again fiercely lambasted Turner's paintings at the 1842 exhibition of the Royal Academy, Ruskin came forth with the first volume of *Modern Painters* to answer the critics' charges that Turner's art was "untruthful." Ruskin thereupon earned the enmity of Eagles and his successor at *Blackwood's*, J. Beavington Atkinson, so that when Ruskin championed the Pre-Raphaelites, the fate of these young painters was sealed in the eyes of *Blackwood's*. Year after year one can observe Eagles and then Atkinson attack Ruskin and the Pre-Raphaelites, assuring the *Blackwood's* reader that these upstarts have been crushed, and the next year see them appear again. *Blackwood's*, in fact, did not publish a large amount of writings on the arts, so when Eagles devotes ten double-column pages to lambasting the supposedly unimportant Ruskin, or Atkinson devotes a full-length review to a single volume of *Modern Painters*, one realizes these men were fighting a

desperate rearguard action, using any weapon in their arsenal — fair or foul — to hold off an apparently unstoppable enemy.

2. [J. B. Atkinson], "Pictures British and Foreign: International Exhibition," *Blackwood's*, 92 (1862), 360.

3. Helene E. Roberts, "Art Reviewing in the Early Nineteenth-Century Periodicals," *Victorian Periodicals Newsletter*, no. 19 (1973), pp. 9–20. For a valuable guide to these materials, see by the same author, "British Art Periodicals of the Eighteenth and Nineteenth Centuries," *Victorian Periodicals Newsletter*, no. 9 (1970), entire issue. For art writing in more general newspapers, magazines, and journals, one can consult *The Wellesley Index to Victorian Periodicals*, which provides important information about authorship, but for periodicals which the invaluable *Index* has not yet included one must search through the individual issues themselves.

4. "English Painters of the Present Day. XXI. — William Holman Hunt," *Portfolio*, 2 (1871), 38.

5. Turner, of course, long had his own exhibition gallery, and Haydon had charged for admission to exhibitions of single pictures. The American landscape painter, Frederick Church, and M. Munkacsy, a painter of large sacred histories, exemplify foreign competitors in the London exhibition scene. In 1860 Hunt exhibited his *Finding of the Saviour in the Temple*, in 1873 *The Shadow of Death*, and in 1885 *The Triumph of the Innocents*, and he continued the practice in later years. The many long reviews his works received demonstrate how effective a method of reaching his audience this exhibition of a single work had become.

6. As the *Illustrated London News* for November 28, 1885, pointed out, "It is only within the last twenty or thirty years that the vital importance of an art education to our manufacturing classes has been recognised. But although the recognition is tardy, it is now very thorough. . . . Birmingham, one of the first towns to recognise the necessity for some such teaching, has just built a magnificent gallery for the housing of her treasures" (p. 550).

7. Turner, who perhaps earned more money from his art than any previous English painter, derived a large portion of his income from engravings after his works. The middle-class market for these editions of his works enabled him to paint as daringly as he wished. One must point out, however, that many of the engravings after Turner were taken from watercolors and drawings originally designed to be reproduced, whereas the later Victorian engravings were meant to make available to a large public major exhibited works that had demonstrated popularity. For valuable information about this practice, see Hilary Beck's *Victorian Engravings*, the catalogue of the 1973 exhibition at London's Bethnal Green Museum.

8. Many of the most important Victorian painters, including Millais, Hunt, Rossetti, Burne-Jones, and Hughes, provided designs for wood-engraving illustrations, and there was also a large group of excellent draftsmen (of whom the finest is perhaps Arthur Boyd Houghton) who devoted their full energies to this mode.

9. "A Few Words about Picture Exhibitions," *Nineteenth Century*, 24 (1888), 32. Harrison also points out that exhibitions prevent the spectator from seeing paintings in their proper setting, and he turns to the French salons, with their scenes of rape and murder, for examples of the end to which the need for exhibitionistic sensationalism brings the artist: "What shall we say to a 'Rape in the Stone Age,' No. 1355, by Jamin? Here a sort of naked Polyphemus has seized and is carrying off a nude, very white studio model, who is posed as the female of the Stone Age. In her fury this elegant nymph has rammed her thumb into Polyphemus's right eye, which she is just gouging out. Polyphemus, howling with pain, clutches the graceful girl in his huge fist, and is just crushing in her ribs, she yelling in agony. To them comes Polyphemus No. 2, a sort of Porte St. Martin torturer; who, seizing his rival behind, is garotting him by strangling him round the throat. Conceive the man who shall purchase this work or art, and sit down to dinner daily in the presence of the last yells of paleolithic man and pre-metallic woman" (pp. 39–40).

10. [J. B. Atkinson], "Decline of Art: Royal Academy and Grosvenor Gallery,"

Blackwood's, 138 (1885), 4. He adds that the Royal Academy, by increasing its "exhibition space . . . is acting the part of certain politicians who lower the franchise, let in the flood of democracy, and with the consequent multiplication of constituents, open additional voting booths" (p. 5).

11. "Pictures British and Foreign: International Exhibition," *Blackwood's*, 92 (1862), 360.

12. "The London Art-Season," *Blackwood's*, 98 (1865), 336.

13. "The Royal Academy and Other Exhibitions," *Blackwood's*, 102 (1867), 80.

14. "The Externals of Sacred Art," *Crayon*, 5 (1858), 334.

15. Roberts, "Art Reviewing in the Early Nineteenth-Century Periodicals," p. 10.

16. Quoted by Roberts, p. 10, from *Art-Journal*, 7 (1845), 68.

17. "The London Art Season," *Blackwood's*, 94 (1863), 71.

18. "London Exhibitions — Conflict of the Schools," *Blackwood's*, 86 (1859), 128.

19. "The Royal Academy. Exhibition the Eighty-eighth: 1856," *Art-Journal*, 18 (1856), 171.

20. "The Royal Academy," *Art-Journal*, 20 (1858), 161.

21. For information about Eagles, consult the *Dictionary of National Biography* and Eric Adams, *Francis Danby: Varieties of Poetic Landscape* (New Haven and London: Yale University Press, 1973).

22. *Materials for a History of Oil Painting* (1847), expanded and reissued in 1869 with the same title; it was later called *Methods and Materials of Painting of the Great Schools and Masters*. Ruskin's fine review of Eastlake's first volume, which took it to task for making no connections between the methods and materials of art and the styles they produced, awakened Lady Eastlake's undying hostility to the author of *Modern Painters*. Its first sign was a number of anonymous attacks on Ruskin in the *Quarterly Review* (to which he had contributed his estimate of her husband's work), and she later became the most passionate advocate and defender of Ruskin's wife when the critic's marriage was dissolved.

23. Mrs. Jameson's various books, which include *Sacred and Legendary Art* in three parts (1848, 1850, and 1852), contain valuable information about medieval and Renaissance iconography. Ruskin did not much care for her work, but for Lord Lindsay's three-volume *Sketches of the History of Christian Art* (1847), which he reviewed, he frequently expressed admiration and indebtedness, although he did not accept many of Lindsay's theories. Ruskin's own iconographic analyses occur in *Modern Painters, The Stones of Venice*, and many other works.

24. See, for example, E. S. Dallas's *Poetics* (1852) and *The Gay Science* (1866). The third and fourth volumes of *Modern Painters* contain the most important parts of Ruskin's own contributions on this subject.

25. Here one should also include pamphlets and manifestoes, such as those written by Hunt and F. G. Stephens, on the occasion of major exhibitions. Stephens's *William Holman Hunt and His Works* (1860), which draws heavily upon the critic's periodical writings (particularly those published in the American *Crayon*), was written specifically for the exhibition of the painter's *Finding of the Saviour in the Temple*, while for his later exhibitions Hunt wrote at least part of each pamphlet himself.

26. "Since the commencement of the Art-Journal, the circulation has gradually increased from 700 (to which it was limited during the year 1839) to nearly 25,000, to which it has reached in the year 1851" (13 [1851], 301). The editor had claimed a monthly circulation of 18,000 in 1850 and 15,000 the year before.

27. "Exhibition of the Royal Academy," *Art-Journal*, 23 (1861), 161.

28. *Ibid.*

29. *Ibid.*

30. *Ibid.*

31. "Art Reviewing in the Early Nineteenth-Century Periodicals," p. 12.

32. *Illustrated London News*, 10 (1847), 297. For this and other reviews of paintings in the Forbes Collection, I am grateful to its curator, Christopher Forbes, and his assistant, Margaret Kelly.

33. *Ibid.*, 68 (1875), 475.

34. *Ibid.*, 88 (1887), 608.

35. *Ibid.*, 102 (1893), 547.

36. *Ibid.*, 54 (1869), 484.

37. T. Brook's *The Awakened Conscience*, in which a family of tramps remorsefully look at a young child saying his prayers, was noticed by the *Art-Journal*, 15 (1853), 150, and both noticed and engraved by the *Illustrated London News*, 22 (1853), 388–89. Richard Redgrave's identically titled painting of a drunkard was described in *Art-Journal*, 11 (1849), 172.

38. *Art-Journal*, 17 (1855), 177.

39. *Ibid.*, 20 (1858), 161.

40. *Ibid.*, 22 (1860), 85.

41. As Tyrwhitt explained in the eighth part of his long series, "Ancilla Domini: Thoughts on Christian Art," "Much of what we have to say here only reflects the thoughts of the author of 'Modern Painters,' but his works have been on the whole carelessly read, and he has complained that people dash at his descriptions and do not attend to his argument." *Contemporary Review*, 10 (1869), 181.

42. Brownlee Brown, "John Ruskin," *Crayon*, 4 (1857), 330.

43. Far more important than the hostility of *Blackwood's* to Ruskin was that of the *Art-Journal*. A detailed history of Ruskin and this periodical would make an interesting contribution to our knowledge of the Victorian art world. The *Art-Journal's* opposition to Ruskin seems to have peaked in the years 1856–1858, when it devoted long feature articles to attacking his ideas and works. His importance in the eyes of the magazine perhaps best appears in the fact that, whereas it usually reviewed books in half a column or less, it once devoted more than ten full columns to a review of the third volume of *Modern Painters* (18 [1856], 113–15, 148–49), while in 1857 it spent thirty columns belaboring a two-page section in *Modern Painters* and some passages from *The Stones of Venice* ("Tintoretto at Venice and Mr. Ruskin," 19 [1857], 265–70, 297–301); this long essay was a response to the high praise for Ruskin which its own "Talk of Pictures and Painters by an Old Traveller" contained [19 (1857), 145–47] — apparently the proprietors felt obliged to publish the passages praising their old enemy in this article by an anonymous author, but they would not let them go unchallenged. A true conservative journal, it began to ease its criticisms when it saw that Ruskin had made himself an established part of the art scene, and finally, it invited him to publish in its pages!

44. See Landow, *Aesthetic and Critical Theories of John Ruskin* (Princeton: Princeton University Press, 1971), pp. 43–86.

45. See Landow, "J. D. Harding and John Ruskin on Nature's Infinite Variety," *Journal of Aesthetics and Art Criticism*, 28 (1970), 369–80.

46. See Harold Bloom, "Introduction," *The Literary Criticism of John Ruskin* (Garden City, N.Y.: Anchor Books, 1965), p. xvi.

47. *The Social History of Art*, 2 vols. (New York: Knopf, 1952), II, 820–22.

48. *Modern Painters*, vol. I, in *Works*, ed. E. T. Cook and Alexander Wedderburn, 39 vols. (London: George Allen, 1903–12), III, 500.

49. For an important introduction to these writings, see E. D. H. Johnson, *The Poetry of Earth: A Collection of English Nature Writings* (London: Gollancz, 1966).

50. Ruskin, who here anticipates the work of Gombrich, is always insistent that art provides the visual vocabularies with which people confront the external world: "I fully believe, little as people in general are concerned with art, more of their ideas of sky are derived from pictures than from reality; and that if we could examine the conception formed in the minds of most educated persons when we talk of clouds, it would frequently be found composed of fragments of blue and white reminiscences of the old masters" (*Works*, III, 345–46).

51. See, for example, *Works*, III, 565.

52. *Works*, III, 395.

53. *Works*, VI, 35.

54. *Works*, III, 134.
55. *Works*, III, 41–42.
56. *Works*, III, 42.
57. *Works*, III, 42–43.
58. *Works*, III, 43.
59. *Works*, IV, 264.
60. *Works*, IV, 264–65.
61. *Works*, IV, 265. It was this section of *Modern Painters* (which demonstrated to Holman Hunt and his friends the possibility of reconciling elaborate symbolism with a detailed realism) that occasioned the severest criticism of Ruskin by the *Art-Journal*, whose writer was apparently unaware of the tradition it draws upon. (See n. 43 above.) For the importance of this passage to Hunt, see Landow, "William Holman Hunt's 'The Shadow of Death,'" *Bulletin of the John Rylands University Library of Manchester*, 55 (1972), 197–239. For the importance of typology in Ruskin's thought, see Landow, *Aesthetic and Critical Theories*, pp. 321–457.
62. See, for example, his superb description of the Goddess of Getting-on in "Traffic" (*Works*, XVIII, 450–53) and his description of the mechanization of pleasure in "Modern Art" (*Works*, XIX, 216–17).
63. P. G. H[ammerton], "Art Criticism," *Cornhill Magazine*, 8 (1863), 336–37.

Architecture, History, and the Spirit of the Age
Phoebe B. Stanton

1. In *Changing Ideals in Modern Architecture, 1750–1950* (Montreal: McGill University Press, 1965), Peter Collins includes a chapter, "The Influence of Historiography," which contains material and discussion parallel to but not duplicating the subject of this essay. The fullest understanding of my argument can be obtained with the assistance of Collins's remarks.
2. Walter Kaufmann, *Hegel: Texts and Commentary* (New York: Anchor, 1966), p. 20.
3. Thomas Carlyle, "Signs of the Times," *Critical and Miscellaneous Essays: Collected and Republished*, 4 vols. (Boston: Brown and Taggard, 1860), II, 153–54, 158.
4. John Stuart Mill, *The Spirit of the Age* (Chicago: University of Chicago Press, 1942), p. 1.
5. The first of these articles, "Normandy, Architecture of the Middle Ages," *Quarterly Review*, 25 (April, May 1821) 112–47, reviewed eight books, one of which was *Specimens of Gothic Architecture*, parts I and II, by A. C. Pugin. The second, "Application of the Various Styles of Architecture," *ibid.*, 27 (April, July 1822) 308–36, reviewed Lewis Cottingham, *Plans, Elevations, and Sections of Henry the Seventh's Chapel* (London, 1822). The articles are not signed but Hill and Helen Chadwick Shine attribute them to Palgrave in their *The Quarterly Review under Gifford: Identification of Contributors, 1809–1824* (Chapel Hill: University of North Carolina Press, 1949).
6. Henry Van Brunt, "On the Present Condition and Prospects of Architecture," *Atlantic Monthly*, March 1886, p. 379.
7. James Fergusson, *An Historical Inquiry into the True Principles of Beauty in Art* (London: Longman, Brown, Green, and Longmans, 1849) p. 169.

Narrative Painting
Melvin Waldfogel

1. Sacheverell Sitwell, *Narrative Pictures* (London, 1937), p. 1.
2. *Ibid.*
3. Young's major reappraisal is *Victorian England: Portrait of an Age* (London, 1936).

4. Quoted from Raymond Lister, *Victorian Narrative Paintings* (London, 1966), p. 90.

5. The standard reference for *ut pictura poesis*, its origin and application to post-Renaissance art is Rensselaer W. Lee, "*Ut Pictura Poesis*: The Humanistic Theory of Painting," *Art Bulletin*, 22 (1940), 197–269; reprinted as a book (New York, 1969). For its influence on Victorian criticism see George P. Landow, *The Aesthetic and Critical Theories of John Ruskin* (Princeton, 1971), pp. 43–53.

6. "The Life and Work of Eugène Delacroix," in Jonathan Mayne, ed., *The Mirror of Art: Critical Studies of Charles Baudelaire* (London, 1955), p. 315.

7. Theodore Reff, "The Pictures within Degas' Pictures," *Metropolitan Museum Journal*, 1968, pp. 125–66, and "Degas and the Literature of His Time," *Burlington Magazine*, 152 (1970), 674ff.

8. Nils G. Sandblad, *Manet, Three Studies in Artistic Conception* (Lund, 1954). See also Reff, "The Meaning of Manet's Olympia," *Gazette des Beaux-Arts*, 62 (1964), 111–22.

9. On Turner and literature see John Gage, *Color in Turner: Poetry and Truth* (London, 1969), pp. 128–48, and Landow, *Aesthetic and Critical Theories of John Ruskin*, pp. 45–50.

10. A work by Henry Moore, brother of the more renowned Albert, is illustrated in *The Art and Mind of Victorian England: Paintings from the Forbes Magazine Collection*, University of Minnesota, Sept. 29–Nov. 8, 1974, pl. 36. Landscape painting of the period is the subject of Allen Staley's *The Pre-Raphaelite Landscape* (Oxford, 1973).

11. *The Works of John Ruskin*, eds. E. T. Cook and Alexander Wedderburn, 39 vols. (London, 1903–12), XII, 371, and XIV, 141–43. Ruskin was obviously referring not to the Impressionists, whose works would have been unacceptable to him, as we know from the Whistler trial, but rather to *valeur* painting, which was prevalent in Paris in the 1860s, was practiced by Manet and Fantin-Latour, and brought to England by Whistler and Legros.

12. Although the academy operated under royal patronage, it received negligible material assistance from the Crown: a building to house its activities and £ 5000 from George III to make up deficits during its first decade. For a contemporary account of institutional and private patronage see John Pye, *Patronage of Great Britain* (London, 1845).

13. Typical narrative works by Hogarth are the series *The Rake's Progress* and *Marriage à la Mode*. In his *Portrait of the Graham Children* intimations of the narrative "before and after" are provided by the menacing cat.

14. Compare Reynolds's *Mrs. R. B. Lloyd* (Rushbrooke Hall: Rothschild Coll.) with Arthur Hughes's mid-Victorian *April Love* (Tate Gallery). Examples of group portraits with a pronounced narrative flavor are Reynolds's *The Daughters of Sir Wm. Montgomery as Graces* (National Gallery, London) and Romney's *Stafford Family* (Duke of Sutherland Coll.).

15. Sir George Hayter's *The Trial of Queen Caroline* (National Portrait Gallery, London), painted in 1820, depicts the proceedings in the House of Lords.

16. Canon Charles Smyth, "The Evangelical Discipline," *The Ideas and Beliefs of the Victorians*, BBC Third Program, 1948 (New York, 1966), p. 98.

17. See John Hayes, "British Patrons of Landscape Painting," part 5, *Apollo*, 86 (1967), 358–65. Pye, cited above, is still useful. Frank Davis, *Victorian Patrons of Art* (London, 1963), contains biographical sketches of major collectors. The most recent study is Frank Hermann, *The English as Collectors* (London, 1972).

18. Margaret Greaves, *Regency Patron, Sir George Beaumont* (London, 1966).

19. Richard Walker, "The Third Earl of Egremont: Patron of the Arts," *Apollo*, 57 (1953), 11–13.

20. Davis, *Victorian Patrons of Art*, ch. 10.

21. Capricorn Editions (New York, 1961), p. 209.

22. Walter E. Houghton, *The Victorian Frame of Mind* (New Haven, 1957), p. 343.

23. *Sesame and Lilies* (London, 1907; reprinted 1913), p. 59. Originally addressed to the worthies of Manchester in 1862 the day after Ruskin had expatiated on the duties and nature of man ("Of Kings' Treasuries"), Ruskin's views on women have recently been excoriated by Kate Millett in "The Debate over Women: Ruskin vs. Mill," *Victorian Studies*, 14 (1970), 63–82.

24. William Gale's *The Convalescent* is illustrated in William Gaunt, *The Restless Century* (London, 1972), pl. 90.

25. References to respectability are legion in the literature. See Houghton, *Victorian Frame of Mind*, pp. 184ff., or G. W. Grossmith's *Diary of a Nobody* (London, 1892), a wry account of a humble clerk's efforts to maintain face.

26. Exhibition date, 1857; present owner, Sir David Scott; illustrated in Jeremy Maas, *Victorian Painters* (London, 1969), p. 121. *Nameless and Friendless* is analyzed in detail by Linda Nochlin, "By a Woman Painted — Artists in the 19th Century," *Ms.*, 3 (1974), 74. Her "Why Have There Been No Great Women Artists?" *Art News*, 69 (1971), 22–39, 67–71, expands on the same theme.

27. Christopher Wood, "The Artistic Family Hayllar," *Connoisseur*, 185 (April 1974), 266–73; 186 (May 1974), 2–9.

28. The letter, which appeared in *The Times*, 25 May 1854, is quoted in *William Holman Hunt*, Walker Art Gallery, Liverpool, 1962, no. 27, which also provides an excellent circumstantial history of the painting.

29. Victoria and Albert Museum, London; illustrated in Jeremy Maas, *Victorian Painters* (London, 1969), p. 119.

30. City Museum, Birmingham; illustrated in Robin Ironside, *The Pre-Raphaelite Painters* (London, 1948), pl. 67.

31. Tate Gallery, London; illustrated in Lister, *Victorian Narrative Paintings*, pl. 43.

32. For the movement from Ireland see Erskine Nicol's *An Irish Emigrant Landing at Liverpool* (National Gallery, Edinburgh); illustrated in Gaunt, *Restless Century*, pl. 127.

33. Victoria's comment is quoted in Robin Mayhead, "The Poetry of Tennyson," *From Dickens to Hardy* (Pelican Guide to English Literature, vol. 6), ed. Boris Ford (Harmondsworth, 1958), p. 241.

614
614

Bibliography

The best introduction to Victorian history for American readers is R. K. Webb, *Modern England: From the Eighteenth Century to the Present* (New York, 1968), with bibliographical footnotes and handy appendixes. There are numerous general surveys, starting with the charmingly antiquated G. M. Trevelyan, *British History in the Nineteenth Century* (London, 1922); among the most useful recent works are Derek Beales, *From Castlereagh to Gladstone* (New York, 1969); Asa Briggs, *The Age of Improvement, 1783–1867* (New York, 1959); David Thomson, *England in the Nineteenth Century* (Pelican History of England, Harmondsworth, 1950); and Anthony Wood, *Nineteenth Century Britain, 1815–1914* (London, 1960). Students at more advanced levels should read G. Kitson Clark, *The Making of Victorian England* (London, 1962), which introduces the leading lines of recent research; Harold Perkin, *The Origins of Modern English Society, 1780–1880* (London, 1969), a stimulating synthesis oriented to social and economic history; and the greatest single piece of writing on the period, G. M. Young, *Victorian England: Portrait of an Age* (London, 1936), itself an expansion of an essay in G. M. Young, ed., *Early Victorian England*, 2 vols. (London, 1934). The best large-scale study, though incomplete, is Elie Halévy, *A History of the English People in the Nineteenth Century*, 6 vols. (London, 1924–47). The two massive volumes of the Oxford History of England for the period are E. L. Woodward, *The Age of Reform, 1815–1870* (2nd ed., Oxford, 1962), and Robert Ensor, *England, 1870–1914* (Oxford, 1936). An essential study of the mid-Victorian period is W. L. Burn, *The Age of Equipoise* (London, 1964).

Richard D. Altick, *Victorian People and Ideas* (New York, 1973), with a useful bibliography, is an able and wide-ranging guide to the social and intellectual backgrounds of Victorian literature. The most penetrating analysis of the Victorian intellectual climate is Walter E. Houghton, *The Victorian Frame of Mind* (New Haven, 1957). D. C. Somervell, *English Thought in the Nineteenth Century* (London, 1929), is a workmanlike general intellectual history. *The Victorian Temper* (Cambridge, Mass., 1959) and *The Triumph of Time* (Cambridge, Mass., 1966), both by Jerome Buckley, describe respectively the literary and aesthetic climate of the age and its pervasive awareness of its place in history.

The "art of Victorian literature" is treated in such works as Wayne C. Booth, *The Rhetoric of Fiction* (Chicago, 1963); Robert Langbaum, ed., *The Victorian Age: Essays in History and in Social and Literary Criticism* (2nd ed., New York, 1967); Georges Poulet, *Studies in Human Time*, tr. Elliott Coleman (Baltimore, 1956); Robert Scholes and Robert Kellogg, *The Nature of Narrative* (New York, 1966); Ian Watt, *The Rise of the Novel* (Berkeley and Los Angeles, 1959); and Erich Auerbach, *Mimesis: The Representation of Reality in Western Literature*, tr. Willard Trask (Garden City, N.Y., 1957). There is no definitive work on Victorian criticism comparable to M. H. Abrams's *The Mirror and the Lamp* (New York, 1953) on the romantics. The best earlier attempt is Alba H. Warren, Jr., *English Poetic Theory: 1825–1865* (1950; reprinted New York, 1966). We may add Lionel Stevenson, "The Key Poem of the Victorian Age," in Max F. Schulz, ed., *Essays in American and English Literature Presented to Bruce Robert McElderry, Jr.* (Athens, Ohio, 1967), pp. 260–89, and Lawrence J. Starzyk, "'That Promised Land': Poetry and Religion in the Early Victorian Period," *Victorian Studies*, 16 (March 1973), 269–90. The great resource in this area is the proliferating collections of reviews, especially the volumes in the Critical Heritage series. Isobel Armstrong, *Victorian Scrutinies: Reviews of Poetry, 1830–1870* (London, 1972), moves from the more theoretical statements treated by Warren to the actual world of Victorian reviewing.

The literature of Victorian religion is dominated by Owen Chadwick, *The Victorian Church*, 2 vols. (London, 1966–70). No one-volume work is really satisfactory, but Desmond Bowen, *The Idea of the Victorian Church* (Montreal, 1968), is at least ambitious; L. E. Elliott-Binns, *Religion in the Victorian Era* (2nd ed., London, 1964), may also be cited. For theology, Bernard Reardon, *From Coleridge to Gore* (London, 1971), is an excellent textbook; on the social side, see K. S. Inglis, *Churches and the Working Class in Victorian England* (London, 1963), and Torben Christensen, *Origin and History of Christian Socialism, 1848–54* (Aarhus, 1962). The mid-Victorian controversies are treated by A. O. J. Cockshut, *Anglican Attitudes* (London, 1959), and M. A. Crowther, *Church Embattled* (Newton Abbot, 1970). The literature of the field is strong on Anglicans, especially the High Church, and on Roman Catholics, particularly Newman (of whom there are numerous biographies); it is weaker on evangelicals and nonconformists, but see Standish Meacham, "The Evangelical Inheritance," *Journal of British Studies*, 3 (November 1963), 88–104.

Victorian political thought is surveyed in Ernest Barker, *Political Thought in England from 1848 to 1914* (2nd ed., London, 1950), and Crane Brinton, *English Political Thought in the Nineteenth Century* (2nd ed., Cambridge, Mass., 1949). Gertrude Himmelfarb's *Victorian Minds* (New York, 1968) is a lively and idiosyncratic treatment of a number of Victorian thinkers. The literature of Victorian science is enormous. Most eminent scientists (like other Victorian eminences) had a "life and letters" published shortly after their deaths, deficient as biography but useful as historical sources. Detailed modern biographies have been written for a number of Victorian scientists, such as L. Pearce Williams, *Michael Faraday: A Biography* (London, 1965); H. Lewis McKinney, *Wallace and Natural Selection* (New Haven, 1972); A. J. Meadows, *Science and Controversy: A Biography of Sir Norman Lockyer* (Cambridge, Mass., 1972); and Leonard G. Wilson, *Charles Lyell, the Years to 1841* (New Haven, 1972). The most convenient guides to the literature of the field are the articles on Victorian scientists in the *Dictionary of Scientific Biography*, 10 vols. to date (New York, 1970–), accompanied by extensive bibliographies.

The history of the theater is surveyed, readably and reliably, by George Rowell, *The Victorian Theatre* (London, 1956). A more comprehensive reference is Allardyce Nicoll, *History of English Drama, 1660–1900*, vols. 5–6 (Cambridge, 1952–59). Contemporary memoirs and biographies are important sources, such as Marie and Squire Bancroft, *The Bancrofts: Recollections of Sixty Years* (London, 1890), and J. W. Cole, *The Life and Theatrical Times of Charles Kean, F.S.A.* (London, 1895). Good modern biographies of actors are Alan S. Downer, *The Eminent Tragedian: William Charles Macready* (Cambridge, Mass., 1966); Shirley S. Allen, *Samuel Phelps and Sadler's Wells Theatre* (Middletown, Conn., 1971); and Laurence Irving, *Henry Irving: The Actor and his World* (New York, 1952).

A standard reference for the arts is T. S. R. Boase, *English Art, 1800–1870* (Oxford History of English Art, vol. X; London, 1959). Two recent books to be enjoyed for illustrations as well as texts are Jeremy Maas, *Victorian Painters* (London, 1969), and William Gaunt, *The Restless Century* (London, 1972). Other surveys include Quentin Bell, *Victorian Artists* (Cambridge, 1967), and Graham Reynolds, *Victorian Painting* (London, 1966). The Dutton Pictureback series has two relevant, well-illustrated volumes: John Nicoll, *The Pre-Raphaelites* (London, 1970), and Robin Spencer, *The Aesthetic Movement* (London, 1972). Nikolaus Pevsner's *High Victorian Design* (London, 1951), based on the 1851 Exposition catalogue, amuses or distresses, depending on one's understanding of design. The leading art critic of the age is treated by George P. Landow, *Aesthetic and Critical Theories of John Ruskin* (Princeton, 1971). The major developments in architecture are covered concisely by R. F. Jordan, *Victorian Architecture* (Harmondsworth, 1966). Major works on the earlier period are Henry-Russell Hitchcock, *Early Victorian Architecture in Britain*, 2 vols. (London, 1954), and Kenneth Clark, *The Gothic Revival* (2nd ed., London,

1950). The most important Gothic architect is treated by Phoebe B. Stanton, *Pugin* (New York, 1972).

The best collection of documentary sources for the Victorian period is G. M. Young and W. D. Handcock, eds., *English Historical Documents, 1833–1874* (London, 1956). Guides to further reading are Lionel Madden, *How to Find Out About the Victorian Period* (Oxford, 1970), and a bibliographical handbook, Josef L. Altholz, *Victorian England, 1837–1901* (Cambridge, 1970).

Index

Index

Actors and actresses: number of, 107; salaries of, 110–113, 187n4; benefit shows for, 111; working conditions of, 112–116, 123; "ponging" among, 113; wardrobes of, 114–115, 188n22; roles played by, 115–117; social life of, 117–118; hostility toward, 118; alcoholism among, 118; training of, 122; use of scripts by, 187n19; imitative practices among, 188n34. *See also* Theatre

Adam Bede, 28

Adams, W. Davenport, on stock company actors, 119

Akenside, Mark, poet and physician, 36

Alexander, George, on training of actors, 121–122

American democracy, Victorian view of, 87

Anglican Church. *See* Church of England

Anthropological Society, 102

Archaeological Association, 102

Archaeological Institute, 102

Archaeology, popularity of, 146

Archer, Frank, actor, 120

Architecture: revivalism in, 146, 149–150, 153, 157, 158, Intro. to Illus. 2; influence of history on, 146–158 *passim*, Intro to Illus. 2; theoretical basis for, 155–156, Intro. to Illus. 2; moral themes in, 157–158, Intro. to Illus. 2; evolution of, 158; excesses of, Intro. to Illus. 1

Aristotle, on poetry, 35

Arliss, George: on actor's workload, 117; on West End managers, 122

Arnold, Matthew: on the critical spirit, 5; as social critic, 19; artistic goals of, 20; on poetry, 36, 52, 53, 54; and society, 85; on social classes, 89; on leadership education, 92

Arnold, Thomas, 45

Art: patrons, 124–126, 165–167, 193n12; monumental art, 127–128; heroic art, 128; politics of, 128–129, 188n1; narrative painting, 159, 160, 163–168, 174;

formalism, 160; popularity of, 161; theory and style of, 161–162

Art collectors, 193n17

Art criticism, 124, 126, 130–134, 189n3

Art exhibitions, 124–125, 126, 127, 189n9

Art galleries, private, 126

Art illustration, 127

Art-Journal, 129, 130–131, 191n43

Art public: democratization of, 124, 127, 128; influence of museums on, 127; influence of press on, 130–131. *See also Art-Journal*; Art, patrons

Art reproductions, 127

Art Reviews. *See* Art criticism

Atheism, 65–66

Atkinson, Joseph Beavington, art critic, 127, 128, 188n1

Atlantic cable, 98

Austen, Jane, 32

Awakening Conscience, 133, 171

Bacon, Francis, 35

Bagehot, Walter, 6, 51

Bailey, P. J., 45

Bancroft, Squire, actor, 111, 112, 117

Bates, Henry Walter, popular science writer, 100

Baudelaire, Pierre Charles, 160

Bentham, Jeremy, 35–36

Biblical criticism: origins of, 59, 62, 66; significance of, 71–74; effects of, 74; mentioned, 173

Bingham, Joseph, 152

Books. *See* Literature

Booth, Charles, on Victorian Architecture, Intro. to Illus. 1

Bowdler, Thomas, 164

Bowler, Henry, *The Doubt*, 174

Brett, John, landscape painter, 132

Bridgewater treatises, 68

British Association for the Advancement of Science, 102

206 Index